STECK-VAUGHN

Pre-GED Writing

Reviewers

Rochelle Kenyon
Assistant Principal
Adult and Vocational Off-Campus
    Centers
School Board of Broward County
Fort Lauderdale, Florida

Dee Akers Prins
Resource Specialist in Adult
    Education
Richmond Public Schools
Richmond, Virginia

Danette S. Queen
Adult Basic Education
New York City Public Schools
New York, New York

Margaret A. Rogers
Winterstein Adult Center
San Juan Unified School District
Sacramento, California

Lois J. Sherard
Instructional Facilitator
Office of Adult and Continuing
    Education
New York City Board of Education
New York, New York

STECK-VAUGHN
COMPANY
ELEMENTARY • SECONDARY • ADULT • LIBRARY

Acknowledgments

Executive Editor: Elizabeth Strauss
Supervising Editor: Carolyn Hall
Design Director: D. Childress
Design Coordinator: Cynthia Ellis
Cover Design: D. Childress
Editorial Development: McClanahan & Company, Inc.
Project Director: Mark Moscowitz
Writers: Roberta Moore, Laurie E. Rozakis
Editor: Amy Levin
Design/Production: McClanahan & Company, Inc.

Photograph Credits: Cover: © Lightscapes/The Stock Market
p.   14   © 1990 Cable News Network, Inc./All Rights Reserved.
p. 140   © Laimute Druskis/Photo Researchers

ISBN 0-8114-4484-8

9 PO 99

Table of Contents

Part

A

Writing Skills

Page 14

Part
B

Handbook

Page 140

To the Student

How to Use This Book

Writing, like speaking, is a form of expression and communication. When you speak clearly, other people can understand what you are saying. Likewise, when you write well, your words can express your ideas clearly so the reader can understand them.

In this book you will learn nine types of writing that you can use in your everyday life. By practicing these types of writing, you will be able to communicate more clearly and effectively. You will also learn to use the Writing Process.

The Writing Process

Writing is a process, a series of steps. All the writing you will do in this book will follow the **Writing Process.** This five-step process is presented in the first section of the book so you can apply it immediately to all your writing. The Writing Process will help you generate ideas and organize them before you begin writing. Then you will follow the other steps in the Writing Process to write, edit, revise, polish, and publish your work.

Your Personal Writing Notebook

Throughout the book you will find some longer writing activities to complete in a separate notebook. Use a three-ring notebook with lined paper as Your Personal Writing Notebook. In this way you can keep all your writing and notes in one place. Refer to your writing samples from time to time to see your progress while you are using this book.

Part A: Writing Skills

Each section in Part A: Writing Skills covers one of nine types of writing. You will learn the writing skills and elements that are unique to that particular type of writing. As you work through each section, you will practice by doing several writing activities. There are three main kinds of writing activities in this book:

Guided Writing. Guided Writing activities are short writing exercises that you can complete in this book. You will write on the lines provided. Then you can compare your writing to sample answers given in the Answers and Explanations on pages 217–244.

Journal Writing. Journal Writing activities are longer. Write these in your Personal Writing Notebook. Share them with others and save them for later reference.

Application. The Application is the last activity in each section. Sometimes there are two Applications. Here you will use all of the skills you learned in the lesson to write an essay on a given topic. The Application pages review each step of the Writing Process. At the end of the Application page, additional topics are listed in case you want further practice in writing essays.

Grammar Skills

Grammar skills are also presented in each section of Part A. The grammar skills covered in each section are the skills most often used with that type of writing. Exercises are presented to allow you to practice the grammar skills. If you need further practice in grammar skills, you can refer to the appropriate page in Part B: Handbook.

Part A Review

Following the ten sections of Part A is a review of the grammar skills covered to that point. If you need further practice in a certain skill, refer to the appropriate page in Part B: Handbook.

Part B: Handbook

The Handbook provides more instruction and practice with grammar skills. After you complete a page of the Handbook, you can return to the section that you were working on in Part A.

Inventory and Posttest

The Inventory is a self-check to see which skills you already know. When you complete all the items in the Inventory, check your work in the Answers and Explanations section in the back of the book. Then fill out the Correlation Chart that follows the Inventory. This chart tells you where each skill is taught in this book. When you complete this book, you will take a Posttest. Compare your Posttest score to your Inventory score to see that your skills have improved.

Answers and Explanations

Answers and Explanations to the exercises are listed at the back of this book on pages 217–244. Some exercise items have more than one possible right answer. In such cases, a sample answer is given.

INVENTORY

Use this Inventory before you begin Section 1. Don't worry if you can't easily answer all the questions. The Inventory will help you determine which writing skills you are already strong in and which skills you need to practice further.

Read and answer the questions that follow. Check your answers on pages 217–220. Then enter your scores on the chart on page 13.

Capitalization and Punctuation

Decide if each underlined part is correct. If so, write _C_ in the blank.
If the part is wrong, write _W_ in the blank.

_____ 1.   In 1945; Japan was a damaged nation.

_____ 2.   Many of its cities were in ruins, and factories had been destroyed.

_____ 3.   It was the end of world war II, and Japan had been defeated.

_____ 4.   By 1982, Japan was the third largest economic power in the world.

_____ 5.   Japan was behind America and Russia.

_____ 6.   today, Japan's exports tell a lot about the country.

_____ 7.   The Country's exports show it has abundant human resources.

_____ 8.   "However," the leader said, "we have few natural resources."

_____ 9.   The country exports cars trucks and steel.

_____ 10.   Other exports include; pianos, watches, and motorcycles.

_____ 11.   Vital imports in contrast are fish and meat.

_____ 12.   The following things are also imported: meat, wood, and iron ore.

_____ 13.   The finance minister said, "we also need oil, gas, and coal."

_____ 14.   According to these facts Japan cannot produce enough food to feed its people.

_____ 15.   Mr. shikso said his country does not have enough good land.

_____ 16.   The country is hilly; the soil is not very fertile.

Verb Tenses

Choose the correct verb to complete each sentence.

17. On January 3, 1959, Alaska _____ the forty-ninth state to join the Union.
    became   will become

18. It _____ the largest state in the Union.   **be   is**

19. Alaska _____ 586,412 square miles.   **covers   covered**

20. It _____ the least settled, though.   **has been   been**

21. The entire state _____ fewer people than New York.
    had   has

22. It also _____ fewer residents than Chicago and Los Angeles.
    will have   has

23. Rich deposits of minerals, oil, and natural gas _____ Alaska much wealth.
    giving   give

24. Its economy _____ a new phase in 1977.   **enter   entered**

25. This _____ when production of oil began on the Arctic coast.
    is   be

26. Experts _____ the oil field contains more than ten billion barrels of oil.
    think   thinks

27. This _____ for 95% of the value of all mining.   **account   accounts**

28. Tourism _____ also an important industry.   **is   has been**

29. About half a million people _____ Alaska every year.
    visit   visiting

30. Tourists _____ more than $750 million a year.   **spend   spent**

31. The state _____ popular state parks.   **maintains   maintaining**

32. Because of Alaska's huge size, people _____ by air and water often.
    travel   travels

33. Alaska _____ more airports than any other state.   **having   has**

34. Airplanes _____ small villages to each other.   **will link   link**

Subject-Verb Agreement

Choose the correct verb to complete each sentence.

35. In the past, to recover from an operation _____ a slow activity.
    was   were

36. No one _____ expected to go home quickly after an operation.
    was   were

37. Now, recovery _____ much faster.
    is   are

38. Today, doctors and nurses _____ that people resume activity quickly.
    advise   advises

39. Health-care workers _____ people to get back on their feet as soon as possible.
    want   wants

40. Now we know that the sooner patients _____ back to their normal activities, the better their health will be.
    go   goes

41. Exercise and physical therapy _____ faster recoveries.
    produce   produces

42. New medicines _____ the danger of infection.
    reduce   reduces

43. Wounds _____ faster, too, thanks to better bandage materials.
    heal   heals

44. Some recent drugs _____ blood clots from forming.
    prevent   prevents

45. Sharp rises in blood pressure _____ controlled by fluids and exercise.
    is   are

46. Today's medical methods _____ operations that would have been impossible a few years ago.
    allow   allows

47. Doctors _____ some hearing problems with sharp beams of light.
    repair   repairs

48. Plastics _____ used to repair parts of noses, ears, and chins.
    are   is

49. Plastic material _____ not react with the body and so is safe to use.
    does   do

Nouns and Pronouns

Decide if each underlined part is correct. If so, write *C* in the blank. If the part is wrong, write the correct word or words in the blank.

_____ 50. A thousand years ago, only the people living around the city of <u>kiev</u> called themselves Russians.

_____ 51. In the thirteenth century, the warlike Mongols conquered <u>they</u>.

_____ 52. By the 1500s, a prince from Moscow had the <u>strengths</u> to proclaim himself czar, or king.

_____ 53. This prince was named <u>Ivan</u>.

_____ 54. He was so fierce that people called him <u>ivan the terrible</u>.

_____ 55. By 1556, he made <u>moscow</u> the capital of Russia.

_____ 56. Over the next 300 years, <u>russia's</u> empire grew.

_____ 57. There were many different people in the country, and <u>they</u> spoke many different languages.

_____ 58. One ruler said <u>their</u> language must be the same.

_____ 59. Many people, however, kept <u>their's</u> own customs and language.

_____ 60. The <u>country</u> was ruled this way until 1917.

_____ 61. That is when the Communists gave <u>they</u> a new government.

_____ 62. The Communists divided the country into separate republics, each with <u>its'</u> own capital city.

_____ 63. In all, there were fifteen <u>Republics</u>.

_____ 64. They formed the <u>Soviet Union</u>.

_____ 65. "<u>Our</u> country has eleven time zones," these people said.

_____ 66. <u>Them</u> had five major climate regions, too.

Adjectives and Adverbs

Complete each sentence by writing the correct word in the blank.

67. It is a well-known fact that widows and widowers do not live as _____ as married people.
   well   good   best

68. Their illnesses are much _____ than those of married people.
   worse   worst   bad

69. They often recover from illnesses very _____.
   slow   slowly   slower

70. They are more likely to die _____, too.
   soon   sooner   soonest

71. Research has shown that all people do _____ when they do not have social ties.
   bad   badly   worst

72. Those who are alone have death rates two to three times _____ than those with many friends.
   higher   more high   highest

73. Even having a pet is _____ than being completely alone.
   better   best   good

74. A fish is a good pet, a bird is better, but a dog or cat is the _____ of all pets.
   best   better   well

75. This is because dogs and cats are _____ to cuddle.
   more better   most better   better

76. _____ people know how important social ties are, but many are still alone.
   More   Most   The more

77. Loneliness can be _____ to bear than illness.
   harder   more harder   most hardest

Plurals and Possessives

Complete each sentence by writing the correct word in the blank.

78. Some people believe that a strange creature lives in the _____ of Nepal.
    mountaines   mountains'   mountains

79. The _____ body is ape-like, but it has the face of a human.
    creatures   creature's   creatures'

80. The _____ body is very big.
    animals   animals'   animal's

81. It stands about eight _____ tall and has thick, white fur.
    feet   foots   feets

82. _____ call it the *Yeti*.
    Natives   Nativs   Natives'

83. The _____ call the creature the *Abominable Snowman*.
    Americans   Americanes   Americans'

84. Some _____ call the creature *Big Foot,* too.
    writeres   writer's   writers

85. _____ articles say the creature only comes to the village to look for food.
    Reporter's   Reporters   Reporters'

86. Several _____ claimed to have seen large footprints in the snow.
    explorers   exploreres   explorer's

87. The _____ body has never been seen, though.
    things   thing's   things'

88. Many people think the big marks in the snow are caused by _____.
    beares   bears   bears'

89. _____ doubt that the creature exists.
    Scientists   Scientistes   Scientist's

90. They doubt _____ existence because they have not found clues.
    it's   its   its'

Spelling and Homonyms

Write the correct word from the list below in each blank.

We _____ that diamonds are the hardest substance. Diamonds become _____
(91)   (92)

only when they have a flaw. Then they can shatter along an _____. Formed by heat,
(93)

diamonds are found in _____ in the ground. Value is based on clarity, color, and
(94)

_____.
(95)

Did you know that most diamonds _____ not used in jewelry? _____ for a
(96)   (97)

small number of stones, that is. Most diamonds have a _____ use. They are used
(98)

in _____ things. This is because _____ hard. They do not _____ easily.
(99)   (100)   (101)

Diamonds are used to drill _____. _____ of diamonds are pressed together.
(102)   (103)

These are used to make home _____ sharpeners. Nearly all the world's diamonds come from
(104)

_____ countries.
(105)

Word List

91.	no	know	now
92.	week	wake	weak
93.	angel	angle	anglle
94.	holes	wholes	whols
95.	wait	wieght	weight
96.	our	are	hour
97.	Except	Accept	Acept
98.	different	diferent	diferrent
99.	making	makeing	makking
100.	their	they're	there
101.	brake	break	brak
102.	metels	metals	mettals
103.	Peaces	Peeces	Pieces
104.	knife	nife	knif
105.	foriegn	foreign	forren

Go on to the next page.

Sentence Structure

Write a word from the list below in each blank.

People used to avoid the sun, _____ they tried to keep their skin untanned.
(106)

They wore hats, _____ they stayed inside on sunny days. Women even wore gloves,
(107)

_____ they carried small umbrellas.
(108)

Today, doctors warn people about the sun, _____ many people still want to get a tan.
(109)

Some people go to beaches and pools to "catch some rays," _____ they smear on gobs of
(110)

suntan lotion. They lie in the sun for hours, _____ they think it will make them look
(111)

good. Many people also go to suntan parlors, _____ that costs a lot of money.
(112)

People do not see how harmful the sun's rays are, _____ doctors warn us. Doctors say the sun
(113)

causes skin cancer, _____ cancer can kill you.
(114)

You should see your doctor if a mole changes shape, _____ this can be a warning
(115)

sign of skin cancer. Also watch if a mole changes color, _____ this is dangerous, too.
(116)

The sun also dries out your skin, _____ it takes away the moisture. The sun feels
(117)

good, _____ it's not good for you.
(118)

Word List

106.	nor	yet	because		113.	for	but	if
107.	or	because	since		114.	because	and	nor
108.	and	so	if		115.	since	or	although
109.	but	which	if		116.	which	because	nor
110.	since	and	which		117.	since	although	which
111.	although	because	unless		118.	because	but	so
112.	even though	since	or					

Sentence Structure

Below are eleven complete sentences and nine fragments. Put an *S* next to each complete sentence. Put an *F* next to each fragment.

_____ 119.   One good way to save money.

_____ 120.   Is to perform minor car repairs yourself.

_____ 121.   Begin by reading through the owner's manual.

_____ 122.   When you buy some simple supplies.

_____ 123.   Buying spark plugs, coolant, and oil at a discount store.

_____ 124.   You will spend less money there.

_____ 125.   Be sure to have your owner's manual handy.

_____ 126.   If you read it over while you are working on the car.

_____ 127.   Your job will be much easier.

_____ 128.   Don't skip any steps.

_____ 129.   Work slowly and carefully.

_____ 130.   You can ask a friend to help, too.

_____ 131.   Spreading newspapers on your work area before you begin.

_____ 132.   Someone who has worked on cars before is best.

_____ 133.   Dispose of all waste products carefully.

_____ 134.   Having put oil down the sewer.

_____ 135.   Instead, putting oil in cans.

_____ 136.   Service stations will show you how to dispose of oil.

_____ 137.   Washing your hands with a good cleaner, too.

_____ 138.   You will be pleased with the money you save.

Sentence Parallelism and Clarity

Fill in the blank with one of the words or phrases listed below.

139. _____, in 1733, the first great weaving invention was the flying shuttle.
At this point in time   Now   start with *In*

140. The shuttle is a _____.
**small piece of wood that is flat   small, flat piece of wood
small and flat kind of piece of wood**

141. It is wood to _____ yarn is attached.
which   whom   that

142. It moves _____ and over yarn tied to a loom.
underneath   under   in the direction of under

143. Faster weaving spurred people to invent a machine that would speed up the twisting,

spinning, and _____.
to clean   cleaning   being cleaned

144. In 1775, the machine for carding, combing, and _____ was invented.
fibers being sorted   sorting fibers   to sort fibers

145. The three basic weaves are plain, twill, and _____.
one called satin   being satin   satin

146. Fancy weaves are made _____ more complex looms.
on   by means of   in order to

147. _____ you visit a weaver, maybe you can see some of the looms in operation.
In the event that   If   On the occasion that

148. _____ many looms today are run by computers, they work very fast.
Because   On account of the fact that   Due to the fact that

149. These methods give today's weavers the advantages of speed, accuracy, and

_____.
making different patterns   various patterns   variety

150. However, nothing can replace the thrill of watching a skilled weaver

_____ a rug on an old-fashioned loom.
making   wanting to make   as he/she is making

Check your answers on pages 217–219.

Inventory for Writing — Essay

This part of the Writing Skills Inventory will help you determine how well you write. You will write an essay that explains something or presents an opinion on an issue. To write your essay clearly, follow these steps.

- [ ] 1. Read all the directions carefully before you begin to write.
- [ ] 2. Read the essay topic carefully.
- [ ] 3. Plan what you want to say before you start to write. List your main ideas and supporting details before you write any sentences.
- [ ] 4. Make sure you stick to the topic.
- [ ] 5. Write your notes and first draft in your Personal Writing Notebook. Then write your final draft on page 12.
- [ ] 6. Review what you have written, and make any changes that will improve your essay.
- [ ] 7. Read over your essay for correct sentence structure, spelling, punctuation, capitalization, and usage.

TOPIC

More and more, people are debating whether gun control helps prevent violent crime. Some people feel that making it harder to obtain guns will reduce the number of violent crimes. Others, in contrast, feel that making it harder for people to get guns will have little effect on violent crime.

Write an essay of about 200 words, stating your opinion about whether gun control will reduce the number of violent crimes. Use specific examples to support your argument.

See model answers on pages 219–220.

INVENTORY
Correlation Chart

Writing Skills

The chart below will help you determine your strengths and weaknesses in grammar and writing skills.

Directions
Circle the number of each item you answered correctly on the Writing Skills Inventory. Count the number of items you answered correctly in each row. Write the amount in the Total Correct space in each row. (For example, in the Capitalization and Punctuation row, write the number correct in the blank before *out of 16.*) Complete this process for the remaining rows. Then add the totals to get your TOTAL CORRECT for the Inventory.

Skill Areas	Item Numbers	Total Correct	Pages
Capitalization and Punctuation	1, 2, 3, 4, 5, 6, 7, 8, 9, 10, 11, 12, 13, 14, 15, 16	_____ out of 16	77 – 79, 150 – 155, 158 – 161
Verb Tenses	17, 18, 19, 20, 21, 22, 23, 24, 25, 26, 27, 28, 29, 30, 31, 32, 33, 34	_____ out of 18	182 – 183
Subject-Verb Agreement	35, 36, 37, 38, 39, 40, 41, 42, 43, 44, 45, 46, 47, 48, 49	_____ out of 15	66 – 67, 186 – 187
Nouns and Pronouns	50, 51, 52, 53, 54, 55, 56, 57, 58, 59, 60, 61, 62, 63, 64, 65, 66	_____ out of 17	28, 170 – 176
Adjectives and Adverbs	67, 68, 69, 70, 71, 72, 73, 74, 75, 76, 77	_____ out of 11	42 – 43, 177 – 181
Plurals and Possessives	78, 79, 80, 81, 82, 83, 84, 85, 86, 87, 88, 89, 90	_____ out of 13	164 – 165
Spelling and Homonyms	91, 92, 93, 94, 95, 96, 97, 98, 99, 100, 101, 102, 103, 104, 105	_____ out of 15	115, 162 – 163, 168
Sentence Structure	106, 107, 108, 109, 110, 111, 112, 113, 114, 115, 116, 117, 118, 119, 120, 121, 122, 123, 124, 125, 126, 127, 128, 129, 130, 131, 132, 133, 134, 135, 136, 137, 138	_____ out of 33	32 – 33, 44 – 47, 54 – 55, 105, 190 – 203
Sentence Parallelism and Clarity	139, 140, 141, 142, 143, 144, 145, 146, 147, 148, 149, 150	_____ out of 12	54 – 55, 105, 196 – 197

TOTAL CORRECT FOR INVENTORY _____ out of 150

If you answered fewer than 135 items correctly, look at the skill areas listed above. In which areas do you need more practice? Page numbers for practice are given in the right-hand column above.

Part A

WRITING SKILLS

Many kinds of writing skills are needed to express yourself clearly in today's world.

Part A of this book will help you develop and sharpen your writing skills. You will practice nine different kinds of writing that you can use in everyday life. The following is a list of some of the ways writing is vital in everyday life.

■ Writing letters, postcards, or notes to friends and family

■ Writing letters or notes to a business about something you bought, or to your child's teacher, or to your landlord

■ Writing a note or message to your boss or to your co-workers

■ Writing a letter to a customer or a client

In Part A of this book, nine different styles of writing are presented. Writing types in this book are taught using the **Writing Process.** The Writing Process has five steps.

Step 1: Prewriting. Plan before you write. Define your purpose, topic, and audience. Make a list of your main ideas and supporting details.

Step 2: Writing the First Draft. Write a strong topic sentence and back it up with facts, examples, and details. End with a concluding paragraph.

Step 3: Editing and Revising. Improve the piece by rereading and making changes such as correcting grammar or rewording unclear sentences.

Step 4: Writing the Final Draft. Recopy the final draft after all corrections are made.

Step 5: Publishing or Sharing the Final Draft. After writing the final draft, read it to a partner or ask someone to read your essay. Have the reader give you feedback on it. Ask someone else to read it just for pleasure.

Each section of Part A includes an explanation and examples of a particular type of writing. Each section also includes Guided Writing and Journal Writing. Guided Writing consists of short activities to complete in the book. Journal Writing activities are longer, and you will write them in a separate notebook. In addition, you will practice grammar skills and other exercises in each section. At the end of each section are two application pages. Here you apply the writing style you learned by writing an essay about an assigned topic.

The nine types of writing that are covered in Part A are listed below.

- **Narrative Writing** is about something that happened to you or to someone else.

- **Descriptive Writing** gives a visual picture of an object, place, or event.

- **Explanatory Writing** informs, gives directions, or explains something.

- **Persuasive Writing** tries to convince the reader to agree with the writer's point of view.

- **Letter Writing** includes writing personal letters to someone you know and business letters to a company or organization.

- **Report Writing** analyzes and summarizes facts and information.

- **Expository Writing** is writing that shows, tells, or proves something.

- **Creative Writing** expresses feelings and ideas that form your personal writing style.

- **Special Writing Situations** include writing a resume and filling out a job application form.

Also in Part A, each section contains one or more pages of practice in specific grammar skills such as how to use punctuation marks and parts of speech. After completing these pages, if you want further practice on the same grammar skill, you can turn to corresponding pages in Part B: Handbook.

The Writing Process

Steps in the Process

Picture yourself sitting down to write an essay. If the thought of writing makes you feel anxious, you are not alone. Here are some thoughts that may help you feel more comfortable.

- Writing is not a natural talent; writing skills can be learned.
- Writing takes practice and patience; with practice your skills will improve.
- Good writers follow a writing process.

In this section you will be introduced to the Writing Process. The **Writing Process** is a series of steps to follow. Following this process is like using a map to get to an unfamiliar place. The writing process has five steps.

Step 1: Prewriting
Step 2: Writing the First Draft
Step 3: Editing and Revising
Step 4: Writing the Final Draft
Step 5: Publishing (Sharing the Final Draft)

Step 1: Prewriting

Prewriting means planning before you begin to write. Your writing will flow more smoothly if you do some prewriting tasks.

Define Your Topic. The first step is to choose a topic. Before selecting a topic, define your **purpose** for writing and the **audience** for whom you are writing. Ask yourself these questions.

Identify Your Purpose. Why am I writing? Possible answers are to tell a story, to give information, to describe something, to explain something, or to persuade someone to do something.

Identify Your Audience. Who will read what I am writing? Possible answers are a friend, a co-worker, a teacher, or a potential employer.

Choose a topic that is not too general or too limited. For example, suppose you are asked to write a two-page essay on carpentry. This is a general topic that could fill a book. But some topics that you could cover in a brief essay are refinishing old furniture or making bookshelves.

A topic that is too narrow or limited is also hard to write about because you may run out of things to say. For example, making picture frames might be too limited a topic for a two-page essay on carpentry.

Choosing a topic that you already know something about or one that you find interesting will make the writing task easier.

Example

Monica Sanchez attended a night class at a community college. Her English instructor asked the students to write an essay on a topic that would help fellow students do well in the class. Monica thought about what might help the other students. First Monica defined her purpose and audience.

Purpose: To explain   **Audience:** Students in my English class

Then she made the following list of possible topics:

1. *Finding your way around the library*
2. *Good study habits*
3. *How to use the library*
4. *Places to study on campus*

Monica selected "How to Use the Library" as her topic.

Guided Writing

In the space below each general subject, write two topic ideas.

1. Subject: Sports
   Purpose: To explain
   Audience: A group of children

   Topic 1: _____

   Topic 2: _____

2. Subject: Exercise
   Purpose: To describe
   Audience: Your friends

   Topic 1: _____

   Topic 2: _____

3. Subject: Movies
   Purpose: To describe
   Audience: Your friends

   Topic 1: _____

   Topic 2: _____

4. Subject: Animals
   Purpose: To persuade
   Audience: Fellow students

   Topic 1: _____

   Topic 2: _____

Generate ideas. After your purpose, audience, and topic are clear in your mind, you are ready to generate ideas about your topic.

Explore your thoughts about the topic. What interests you about the topic? Do you already have information, or will you need to do research?

Brainstorm ideas. Ask yourself a series of questions about the topic to get your ideas flowing. Questions such as What? Who? Where? How? When? Why? will help you focus on your topic.

Talk to other people. Discuss the topic with other people. If you have strong opinions on a topic, you might want to discuss the topic with someone whose views are different. If you are unfamiliar with a topic, ask an expert or talk to several people to collect information.

Read and research. Read magazine or newspaper articles, watch videotapes, or go to the library to get information.

Check your answers on page 220.

Outline or Map Your Ideas

While you are generating ideas, write them down so you can refer to them when you begin to write. First, make a list of your ideas. Next, organize the ideas in the order in which you want to write about them. Writing an **outline** and drawing an **idea map** are two ways to organize your ideas.

Example

Monica asked the librarian some questions. She also talked with some other students. Then she made notes for her essay.

<u>Main Desk</u>   <u>Services</u>

staff, pamphlets   books, periodicals, references

Then she wrote an outline to organize her ideas.

Main Desk   Periodicals
   staff — librarians   locating magazine articles
   pamphlets   locating newspaper articles
Finding Books   Reference Section
   card catalog   types of reference materials
   electronic catalog   how to use them
   books on shelves   Conclusion

Monica could have written this idea map instead of writing an outline.

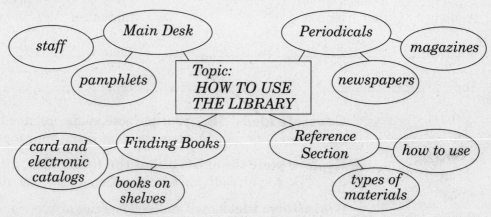

Guided Writing

Brainstorm and list your ideas for this essay topic: the advantages (or disadvantages) of a small (or large) family.

_____

_____

Journal Writing

In your Personal Writing Notebook, draw an idea map for the same topic. Then organize these ideas into an outline.

Step 2: Writing the First Draft

In Step 1 of the Writing Process, you created a plan for what you are going to write. In Step 2 you will follow your plan and write the first draft. A **first draft** is the first version of your piece. Sometimes you'll need to write two or three drafts before a piece is final. With each draft you will improve the piece.

When writing the first draft, the main goal is to get your ideas on paper in an organized way. As you write, choose words and develop sentences that best express your ideas. Perfect word choice, spelling, and punctuation are not necessary at this stage.

The first draft of the essay will have several paragraphs. Each paragraph will consist of a topic sentence and supporting details. The **topic sentence** states the main idea that will be developed in the paragraph. The **supporting details** are sentences that relate to the main idea.

Writing Topic Sentences

The first topic sentence you write is an opening statement that tells the **main idea** of the entire piece. It tells the reader your purpose for writing the essay. If you write a good opening statement, you can refer back to it as you continue writing to make sure you have not drifted away from your point.

A good opening statement should be a clearly written summary of the main idea. It should be general enough to introduce the points you will cover in the rest of the piece. Avoid making opening statements that are vague (unclear) or statements that simply announce the topic.

Example

Monica reviewed her outline for her essay on using the library. Then she wrote her main idea:

Students will feel comfortable using the library if they understand how its services work.

Monica wrote three possible opening statements:

1. *This article is about how to use the library.*
2. *Using the library is not as hard as you may think.*
3. *The library can be a scary place until you get to know how to use its many services.*

Sentence 1 just announces what the article is about in general terms. Sentence 2 states the main idea, but it is vague. Since Monica's goal was to make students feel comfortable using the library by explaining how library services work, she decided that the third sentence was the best opening topic sentence.

Exercise ▊ Each topic below is followed by three opening statements. Place an *X* in front of the best statement to introduce each topic.

1. **Topic:** The Case Against Gun Control

    _____ A. Owning guns is a constitutional right of all Americans.

    _____ B. I don't believe in gun control.

    _____ C. I am going to write about gun control.

2. **Topic:** Every Citizen Should Vote

    _____ A. Voting is not a right; it is a duty of every citizen.

    _____ B. Voting in elections is a strong American tradition.

    _____ C. Some people don't believe in voting.

3. **Topic:** Avoiding Sun Exposure

    _____ A. Many people like to spend hot summer days outside.

    _____ B. You don't have to stay inside to avoid the danger of too much sun.

    _____ C. There are all kinds of sunscreens on the market.

Developing Supporting Details

Each paragraph in an essay has a topic sentence and other sentences that support the topic sentence. Your outline or idea map will guide you through the main points of the essay. As you get to each main point, begin a new paragraph.

There are several types of detail sentences you can write to support a topic sentence. Details may:

- be statements of **facts** or **reasons** that prove or disprove a point.
- be **examples** that explain or prove a main idea.
- be listed in **time order**, according to the order in which they occur.
- be listed in **order of importance**, from the most (or least) important to the least (or most) important.
- show **cause and effect**, how one thing causes another thing to happen.
- **compare or contrast** to show how things are alike or different.

As you write paragraphs, use several types of details to support your topic sentences.

Here are the first three paragraphs of Monica's essay. Compare these paragraphs to the outline and map of Monica's essay. Notice that she wrote a topic sentence for each main topic and then wrote supporting details to explain her statements.

Example

Paragraph 1

    The library can be a scary place until you get to know how to use its many services. The basic services in the Central Community College Library are the main information desk, the card catalog, the electronic catalog, the periodical section, and the reference section.

Paragraph 2

    The main information desk is staffed by a professional librarian and an assistant librarian. They will answer any questions you have about how to use the library. They also have pamphlets that explain the procedures for using all the library services.

Paragraph 3

    The card catalog and the electronic catalog are the basic tools for finding library books. These catalogs list all the books in the library. Books are listed in alphabetical order by subject, title, and author. In the card catalog, the entries are on small cards arranged in drawers. The electronic catalog lists each entry on a computer. Instructions on how to use the catalog are posted next to each computer.

Exercise   The following sentences and paragraphs contain different types of supporting details. Identify the types of details used. Circle the correct type.

Paragraph 1 Topic Sentence: Spectator sports are the great American pastime.

1. Whether we are watching on TV or in person, we never seem to get enough of the excitement of sports.

    time order   fact/reason

2. Some people think baseball is the most popular of all sports, but soccer is gaining new fans every day.

    compare/contrast   cause/effect

3. Another sport that has become more popular is tennis. It used to be the sport of the rich, but now people everywhere are playing and watching.

    cause/effect   examples

Paragraph 2 Topic Sentence: Rap music began on the street corner, but it has now entered the mainstream.

1. Rap music tops the charts on almost every major radio station that plays rock.

    fact/reason   examples

2. When rap first began, most of the artists dressed in sneakers and sweat suits. Now they are wearing expensive clothes and jewelry.

    compare/contrast   examples

3. Rap artists have been featured in major motion pictures. They are able to get recording contracts with major record labels. The Grammy Awards even created a special category to honor rap music artists.

    compare/contrast   order of importance

Organizing Details

When you write supporting details, organize them so that the reader will follow your train of thought in the clearest, most logical order.

Exercise A ■ Each set of sentences below has a topic sentence and supporting details. Find the topic sentence and write *1* by it. Then number the details in order.

Paragraph 1

_____ Good study skills take time to develop.

_____ The last rule is turn off the telephone, the TV, and the headphones.

_____ Next, find a quiet place where you can avoid distractions.

_____ First, set aside enough time to get all your assignments done.

_____ Make sure you have all the books and supplies you need.

Paragraph 2

_____ If you don't eat before an interview, you might feel weak and less talkative.

_____ Don't let nervousness spoil your appetite.

_____ Your physical condition can be important to a job interview.

_____ Otherwise you might not be alert during the interview.

_____ Go to bed early the night before.

Exercise B ■ Identify the types of supporting details used in Exercise A.

Paragraph 1 _____

Paragraph 2 _____

Journal Writing ■ In your Personal Writing Notebook, write supporting details for each of the following topic sentences. Use facts and reasons, examples, time order, cause/effect, compare/contrast, and order of importance.

1. Morning people and night people are like oil and water.
2. Learning to organize your time will change your life.
3. Friendship is one of the most important things in life.

Writing the Conclusion

The last paragraph of your essay is the **conclusion**. The topic sentence of the last paragraph should signal that the piece is drawing to a close. The supporting details should highlight what you want the reader to remember.

Certain words and phrases signal a conclusion. The most commonly used are *in conclusion, to conclude, finally, last, as a result, consequently,* and *therefore*. Here are four methods for writing conclusions and an example of each method.

End with a summary and a final thought.

Example

Therefore, the facts speak for themselves. The campus library has the greatest number of resources to help you with your studies. And there is one last feature of the library that should be mentioned. It is the quietest and most comfortable place on campus to study.

End with a prediction for the future.

Example

Once you visit the library and get to know how to use its many services, you will wonder how you ever lived without it.

End with a recommendation.

Example

Finally, I recommend that you visit the library as soon as possible. If you don't, you will be cheating yourself out of a chance to get to know the best friend a student can have on this campus.

End with a question.

Example

Now that you have heard all about what the library has to offer, are you still feeling a little insecure about using it? If so, consider talking with one of the librarians. Their job is to make you feel at ease.

Exercise ■   Write the method of conclusion used in each paragraph below.

summary and final thought   recommendation   prediction   question

1. In conclusion, I ask, how many more people will die needlessly before our lawmakers ban the sale or ownership of handguns and automatic weapons?

_____

2. Sadly, it seems that Congress will continue to focus on getting rid of guns instead of focusing on getting rid of the drug dealers and other criminals who use guns.

_____

3. In conclusion, it is important to keep the gun control issue alive. Write to your representative, support gun control laws, and influence your local government to take action.

_____

Check your answers on page 221.

Step 3: Editing and Revising

The next step of the writing process is to review and evaluate your work. This is your chance to polish your work before writing the final version. When you edit, look at **content**, **style**, and **grammar**. The following checklist contains questions to ask yourself as you edit your work. Read each question, then read your work. If your answer to a question is *no*, change or **revise** that part of the work. This checklist is also on page 249.

Editing Checklist

		YES	NO
Content	Does the content reflect your original purpose?	☐	☐
	Is the content right for your intended audience?	☐	☐
	Is the main idea stated clearly?	☐	☐
	Does each paragraph have a topic sentence?	☐	☐
	Are topic sentences supported by details?	☐	☐
	Are details written in a logical order?	☐	☐
	Is the right amount of information included? (Check for details that are missing or not needed.)	☐	☐
Style	Will the writing hold the reader's interest?	☐	☐
	Are thoughts and ideas expressed clearly?	☐	☐
	Are any ideas repeated?	☐	☐
	Are some words used too many times?	☐	☐
Grammar	Are all sentences complete sentences?	☐	☐
	Are any sentences too long and hard to understand?	☐	☐
	Are any sentences too short and choppy?	☐	☐
	Are nouns and pronouns used correctly?	☐	☐
	Are verbs used correctly?	☐	☐
	Are adjectives and adverbs used correctly?	☐	☐

Example

This is the first draft of Paragraph 3 of Monica's essay.

The card and elctronic catalogs list all the books in the library. You will not find books listed if they don't have them. For example, if you want to find books on the subject of education, look in <u>E</u> drawer of the subject index. You will find all the books on education listed by author and title. If you use the electronic catalog, you will type in the word <u>education</u> on the computer. You will get a list of all the books on education.

Monica read her draft and answered the questions on the checklist. She found four mistakes in the third paragraph. Her edited and revised versions are shown on the next page.

Edited Version

The card and elctronic catalogs list all the books in
e

the library. ~~You will not find books listed if they don't have~~

~~them~~. For example, if you want to find books on the subject

of education, look in E drawer of the subject index. You will

are alphabetically
find all the books on education listed by author and title.

If you use the electronic catalog, you will type in the word

education. ~~You will get a list of all the books on education.~~

place details in logical order

delete unnecessary detail

add detail

delete repeated idea

Revised Version

The card and electronic catalogs list all the books in the library. For
example, if you want to find books on the subject of education, look in the
E drawer of the subject index. If you use the electronic catalog, you will
type in the word <u>education</u>. All the books on education are listed
alphabetically by author and title.

Exercise ■ The topic of the following paragraph is that smoking should not be allowed in public
places. The paragraph contains mistakes in content, style, and grammar. Match the
number of the sentence to the lettered items from the Editing Checklist. A sentence
may have no errors.

(1) There are far fewer smokers today than there were in the past. (2) The time has come to
outlaw smoking in all public places. (3) Smoke is a hazard to the healthy nonsmoker. (4) In public
places pollutes the air, irritates the eyes. (5) It can also cause sneezing attacks and allergy attacks.
(6) Nonsmokers should stand up and be counted. (7) Since nonsmokers is the majority, they must
push for laws that protect their rights.

Sentences   **Editing Checklist**

1. _____   a. style error — same word used too many times

2. _____   b. content error — supporting detail out of order

3. _____   c. grammar error — wrong verb

                  d. content error — topic sentence out of order

4. _____   e. style error — idea not clearly expressed

5. _____   f. grammar error — incomplete sentence

                  g. no error

6. _____

7. _____

Journal Writing ■ Now that you have found the mistakes, edit and revise the paragraph. Write
the revised version in your Personal Writing Notebook.

Check your answers on page 221.   *Section 1: The Writing Process*

Step 4: Writing the Final Draft

After editing and revising your work, prepare a **final draft**. Proofread the revised version to make sure that you did not miss any errors, such as spelling, punctuation, and paragraph indentation. To **proofread**, look at each word and punctuation mark to make sure it is correct. Use the following checklist when preparing your final draft. This checklist is also on page 250.

Proofreading Checklist

	YES	NO
Is correct punctuation used in every sentence?	☐	☐
Is correct capitalization used in every sentence?	☐	☐
Are all words spelled correctly?	☐	☐
Are new paragraphs clearly shown? (Check to see if paragraphs are either indented or have an extra line space in between.)	☐	☐
If handwritten, is the handwriting as neat as possible?	☐	☐
If typed, is the typing neat and without errors?	☐	☐
Is there enough space between words and lines?	☐	☐
Are the margins too wide or too narrow?	☐	☐

There are special symbols you can use to mark mistakes when you are proofreading. These marks help you spot the errors to fix when you rewrite or retype your final draft. The basic proofreader's marks are shown below.

Proofreader's Marks

b̲ B	change to a capital letter
B̸ b	change to a lowercase letter
the end⊙	insert a period
red, white∧ and blue	insert a comma
Will you go *?*	insert a question mark
and Sue Will you∧go?	insert word(s)
ⓢₚ ⟮there⟯ car	check spelling
end.¶ We will	insert a paragraph indent
end.⊃ We will	remove a paragraph indent
go on̸ away	delete a word
and# a half	add a space between words
to̸ day	delete a space between words

Monica read the revised copy of her essay. She proofread it and made changes using the proofreader's marks. Then Monica wrote the final version of her essay. Compare the two paragraphs below.

Proofread Version

The card and electronic catalogs list all the books in the library. For example, if you want to find books on the subject of education, look in˄ the E drawer of the subject index. If you use the electronic catalog˄, you will type in the word education on the computer. All the books on education are listed alphabetically by author and title.

Final Version

The card and electronic catalogs list all the books in the library. For example, if you want to find books on the subject of education, look in the E drawer of the subject index. If you use the electronic catalog, you will type in the word education on the computer. All the books on education are listed alphabetically by author and title.

Exercise ▮ Below is a paragraph from a job application cover letter. Use proofreader's marks to make corrections. The paragraph contains eight errors.

I am enclosing copy of my resume in resonse to your ad in the <u>Boston Journal</u> on June 26, 1992. I hope you will find my exereience and skills in line with the qualifications for the telemarketing sales position. I available to come to your office for a job interview please call me at 555-6242.

Journal Writing ▮ In your Personal Writing Notebook, rewrite the final version of the paragraph from the exercise above.

Step 5: Publishing (Sharing the Final Draft)

The final step in the Writing Process is **publishing** or **sharing the final draft**. Before sharing the entire piece, if you wish, read it aloud to yourself. As you read, think about what you enjoyed most about doing the writing and what you found to be the hardest part. Make notes.

Then read to a partner or ask someone else to read your work. Ask for honest feedback. Is the writing clear? Is the piece interesting to read? Is your message clear? What parts need improvement? Make notes on the feedback. Use the notes to help you improve your writing.

Put a date on your final draft and notes and keep them in a special folder or notebook. Keep an ongoing record of everything you write. Review all your work from time to time and make notes about your progress.

For more practice on the writing process, see pages 142–149.

Check your answers on pages 221–222.

Narrative Writing

Point of View in Narrative Writing

Narrative writing is a form of writing in which you tell a story about you or someone else. If you are writing about yourself, the piece is called a **personal narrative**. This might be in the form of a diary, a personal letter, an autobiography, or an application letter for a job. When writing about yourself, use the **first-person point of view**. This means that you refer to yourself by using the personal pronouns *I*, *me*, *my*, or *mine*.

A personal narrative in the form of a letter appears below.

Example

> Dear Tina,
>
> As promised, *I* am writing to tell you about *my* new job. This letter will be short. *I* am pretty tired at the end of *my* first week.
>
> Last Monday was *my* first day. Believe *me*, *my* head was spinning! *I* have to answer the telephones, so *my* first job was to learn everyone's name. *My* boss is very nice. She will train *me* for six months. After that *I* will have *my* own accounts.
>
> Wish *me* luck. Please write soon to let *me* know what is new in your life.
>
> Your friend,
> Maria

When you are writing about someone else, the point of view is the **third person**. Use the pronouns *she, her, he, him, his, hers, they,* and *them*. (The **second person** point of view is you, the one who is reading the narrative.)

Example

> Tina and Maria are close friends. *They* went to the same school. When Tina was 15, *she* moved away because *her* father took a new job. *He* did not want to move *his* family, but the new job offered *him* more money. Maria was sad to see Tina's family leave, but *she* was happy for *them*.

Grammar: Pronouns

A **noun** in a sentence names a person, place, thing, or idea. A **pronoun** is a word that can replace a noun in a sentence. A pronoun can be used as a subject, an object, or a possessive (to show ownership).

▎**Example**   *subject* *object*   *possessive*   *subject* *object* *possessive*

He bought **me** a wallet for **my** birthday.   **She** drove **him** to **his** job every day.

Exercise A ▎ The following sentences are written from the third person point of view. Write pronouns in the blanks to take the place of the underlined nouns.

1. On New Year's Day, <u>Sam</u> will marry <u>Alice</u>. _____ _____
   he   him   her   them

2. <u>Tomas</u> will be going to <u>Sam and Alice's</u> wedding. _____ _____
   he   they   their   my

3. Invitations should go to <u>Sally, Keisha, and Corinne</u>. _____
   him   them   they   her

4. The bills for the wedding will be sent to <u>Diego</u>. _____
   them   he   him   his

5. <u>Sam and Alice</u> are going to the mountains for a honeymoon. _____
   Them   They   Their   My

Exercise B ▎ The following paragraph is written from the first-person point of view. Write a pronoun from the list for each blank.

1.	they	me	I	5.	us	them	we
2.	We	I	You	6.	him	our	us
3.	me	mine	my	7.	he	we	us
4.	I	them	we	8.	Their	Your	Our

The apartment belongs to Terri and _____ . _____ can both save money by
                                              1   2

sharing the rent. This tiny bedroom is _____ . _____ let Terri have the big one.
                                               3   4

The furniture was loaned to _____ by _____ friends. Last week _____
                                  5   6   7

painted the living room. _____ goal is to paint all the rooms.
                                8

Journal Writing ▎ In your Personal Writing Notebook, write two paragraphs. Write one paragraph from the first-person point of view. Write one paragraph from the third-person point of view.

For more practice on pronouns, turn to pages 172–176.

Check your answers on page 222.

Writing A Personal Narrative

A narrative about yourself is called a **personal narrative**. One type of personal narrative, a **diary** or **journal**, is a written record of things that happen to you and thoughts about your life. This type of personal narrative is something that you may choose not to share with other people. Some personal narratives are written for others to read. One type is an **autobiography**, which is the story of your life. Another type is an **anecdote**, which is a short narrative about an event that happened to you. Here is an example of an anecdote written by a soldier after the Persian Gulf War.

Example

I left in September for the Gulf. I knew that my wife, Colleen, was going to have twins, but we didn't find out she was going to have triplets until she actually had them. They were born on October 6. I found out about five days later through a Red Cross message.

I thought the Red Cross had made a mistake. So I called my mother and she said yes, we had triplets. I was so stunned that I almost passed out. I felt afraid, nervous, great — everything rolled into one.

I didn't really believe I had three babies until I got home and held all three. When I held the first two, I started crying. Almost every night, I rock them to sleep in my lap. The best thing is when I'm holding them and they smile at me.

Journal Writing

In your Personal Writing Notebook, practice writing a personal narrative by writing something about yourself. Write something autobiographical, or write an anecdote about something you did recently.

Writing About Others

When you write about other people, you tell about something they did or something that happened to them. A narrative about another person's life story is a **biography**.

Example

My mother's life shows that the future is never certain. She got married when she was eighteen and had three children. She never thought much about what she wanted to do with her life, other than raising her family.

When I was ten, my father got sick. After my father died, my mother didn't know how she was going to take care of us. She took a job caring for patients in a nursing home. Her boss encouraged her to go back to school. Now she is a registered nurse. We have a good family life and she also has a career, even though she had not planned her life that way.

Journal Writing

In your Personal Writing Notebook, practice writing about someone else. Write a biographical paragraph, or tell a story about something that happened to someone you know.

Grammar: Subjects and Predicates

A narrative essay is made up of several paragraphs. Each paragraph begins with a topic sentence, followed by sentences that give supporting details. A sentence has to express a complete thought. A sentence also must have a subject and a predicate. The **subject** of the sentence is the person or thing that the sentence is about. The subject is a noun or a pronoun. The **predicate** is a verb and usually shows an action. It tells what the subject does or what is being done to the subject. The **complete subject** may be one or several words. The **complete predicate** can also be one or more words.

Example

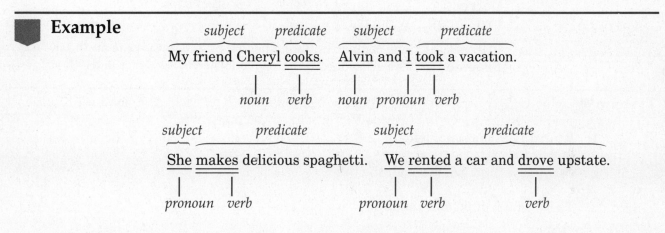

Exercise A Put one line under the complete subject and two lines under the complete predicate in each of the following sentences.

1. Some people like to give parties.

2. Joanne and I gave a New Year's Eve party.

3. Alex invited everyone over for his birthday.

4. Barbara cooked and packed a picnic lunch for eight.

Exercise B In each sentence below, put one line under the subject and two lines under the verb.

1. My sister plans to be a track star.

2. She runs and exercises every day.

3. Our father trains and coaches her for track meets.

4. My mother and I attend and give our support.

5. She runs for the Ohio State University track team.

6. Last week the team won a meet against Memphis State.

7. My sister competed in three events.

8. She got first place in two events.

For more practice on subjects and predicates, see pages 186, 190.

Check your answers on page 222.

Grammar: Writing Complete Sentences

A sentence fragment is a group of words that does not express a complete thought. It may look like a sentence, beginning with a capital letter and ending with a punctuation mark. To avoid sentence fragments, make sure every sentence has a subject and a verb and expresses a complete thought.

Example

Correct:	The A-1 Software Company on 6th Street hired me last week.
Fragment:	The A-1 Software Company on 6th Street. (needs a verb)
Correct:	I will have two weeks of vacation each year.
Fragment:	Will have two weeks of vacation each year. (needs a subject)
Correct:	The company offers a health plan for everyone on the payroll.
Fragment:	For everyone on the payroll. (needs a subject and a verb)

Exercise Put an *S* by each complete sentence below. Put an *F* by each fragment.

_____ 1. Waited two hours and left.

_____ 2. Judy plays practical jokes all the time.

_____ 3. These white, pink, and yellow flowers.

_____ 4. My boss is a smart person.

_____ 5. They dropped crumbs all over the floor.

_____ 6. As long as he could.

Guided Writing A Below, write each of the complete sentences from the Exercise above. Draw one line under the subject and two lines under the verb.

1. _____

2. _____

3. _____

Guided Writing B Rewrite each sentence fragment from the Exercise above to make it a complete sentence.

1. _____

2. _____

3. _____

For more practice on writing complete sentences, see pages 190–191.

Grammar: Run-on Sentences

A **run-on sentence** has two or more complete thoughts that are not separated by punctuation. Sometimes a run-on sentence has two complete thoughts separated by a comma when they should be separated by a period. Correct a run-on sentence by separating the two complete thoughts with a period or by joining them with a comma and a connecting word.

Example

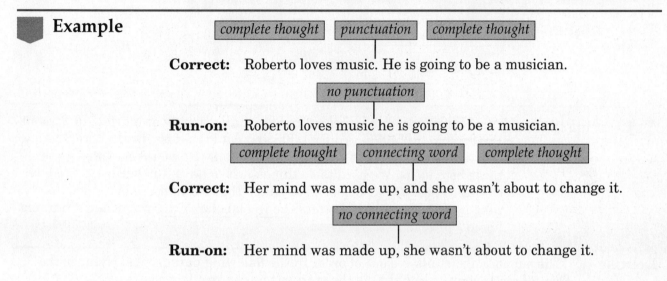

Correct: Roberto loves music. He is going to be a musician.

Run-on: Roberto loves music he is going to be a musician.

Correct: Her mind was made up, and she wasn't about to change it.

Run-on: Her mind was made up, she wasn't about to change it.

Exercise A ■ Correct each of the following run-on sentences. Fill in the blank with one of the connecting words listed below.

so	and	because	unless	but
since	if	although	even	when

1. I am taking classes at night, _____ I have to work during the day.

2. It will take me a long time to finish, _____ it will be worth doing.

3. Then I am going to move to the city, _____ there are more jobs there.

4. My mother will worry, _____ it is time for me to leave the nest.

5. She will be proud of me _____ I become a big success.

Exercise B ■ Correct the following run-on sentences by adding one of the connecting words listed in Exercise A or by separating the two thoughts into two complete sentences.

1. Last year I took a trip to Florida my sister's two kids went with me.

2. I took all their games and toys, the kids still drove me crazy.

3. They were never sleepy at the same time one of them was always crying.

For more practice on correcting run-on sentences, see pages 192–193.

Check your answers on page 222.   *Section 2: Narrative Writing*   **33**

Supporting Details in Narrative Writing

In most narratives, the details of a story are told in the order in which they happened. This holds the reader's interest. It is also a good way to make sure the details are told in a way that is clear to the reader. Below are clue words you can use to relate events in time order.

Time Order Words			
first	then	soon	until
second	after	later	before
next	after a while	during	after that
specific time: at noon, last week, last year			

Example   My friends and I meet every Saturday morning at Marla's apartment. First we sit around her coffee table and eat breakfast. During breakfast we talk about what each of us would like to do. Next we take a vote on the three best ideas. We used to do things just to have fun, but lately we have changed. Last week someone suggested that we ought to make soup and take it to the homeless shelter. The week before that, we visited a nursing home and read to the patients.

Exercise   The supporting details are out of order in the following paragraphs. Number the sentences in the order that tells the story in the clearest way.

1. Topic Sentence: My father came to the United States when he was eighteen years old.

_____ A. The first English words he learned were *beef*, *veal*, *chop*, and *steak*.

_____ B. I guess that being a butcher made him want to help animals.

_____ C. For a while he worked in a butcher shop.

_____ D. Later he studied English and earned his GED diploma.

_____ E. By the time I was born, he had finished college and become a veterinarian.

_____ F. He had dropped out of high school at sixteen and did not speak English.

2. Topic Sentence: Going camping was the worst experience of my life.

_____ A. I had no idea the woods got so dark at night.

_____ B. Everything was fine until the sun went down.

_____ C. We left at noon on Friday.

_____ D. After everyone went to sleep, I sat up with a flashlight.

_____ E. I later decided that my first camping trip will also be my last.

_____ F. The sounds of strange animals kept me awake all night.

3. Topic Sentence: My most unforgettable experience was seeing myself on TV.

______ A. A TV news truck arrived, and people told the reporter what I had done.

______ B. I happened to be walking on a busy street when a car went out of control and ran up on the sidewalk.

______ C. There was a little boy in the car's path.

______ D. I grabbed the little boy and pulled him to safety.

______ E. The news reporter interviewed the little boy and me.

______ F. There I was on the six o'clock news, a hero for a day.

Guided Writing Use your imagination to complete each paragraph below by adding details to support the topic sentence. Use time order words from the list on page 34.

1. Topic Sentence: Before I was in high school, I had attended six different schools.

____

____

____

____

2. Topic Sentence: Denise and Carol got caught in a terrible snowstorm.

____

____

____

____

3. Topic Sentence: My last birthday was the best one I have ever had.

____

____

____

Journal Writing Choose one of the three topics below and write a brief narrative. Write the narrative in your Personal Writing Notebook.

Topics: a childhood memory; an unforgettable experience; a hard decision

Check your answers on pages 222–223.

Application

Write a Narrative Essay

Apply what you have learned about narrative writing by writing two essays. Write the first essay about someone else. Write the second essay about yourself.

Essay Topic 1:   A short biography of someone you know well or someone who is known to the general public

Essay Topic 2:   An important event in your past or present life

As you write each essay, follow the steps in the **Writing Process.** The steps are reviewed below.

Prewriting

Define Your Topic, Purpose, Audience. For Essay 1, make a list of people whose lives you think are interesting. Then shorten the list. Choose someone you already know a lot about, or someone whose life you can easily learn about. In this case your purpose is to practice what you have learned about narrative writing. The audience will be your instructor. It is up to you whether you wish to show your work to your classmates.

Develop Main Ideas. Before you begin writing, list or make a map of the main ideas you want to cover in your essay. If you are writing about a public figure in Essay 1, you may want to do some research before you start writing. If you are writing about someone else, you may want to talk with that person or interview others before you start to write.

Organize Your Ideas. Write an outline or create an idea map like the example below. If you need help with outlining or mapping, review page 18.

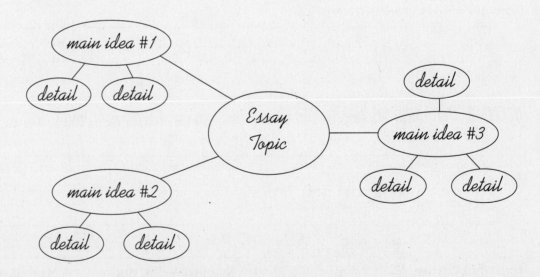

Writing the First Draft

Write the Topic Sentence. Your first topic sentence will state the main idea of the essay. Try writing it several different ways until you have a clear sentence that will catch the interest of the reader.

Develop Supporting Details. As you write each paragraph, make sure that it has a good topic sentence. Each sentence in the paragraph should support the topic sentence. Place sentences in a logical order that helps the reader understand the narrative.

Write the Conclusion. Write a topic sentence that lets the reader know that the essay is coming to an end. Use the concluding paragraph to leave the reader with a final thought or question, or summarize your point.

Editing/Revising

Review. Read the entire essay to see if you accomplished what you set out to do.

Edit/Revise. Refer to the Editing Checklist on page 24. Answer each question on the checklist as you read your essay. Then edit and revise the entire essay, marking any mistakes in content, style, and grammar. In addition, check to see that you followed the guidelines for narrative writing that you just learned:

- ☐ Did you write complete sentences?
- ☐ Did you avoid writing run-on sentences?
- ☐ Did you use connecting words when your sentences were too long?
- ☐ Did you organize the narrative details in the order in which they occurred?

Writing the Final Draft

Proofread. Reread your revised essay. Check for correct spelling and punctuation and for neatness. Use the proofreader's marks on page 26 to correct any errors you find. If necessary, rewrite or retype your work.

Sharing Your Final Draft

Publish. Read to a partner or let someone read your final draft. Ask this person if your message was clear. Make notes on the comments you receive. Think about what you liked and what you did not like about writing the two essays. What did you find the easiest to do? What did you find the hardest to do? Make notes on your thoughts and feelings about your writing.

File. Place your notes and the essays in your notebook or portfolio for future reference.

Apply

For further practice in narrative writing, go to your Personal Writing Notebook. Write a paragraph each day about yourself.

Descriptive Writing

Elements of Descriptive Writing

The purpose of **descriptive writing** is to create a clear picture in the mind of the reader. One way to do this is to include specific details about the subject. This is different from the way we describe things when we speak. When you tell a friend that a movie was "great" because "it had a lot of action," that may be all he or she wants to hear. When people read about something, however, they will be more interested if you describe things in specific terms.

When you describe specific details, use words that create images in the reader's mind. Read the two sentences below.

Example

I sat on the porch on a hot summer day.

I slouched on the rusty porch swing, trying to catch a breeze from the sycamore tree that shaded me from the scorching noonday sun.

Descriptive Details

You can make your writing clearer or more vivid if you look for details. Good writers notice things that others may never see. Writers use these descriptive details to create pictures in the reader's mind. They use specific words in place of general words.

Example

General: She handed me a <u>cup of coffee</u>.
Specific: She handed me a <u>mug of steaming coffee</u>.

General: Gus has <u>short</u> hair.
Specific: Gus's hair is layered and <u>cut close to his head</u>.

General: I could smell <u>food cooking</u>.
Specific: I could smell <u>onions frying</u>.

Guided Writing Practice creating specific word pictures. Write a sentence that has two details for each item below.

1. (a car) _____

2. (a streetlight) _____

3. (a cake) _____

4. (a tree) _____

5. (a bowling ball) _____

Check your answers on page 223.

Precise Words

Descriptive details come to life for the reader when you use precise words. As you choose a word, ask yourself if a more precise word could paint a more specific word picture.

Example

General: The <u>man</u> wore a <u>hat</u>.
Precise: The <u>welder</u> wore a <u>hard hat</u>.

General: She <u>closed</u> the door.
Precise: She <u>slammed</u> the door.

Exercise

Below is a list of general words and a list of precise words. Find a precise word in the right column that could replace the general word in the left column. Write the letter in the blank.

_____ 1. shirt   a. devour   _____ 6. vegetable   f. station wagon

_____ 2. jump   b. waltz   _____ 7. doctor   g. eggplant

       c. leap   h. shock

_____ 3. child   d. six-year-old   _____ 8. car   i. stare

_____ 4. dance   e. T-shirt   _____ 9. look   j. surgeon

_____ 5. eat   _____ 10. surprise

Guided Writing

Revise each sentence to make the description more specific. Use precise words in place of the underlined words.

1. **General:** He has a <u>young child</u>.

   Precise: _____

2. **General:** After dinner we had <u>dessert</u>.

   Precise: _____

3. **General:** I gave my daughter a <u>pet</u>.

   Precise: _____

Journal Writing

In your Personal Writing Notebook, write a descriptive paragraph on one of the topics listed below. Concentrate on providing specific details and using precise, vivid words.

My Favorite Clothes   **The View from My Window**

Sensory Details

Another way to create word pictures is to use words that appeal to the five senses: *sight, hearing, taste, smell,* and *touch*. Details that appeal to the senses are called **sensory details**. Sensory details make descriptions come to life. Notice the words that appeal to the five senses in the paragraph below.

Example

This morning I ran across a pair of **musty sneakers**. Why, I asked myself, are they still in the closet? I knew the answer. I was wearing them the day my grandfather took me to Coney Island. When I look at those **dirt-encrusted, cola-stained** sneakers, it all comes back to me. I can feel the **sweet cotton candy** melting on my tongue. I can taste those **salty fries**. My stomach churns at the memory of that **roaring roller coaster**, the Cyclone. I remember grabbing hold of my grandfather's **big, rough hand**, and pulling him toward the **soft, gentle music** of the carousel.

`smell` `sight` `touch` `taste` `sound` `sound` `sight` `touch`

Exercise Write the sense that is affected by the sensory details in each of the following sentences.

_____ 1. The deep blue sea had shades of turquoise.

_____ 2. The waves tickled my toes.

_____ 3. The waves lapped gently on the shore.

_____ 4. The sea air had a slightly salty smell.

_____ 5. We drank ice-cold lemonade at the beach.

Guided Writing Write a sentence that describes each item. Use specific details that appeal to the sense listed beside the topic.

1. (**Sight:** sunset) _____

2. (**Hearing:** factory) _____

3. (**Taste:** hamburger) _____

4. (**Touch:** handshake) _____

5. (**Smell:** new baby) _____

Journal Writing In your Personal Writing Notebook, write a paragraph describing a place you have been. Use as many sensory details as possible.

Figurative Language

When you describe exactly how something looks, tastes, feels, smells, or sounds, you are using **literal language**. As you learn to use descriptive details in your writing, you may find it useful to describe someone or something by using an imaginary comparison. This is called **figurative language**. Here are three ways that you can use figurative language to make comparisons.

Example

1. Use *like* or *as*.

   Literal: She was so upset that she cried.
   Figurative: She was so upset that she cried like a baby.

2. Say that something is something else.

   Literal: The snow covered the field.
   Figurative: The snow was a soft white blanket over the field.

3. Give human qualities to things that are not human.

   Literal: The rain fell on my face.
   Figurative: The rain caressed my face.

Guided Writing The following sentences are written in literal language. Rewrite them using figurative language that appeals to the sense listed.

1. (Sight) My apartment is small.

   _____

2. (Touch) Rich has beautiful hair.

   _____

3. (Hearing) The wind was loud last night.

   _____

4. (Taste) The cold lemonade was refreshing.

   _____

5. (Smell) I could smell her perfume before she opened the door.

   _____

Journal Writing In your Personal Writing Notebook, write a description of one of the topics below. Use figurative language that appeals to the five senses.

My Favorite Season   **A Day at the Park**

Grammar: Adjectives and Adverbs

In descriptive writing you often use adjectives and adverbs.
Adjectives are words that describe nouns and pronouns. Adjectives answer the following questions.

What kind?	This <u>large</u> diner has just opened.
How many?	I'll have <u>two</u> eggs with toast.
Which one?	It is the <u>first</u> item on the menu.

Adverbs are words that describe verbs, adjectives, and other adverbs. Adverbs answer the following questions.

How?	He walked <u>quickly</u>.
When?	He left <u>early</u>.
Where?	He went <u>there</u>.
To what extent?	He went to a <u>very</u> popular restaurant.

It is easy to confuse adjectives and adverbs. With adjectives and adverbs that are similar, the adverb usually ends in *-ly*. Be careful not to use an adjective when an adverb is needed.

Example

Correct: She ran to the store <u>quickly</u>.
Incorrect: She ran to the store <u>quick</u>.

The first sentence is correct because the word *quickly* describes the verb. It tells how she ran.

Exercise Choose the correct adjective or adverb to complete each of the following sentences.

1. Lilly's Kitchen is a _____ restaurant.
   fine (adj.)   **finely** (adv.)

2. The bakery's bread is _____ every day.
   fresh (adj.)   **freshly** (adv.)

3. The dining room is lit _____ .
   bright (adj.)   **brightly** (adv.)

4. The tables are decorated _____ .
   beautiful (adj.)   **beautifully** (adv.)

5. The food is always _____ .
   delicious (adj.)   **deliciously** (adv.)

6. I eat at Lilly's _____ .
   regular (adj.)   **regularly** (adv.)

Grammar: Comparing with Adjectives and Adverbs

Adjectives and adverbs can show comparison. To compare two things, use the **comparative** form. To compare three or more things, use the **superlative** form. Read the examples below.

▼ **Example**

adjective	comparative	superlative
long	longer than	longest
careful	more careful than	the most careful

adverb	comparative	superlative
fast	faster than	the fastest
quickly	more quickly than	the most quickly

Adjective: This is a <u>good</u> supper.
Comparative: This meal is <u>better</u> than lunch.
Superlative: This is the <u>best</u> supper I've eaten in months.

Some adjectives and adverbs change completely in their comparative and superlative forms. Read the examples below.

▼ **Example**

adjective	comparative	superlative
good	better than	the best
bad	worse than	the worst

adverb	comparative	superlative
well	better than	the best
little	less than	the least
badly	worse than	the worst

Adverb: I bowled <u>badly</u> Friday.
Comparative: I bowled <u>worse</u> today than on Monday.
Superlative: Of all my scores, I bowled the <u>worst</u> today.

Exercise ▪ Complete the paragraph with the correct form of each adjective or adverb from the choices listed above the paragraph.

1. hot, hotter, hottest
2. new, newer, newest
3. quickly, more quickly, most quickly
4. important, more important, most important
5. easy, easier, easiest

It was the _____ day of summer, and it was my job to train the _____
    1   2

employee in our mail room. Ramos learned _____ than the last person.
                                                                              3

When the _____ job of the day arrived, he made the work seem
                              4

_____.
         5

For more practice on adjectives and adverbs, turn to pages 177–181.

Check your answers on page 224.

Grammar: Varying Sentence Structure

To be an effective writer, vary the kinds of sentences you write. Changing the pattern of some of your sentences will help make your writing more interesting. You can learn to write sentences in different patterns by following some basic techniques.

Here are three ways to vary sentence structure.

1. Write compound sentences.
2. Write complex sentences.
3. Use adjectives, noun phrases, and verb phrases in a series.

Compound Sentences

A **compound sentence** has two complete thoughts that are closely related. Each of these thoughts could stand alone as a sentence. Connect related ideas by using a **comma** and a connecting word called a **conjunction**. The four most commonly used conjunctions are *and, but, or,* and *so.*

Example

1. Rosa takes care of stray animals.
   Rosa sometimes finds new homes for strays.

   Compound Sentence: Rosa takes care of stray animals, or sometimes she finds new homes for them.

2. Rosa's favorite pet is a sad-eyed puppy.
   Rosa also loves the dingy white alley cat she found.

   Compound Sentence: Rosa's favorite pet is a sad-eyed puppy, but she also loves the dingy white alley cat she found.

3. The cat roams all over the house.
   The parakeet has to be kept in its cage.

   Compound Sentence: The cat roams all over the house, so the parakeet has to be kept in its cage.

4. I help Rosa with the animals.
   She pays me a small amount for my work.

   Compound Sentence: I help Rosa with the animals, and she pays me a small amount for my work.

Exercise Combine the following pairs of sentences to make compound sentences. Use a comma and one of the conjunctions *and, but, or,* or *so* to connect each pair of statements.

1. The skies opened up. Lightning streaked across the clouds.

_____

_____

2. Last year we had floods. This year was not as bad.

_____

_____

3. The storm caused severe damage. Several people were injured.

_____

_____

4. Windows were shattered by the wind. We went into the basement.

_____

_____

5. We read books. We played cards.

_____

_____

Guided Writing ■ Complete each sentence below by adding a related second thought to make a compound sentence. Use the conjunction listed above the sentence.

1. **but**
The steak was tender, _____

2. **and**
The street was deserted, _____

3. **so**
The couch was new, _____

4. **but**
The soldiers marched bravely, _____

5. **so**
The sky looked threatening, _____

6. **and**
The fruit was ripe, _____

7. **but**
The snow was knee-deep, _____

8. **or**
I should get gas soon, _____

9. **or**
We could see this movie, _____

For more practice on compound sentences, turn to pages 194–195.

Check your answers on page 224.   *Section 3: Descriptive Writing*   45

Complex Sentences

Another way to vary your writing is to use complex sentences. Remember that a compound sentence has two complete thoughts that are connected by a conjunction.

A **complex sentence** has two parts. It has one complete or **independent** thought and one incomplete or **subordinate** thought. Each part is called a **clause**. The independent clause has a subject and a predicate. It can stand alone. A subordinate clause cannot stand alone. A subordinate clause may come before or after an independent clause in a complex sentence.

Example

Wherever you go, you will see tall buildings.
You will see tall buildings wherever you go.

Use complex sentences to show how ideas are related and to make your writing more interesting.

Many subordinate clauses begin with a connecting word called a **subordinating conjunction**. Here are some examples.

after	although	as	before	because	if	since
unless	whenever	until	when	whatever	while	

Exercise Complete the paragraph with the correct subordinating word or words from the choices listed above the paragraph.

after	as though	because	if	unless
as soon as	when	whenever	whichever	even if

_____ you have a chance, you should take a drive to the mountains. Go on a
1

sunny day, _____ you can really appreciate the scenery. _____
2   3

you go, don't forget to take your camera. _____ you go in the fall, you will see the
4

spectacular autumn colors. The reds and golds light up the forest _____ it were on
5

fire. Follow the signs, _____ they point out the best route. _____
6   7

you get lost, you will still enjoy the day. _____ you are in a hurry, don't worry
8

about it. _____ way you go, you can get back to the highway. _____
9   10

one trip, you'll want to go back every year.

For more practice on complex sentences, turn to pages 198–199.

Check your answers on page 224.

Using Words in a Series

Another way to vary your sentence structure is to use a series of adjectives, noun phrases, or verb phrases.

Example	**Adjectives**	The ballpark was noisy. The ballpark was crowded. The ballpark was hot.
	Series	The ballpark was noisy, crowded, and hot.
	Nouns	The living room had a picture window. The living room had wood floors. The living room had a view of the park.
	Series	The living room had a picture window, wood floors, and a view of the park.
	Verbs	The car spun around. It hit a tree. The car landed in a ditch.
	Series	The car spun around, hit a tree, and landed in a ditch.

Exercise Revise each group of sentences into one sentence that uses adjectives, nouns, or verbs in a series. Omit the words that are not needed. Use commas between three or more words or phrases in a series.

1. The bus driver signaled.
   She turned into the traffic.
   She slowly made her way along the street.

   _____

   _____

2. Jose has a red car.
   It has bucket seats.
   It has chrome trim.

   _____

   _____

3. The sofa was old.
   The sofa was plaid.
   The sofa had worn-out cushions.

   _____

   _____

Application

Write a Descriptive Essay

Put together all the things you have learned about descriptive writing. Apply what you have learned by writing a descriptive essay on the following topic:

My Favorite Movie Character

As you write, make sure you follow the **Writing Process**. The steps are reviewed below.

Prewriting

Define Your Topic. The subject of your essay is your favorite movie character. The character you select is your topic.

1. Make a list of several movie characters you like.
2. Think about each character on your list. Get a clear picture of him or her in your mind.
3. Think of three things you can describe about the character such as personality, what the character did, and what he or she looked like. Don't limit yourself to these. Use your imagination in deciding what you want to write about the character.
4. If you cannot think of at least three things about the character, cross off the name. Select another character to write about.

Identify Your Audience and Purpose. Assume your audience is a group of people who are similar to you in their taste in movies. You are telling them about this character because you think that, after reading your description, they will want to see the movie your character is in.

Develop Main Ideas. List or make an idea map of the main ideas you want to cover in your essay.

Organize Your Ideas. List the descriptive details under each main point, or make an idea map to organize the main ideas you want to cover.

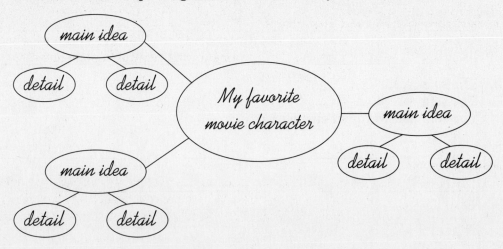

Writing the First Draft

Write the Topic Sentence. Try writing several topic sentences until you have a strong one that will make the reader want to continue reading.

Develop Supporting Details. Make sure that each main point starts a new paragraph. Each paragraph should begin with a topic sentence.

Write the Conclusion. Develop a strong concluding paragraph that goes with the rest of the essay.

Editing/Revising

Review. Read the entire essay once to see if you accomplished what you set out to do.

Edit/Revise. Read each paragraph carefully, and revise your work using the Editing Checklist on page 24. In addition to the items on the general editing checklist, check to see that you followed the specific guidelines for descriptive writing that you just learned:

- [ ] Did you use descriptive details?
- [ ] Did you use precise words?
- [ ] Did you use sensory details?
- [ ] Did you use figurative language?
- [ ] Did you use adjectives and adverbs?
- [ ] Did you vary your sentence structure?

Writing the Final Draft

Proofread. After you have completed all the necessary revisions, reread the essay. Check for correct spelling, punctuation, and neatness. Use the proofreader's marks on page 26 to correct any errors you find. Rewrite or retype your work if necessary.

Sharing Your Final Draft

Publish. Read your essay to a partner or have someone read it. Ask this person if your message was clear. Ask someone else to read the essay just for enjoyment.

File. Save the essay and your notes in your notebook or portfolio for your future reference.

Apply

For further practice in descriptive writing, go to your Personal Writing Notebook. Write a paragraph each day that describes something to someone else. If you need an idea, use one of the ideas below.

1. a car
2. a party
3. a friend

Explanatory Writing

Elements of Explanatory Writing

Explanatory writing explains, informs, or gives directions. It relates ideas and facts. Most of the writing that you do every day is explanatory writing. Telephone messages and travel directions are explanatory writing, and so are job applications and insurance claims. You can also find explanatory writing in textbooks, newspapers, and magazines.

Explanatory writing contains clear and complete facts. Good writers use precise words and arrange their ideas to help the reader follow the point. Read the two telephone messages below and decide which one is clearer.

Example

Mr. Rice,

Call Barbara Slade because she won't be in.

Luis

Mr. Rice,

Barbara Slade called to say that she cannot be at the store today. She said that her mother is ill, and she would like you to call her when you have time. She called at 9:00. Her number is 555-4391.

Raoul

1. List three facts missing from the first message.

_____

_____

_____

2. What two facts are out of order in the first message?

_____

_____

The first message is missing three important facts. The writer does not say why Barbara will be absent from work, when she called, and how Mr. Rice can reach her. There are also two facts out of order. First, the writer asks Mr. Rice to call Barbara Slade. This does not make sense, because the writer has not yet said that Barbara will be absent from work. The second message first explains <u>when</u> Barbara will be absent and then gives her excuse. The writer also gives the time Barbara called and her telephone number.

Read the following explanatory paragraph that tells how laughter can help you live longer.

Example

Some doctors think that laughter can be good for you. They found that laughing reduces stress and high blood pressure. A good laugh has the same effect as mild exercise. Both can double your pulse rate and blood pressure. Laughter also tones your muscles. This is because muscles contract during laughter. Some doctors even think that laughing sends chemicals to the brain that make you feel good. The facts are not all known, but we do know a good laugh can't hurt!

Time-order Transition Words

One way to explain your ideas clearly is to include transition words in your paragraphs. **Transition words** connect ideas. They signal ways that ideas are linked. **Time-order transition words**, for example, show the order of ideas. Common time-order transition words are listed below.

first	second	third	fourth
next	then	last	after
before	soon	later	during
meanwhile	when	while	earlier

Example

Transition word:	First, go north on Main Street for two miles.
No transition word:	Go north on Main Street for two miles.
Transition word:	Next, turn left onto King Street.
No transition word:	Turn left onto King Street.
Transition word:	Finally, take a left by the park.
No transition word:	Take a left by the park.

Exercise Write time-order transition words in the passage below. Use each of these words once: *when, meanwhile, second, last, then, first.*

_____, go north to the corner. _____, turn right at the food

store. _____ look for the sign for Smith Street. _____ you see the

sign, walk a block more. _____ turn left. _____, stop at the dress

shop. Our apartment is on the second floor.

Guided Writing Below is a list of directions. Link the sentences by adding time-order transition words to make the directions clearer. Begin with the word *first*.

Walk one block to Price Street.	You will see the post office.
You will pass the gas station.	There is a bank.
Turn left.	Walk four more blocks.
Turn right at the train tracks.	We are the third house on the right.

_____

_____

_____

Transition Words in "How-to" Writing

Time-order transition words help link ideas in explanatory paragraphs that give directions. Time-order transition words are also used in "how-to" papers. "How-to" papers explain how things are made or done. Read the paragraph below about how to save energy. Notice that the writer uses time-order transition words to join the steps.

Example First, turn off unnecessary lights. Second, turn down the heat. Then put on a sweater. Soon you will not feel cold. Third, use a fan in the summer. Last, cover windows with drapes and shades. They help keep out drafts. Before you know it, you will have saved a lot of energy!

Exercise A Write time-order transition words in the blanks in the passage below. Use each of these words once: *next, during, after, second, last, then, first.*

_____, the peanuts are shelled. _____, they are sorted for size and value.

_____, they are roasted. _____ they are cooked, the red outer skin is removed.

_____ the nut is split and the small piece called the "heart" is taken off. The heart makes

the peanut butter sour. _____, the nuts are mashed. _____ the last step of

mashing, workers add honey, sugar, and salt.

Exercise B The sentences below are out of order. Number the seven sentences in time order. Write the number of each sentence in the blank.

_____ Next, I have a cup of tea and a piece of toast. _____ When I wake up, I jog for half an

hour. _____ Before I leave, I call my friend. _____ While I eat, I watch the news. _____ Third, I get

dressed. _____ Last, we meet on the street. _____ Second, I take a bath.

Grammar: Verb Tenses

Verbs are words that show action. Verbs are used to show time in a sentence. Verbs show a change in time by changing form. Verbs can change their endings, change form wholly, or add a helping word. English has six verb tenses. There are three simple tenses and three perfect tenses. The **simple tenses** show present, past, and future time.

Example

Present tense:	I <u>call</u> my friend daily.	She <u>is</u> my friend.
Past tense:	You <u>smiled</u> at me yesterday.	They <u>gave</u> a party.
Future tense:	He <u>will work</u> late tonight.	We <u>shall call</u> home.

The three **perfect tenses** show actions that have ended or that will end soon. They also can show the effect of these actions.

Example

Present perfect:	My friend <u>has offered</u> to help me.
Past perfect:	The storm <u>had ended</u> when the power went off.
Future perfect:	I <u>will have been</u> here three days by Tuesday.

Exercise A ◢ Identify the tense of each of the underlined verbs in the sentences below. Write <u>past</u>, <u>present</u>, or <u>future</u> in the blank.

_____ 1. We <u>will give</u> a party after work today.

_____ 2. Marge <u>buys</u> chips, dips, fruit, and soda.

_____ 3. I <u>called</u> all our friends last night.

Exercise B ◢ Circle the best way to correct the underlined part of each sentence.

1. We <u>has grown</u> plants on the porch since last year.

   (1) have grown
   (2) will grow
   (3) grew
   (4) grows

2. Before you came home, I <u>have cleaned</u> up.

   (1) had cleaned
   (2) will clean
   (3) cleaning
   (4) cleans

3. Charles <u>did visited</u> his aunt.

   (1) visiting
   (2) has visited
   (3) have visited
   (4) visit

4. Steve <u>has swum</u> across the lake before you came.

   (1) swimming
   (2) had swum
   (3) will be swimming
   (4) swim

For more practice on verb tenses, turn to pages 182–183.

Check your answers on page 225.   *Section 4: Explanatory Writing*   53

Grammar: Writing Clear Sentences

You saw that using the wrong verb tense can make a sentence unclear. Placing sentence parts in the wrong place or leaving out words can also confuse the reader.

Words in the wrong place. Sentences are unclear when the writer puts describing words in the wrong place. Place describing words as close as possible to the part of the sentence they describe.

For example: John saw the train passing through the open window. The train did not pass through the open window. The phrase "through the open window" should be closer to the word it describes, saw. Move the phrase so the sentence reads: Through the open window, John saw the train passing.

Exercise A ◆ Some sentences have describing words in the wrong place. Circle the sentences that are wrong.

1. Save a room for the couple with a bath.

2. I found a letter in the mailbox that is not mine.

3. To get to the plant, we went nearly ten miles.

4. We bought a cat for my son we call Fluff.

Leaving out words. What is wrong with the next sentence? Coming up the stairs, the clock struck one. A clock cannot come up the stairs. The sentence does not say who did the action. There are two ways to correct the sentence.

Correct: Coming up the stairs, he heard the clock strike one.

Correct: As he was coming up the stairs, the clock struck one.

Exercise B ◆ Circle the best way to correct each sentence.

1. When driving, a fatal crash was seen.

    (1) When driving a fatal crash, we saw it.

    (2) A fatal crash, when driving, was seen.

    (3) When driving, we saw a fatal crash.

    (4) A fatal crash was seen when driving.

2. While passing a large rock, a noise made me jump.

    (1) While I was passing a large rock, a noise made me jump.

    (2) While a large rock was passing, a noise made me jump.

    (3) A noise made me pass a large rock.

    (4) While a large rock was passed, a noise made me jump.

For more practice on clear writing, turn to page 200.

Check your answers on page 225.

Grammar: Parallel Sentence Structure

Your writing will be clearer if you put all the ideas in a sentence in the same form. **Parallel structure** is a way to join equal and linked words and phrases. Use parallel adjectives, nouns, verbs, and adverbs in a list.

Example

Parallel: TV is good for <u>news</u>, <u>movies</u>, and <u>sports</u>. (nouns)
Not parallel: TV is good for <u>news</u>, <u>movies</u>, and <u>to watch sports</u>.

Parallel: The room was <u>clean</u>, <u>nearby</u>, and <u>low-priced</u>. (adjectives)
Not parallel: The room was <u>clean</u>, <u>nearby</u>, and <u>did not cost a lot</u>.

Parallel: The cat likes to <u>sleep</u>, <u>scratch</u>, and <u>eat</u>. (verbs)
Not parallel: The cat likes <u>to sleep</u>, <u>scratch</u>, and <u>eating</u>.

Parallel: For an interview, dress <u>neatly</u>, <u>carefully</u>, and <u>plainly</u>. (adverbs)
Not parallel: For an interview, dress <u>neatly</u>, <u>carefully</u>, and <u>plain</u>.

Exercise ◤ Some sentences below are not parallel in structure. Circle any correct sentences.

1. Mr. Paul promised me a good job and to pay me a fair wage.

2. Hard workers are intense, driven, and carefully.

3. My friend is kindly, friendly, and resting.

4. Cleaning up a little every day is better than saving the mess for the weekend.

5. They like watching football, playing baseball, and to shop.

Guided Writing ◤ Practice writing parallel sentences. Correct each of these sentences.

1. It is good for people to run, swim, and go jogging.

   _____

2. Running, for example, helps you stay fit and be in good health.

   _____

3. Swimming can help in toning your muscles and to lower your blood pressure.

   _____

4. You can start by walking a block a day and to eat good food.

   _____

5. Exercise can help you look better, be stronger, and wise.

   _____

For more practice on parallel structure, turn to pages 196–197.

Check your answers on page 225.

Developing Explanatory Essays

Recall that explanatory essays explain, inform, or give directions. To write a clear essay, you must develop your ideas in a way the reader can follow. One good way to develop an essay is first to state your main idea. Then support the main idea with clear examples and details. Read these two examples. Which is better?

Example   There are a lot of stories of roaches. Most of these stories are true. Many of us get upset when we hear these stories. They can get you angry. I have heard a lot of these stories. People pass these stories to each other. That is why there are so many stories about roaches.

Example   Few insects are harder to kill than roaches. They can live nearly a month without food. They can go two weeks without water. Almost no place is safe from them. They can crawl through a crack as thin as a dime. They are not picky about food. They eat our kind of food, as well as glue, hair, and paper. If you move to catch a roach, it will run away in less than half a second. A roach can stand still for days. It can even fly. No wonder it is so hard to kill roaches!

Example 2 is better because this writer uses details and examples to develop the point that roaches are hard to kill. Example 1 says the same thing over and over but does not give any clear support for the point. Use this chart to help you think of ways to develop your essay:

Details
Senses (looks, smells, tastes, feels, sounds)
Examples
Names (of things, people, places)
Numbers (amounts, value, prices)
Reasons (why things turned out as they did)

This chart of details (SENNR) can help you think of ways to develop your essay. You do not have to put all these items in every essay, but you may if you wish. The details do not have to be listed in this order. If you use many of these items, though, your writing will better inform your reader and explain your point.

Exercise   Put an X in the blank next to each sentence that is specific.

_____ 1.   A full-grown brown bear can weigh more than one thousand pounds, stand twelve feet tall on its back legs, and outrun a horse.

_____ 2.   I have never seen a bear in my life, and I hope I never do!

_____ 3.   The cool water flowed over my open palm, and the sun beat down on my hair.

_____ 4.   The day was hot.

_____ 5.   The fierce "killer bees" came into this country from Brazil in the mid-1950s.

_____ 6.   You can learn a lot from bees and the way they live.

_____ 7.   My mother was born in St. Kitts in a neat wood cabin with a dirt floor.

_____ 8.   In the heat, the swirls of dust and gas collect near the roof of the cave.

Guided Writing ■ Complete each sentence with a specific SENNR detail.

1. The place I feel most at home is _____

2. Getting a good job depends on _____

3. One way to stay healthy is to _____

4. After work, I like to _____

5. One of my problems is _____

6. The game was good because _____

7. When I think of my past, I recall _____

8. One reason people give up smoking is _____

9. One of my strengths is _____

10. One of my hobbies is _____

Journal Writing ■ For each topic below, write four details you could use to develop the topic into an essay. Refer back to the SENNR chart on page 56 for types of details. Write in your Personal Writing Notebook.

1. The things we throw out say a lot about the way we live.

2. How to travel by bus

3. The problems with junk food

4. How to go on a diet

5. What dreams tell us

Application

Write an Explanatory Essay

Apply what you have learned about explanatory writing by writing an explanatory essay on this topic:

A Skill I Perform Well

As you write, make sure you follow the **Writing Process.** The steps are reviewed below.

Prewriting

Define Your Topic. The subject of your essay is a skill you perform well. The skill you pick to write about is your topic.

1. First, list several skills that you perform well.

2. Read your list. Think about each skill you wrote. Get a clear picture of each skill in your mind.

3. Think of three things you could explain about each skill, such as how you learned it, what makes you good at it, and what others say about your skill. If you cannot list at least three things about a skill, cross it off your list. Select another skill to write about.

4. Pick the skill you know the most about, the one you feel you can write about the best.

Identify your Audience and Purpose. Suppose your audience is a group of people who share your background but do not know a lot about your skill. Your purpose is to explain your skill to them.

Develop Main Ideas. List or make a map of the main ideas you want to cover in your essay.

Organize Your Ideas. Arrange your ideas in a way that will help you best make your point. If you are writing directions, list your steps in the order they must be done. If your essay explains or informs, list your ideas from the most important to the least important.

Writing the First Draft

Write the Topic Sentence. Try writing several topic sentences until you have one that will grab your reader's interest and state your topic best.

Develop Supporting Details. As you write details, keep in mind the five kinds: senses, examples, names, numbers, and reasons. Use as many of these types as you can.

Write the Conclusion. Write a strong ending that ties up all the points you made. Do not bring up any new points here.

Editing/Revising

Review. Read the entire essay for sense to make sure you accomplished what you set out to do.

Edit/Revise. Read each paragraph carefully, and revise your work using the Editing Checklist on page 24. Also check to see that you followed the guidelines for explanatory writing that you just learned:

☐ Did you use time-order transition words?

☐ Did you use the correct verb tenses?

☐ Did you write clear sentences?

☐ Did you use parallel structure?

☐ Did you develop your ideas?

Writing the Final Draft

Proofread. When you have finished your revisions, check for correct spelling and punctuation. Use the proofreader's marks on page 26 to correct any errors you find. Rewrite or retype your work if necessary.

Sharing Your Final Draft

Publish. Read to a partner or have someone read your final essay. Ask this person if your message was clear. Then ask someone else to read the essay just for pleasure.

File. Save the essay and notes in your notebook or portfolio for your future reference.

Apply

For further practice writing explanatory essays, go to your Personal Writing Notebook. Each day write a paragraph that explains something. If you need an idea, use one below.

1. Cooking dinner

2. Fixing a leak

3. Changing a tire

4. Winning at bowling

Persuasive Writing

Elements of Persuasive Writing

The purpose of **persuasive writing** is to convince the reader to agree with your point of view. When you write a persuasive essay, choose your words with care. Avoid words that distort your meaning or that might insult the readers. Convince your readers by giving them facts, opinions, and reasons that relate to the point you are discussing. Good newspaper ads, letters to the editor, and editorials use these methods.

The first step in writing a persuasive essay is to select a topic that can be argued. For example, no one is likely to disagree with the position that children need to be cared for. But people <u>will</u> argue about how to reach this goal. Should children be in day-care centers or at home with their parents? This is a topic that can be the basis for a persuasive essay.

Next, think about how to appeal to your readers. There are three main ways to persuade people in writing. You can: (1) appeal to their reason; (2) appeal to their emotions; and (3) appeal to their ethics (sense of right and wrong). Below is an appeal to reason.

Example
                          The Plus Side of Failure

Failure is a better teacher than success. Unlike success, failure can be a chance for you to grow. Success makes you repeat what you have done; failure can make you change. Looking back at a failed job interview, for example, can help you correct some of your flaws. On the next interview, you might prepare better and be on time. Failure helps you learn to deal with the real world, too. It shows you that you can have a good time even if you don't win, and that even if you don't get the prize at the party, you can enjoy yourself. It shows you how to master anger and defeat. Every person has the right to fail.

Guided Writing ■ The essay you just read appeals most to reason. On the lines below, write some sentences that could be added to this essay to make it appeal to emotions and ethics (right and wrong) as well.

1. appeal to emotions _____

   _____

2. appeal to ethics _____

   _____

Using Connecting Words

Use connecting words called **conjunctions** to join ideas. This helps your reader follow your line of thought. It makes your reader more willing to see that your point is solid. The words in the list below will help you make your point.

Connecting Words and Phrases

therefore	as a result	due to this
so	in short	in brief
in summary	finally	

Example

No connecting word: People have the most energy at 10:00 A.M. You should read and do other memory tasks at that time.

Connecting word: People have the most energy at 10:00 A.M. <u>Therefore</u>, you should read and do other memory tasks at that time.

No connecting word: Your body goes into an energy slump at 2:00 P.M. You should do easier tasks in the afternoon.

Connecting word: Your body goes into an energy slump at 2:00 P.M., <u>so</u> you should do easier tasks in the afternoon.

Exercise Fill in the blank with the connecting word that best joins the two thoughts in each sentence below.

1. Bran cereal and whole-grain bread are high in fiber. _____ , they are good choices for breakfast.
   In summary   **Finally**   **Therefore**

2. People react to coffee in many ways, _____ whether you should drink coffee is up to you.
   in summary   **in brief**   **so**

3. Walking, running, and jogging will give you more energy. _____ , any exercise that speeds up your heart rate is good.
   Finally   **In brief**   **Therefore**

4. _____ , avoid foods high in fat such as ice cream, peanuts, and candy.
   Due to this   **Finally**   **As a result**

Journal Writing Suppose that you have been upset because a friend drinks, smokes, or eats too much. In your Personal Writing Notebook, write a note to convince your friend to give up the bad habit. Link the sentences with connecting words to make your points more convincing.

Check your answers on page 226.

Writing Compare and Contrast Sentences

One good way to help persuade your readers to agree with your point of view is to write sentences that compare and contrast. To **compare** is to show how things are the same. To **contrast** is to show how things are <u>not</u> the same.

Example

Compare

The belt is the same price as the shoes.

The belt and the shoes match.

Contrast

The belt costs $5 less than the shoes.

The belt is a darker brown than the shoes.

Exercise Write *compare* if the sentence shows how two things are the same. Write *contrast* if the sentence shows how two things are not the same.

_____1. People who are out of work are less healthy than those with jobs.

_____2. A half cup of ice cream has the same fat content as ten peanuts.

_____3. Japan exports more cars to the U.S. than France does.

_____4. *As the World Turns* has more viewers than any other soap opera on TV.

Compare and contrast sentences make your point clearly when the ideas are smoothly joined. Here are some words and phrases you can use to link ideas that compare and contrast. Sometimes these words and phrases are linked with commas or with semicolons. Read the rules for using commas and semicolons on pages 151–154.

Words that compare: *and, same as, as*

Words that contrast: *but, yet, than, still, however, likewise, in the same way, in contrast to, at the same time, on the other hand*

Example

I like to shop on weekends <u>as</u> much <u>as</u> I like to shop during the week.
The stores are crowded; <u>however</u>, I can still buy what I need.

Guided Writing Complete each sentence with the linking word or phrase given to compare or contrast.

1. I liked the last movie I saw, but _____ .

2. The movie was as _____ .

3. The movie had great action scenes, yet _____ .

4. The movie told the ending in the first scene, in contrast to _____

Remember these three points when you write sentences that compare and contrast.

1. Avoid obvious statements. If you are writing about two books, for example, it would be pointless to write that both have words.

2. Stick to two subjects at a time. You cannot compare and contrast more than two topics in one sentence.

3. Select subjects that are members of the same group. For example, two athletes, two jobs, and two people are all similar enough to be good topics.

To compare and contrast, first make a list of the things the two subjects share. Here is a list someone wrote about how males and females learn:

How males learn	How females learn
Boys speak later than girls.	Girls learn speech first.
Boys stutter more.	Girls speak better.
Boys catch up by age eight.	Girls speak better from age ten.
Teenage boys do better on mazes.	Teenage girls do worse on mazes.
Men are better at mazes.	Women are better at language.

Here is how one writer used the list:

Example

  People wonder why men and women seem to do better at some tasks. Experts have proved some facts about male and female learning styles. First, girls learn to speak earlier and better than boys, and boys have more speech problems. Far more boys than girls stutter, for example. Boys catch up by age eight, though. From age ten on, girls again speak better than boys, and women do better than men on speech and language tasks. Meanwhile, teenage boys do better than teenage girls on tests with mazes. Later, men do better than women on mazes. Even after much research, no one can tell why there are these differences in males and females.

Guided Writing 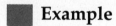 Write one sentence that compares and one that contrasts for each topic.

1. two friends

   compare _____

   contrast _____

2. two places you have lived

   compare _____

   contrast _____

Using Specific Versus Vague Language

It is important in all your writing to choose your words with care. In descriptive writing, precise words create an interesting word picture. In persuasive writing, specific words help show your reader the value of your point of view. Writing with vague words has little meaning. By using specific words in a phrase, you create a clear picture in your reader's mind.

Example

Vague: Many people work too hard.

Specific: The fifteen tool-and-die machinists at the Ace plant work ten hours a day, seven days a week.

The first sentence may seem to give you a fact, but look closely at the words. What does "many people" mean? What does "too hard" mean? The second sentence states the same idea with specific words.

Guided Writing Revise each sentence to make it more persuasive. Replace each underlined word with a more specific word or phrase.

1. **Vague:** Sabrina's new <u>dog</u> is <u>great</u>.

   Specific: _____

2. **Vague:** My leg was <u>hurt</u> in the crash.

   Specific: _____

3. **Vague:** Mr. Mori drives a <u>truck</u> <u>part-time</u>.

   Specific: _____

4. **Vague:** The <u>man</u> <u>went</u> to the boss's office for an answer.

   Specific: _____

5. **Vague:** They were <u>eating</u> candy in the next row and making <u>noise</u>.

   Specific: _____

Words and phrases often become vague through overuse. "Quick as a wink" and "good as gold" have become so well-known that readers skim over them. Replace these vague phrases with specific words.

Example

Vague	Specific
blind as a bat	very nearsighted
hit the ceiling	became visibly angry

Exercise ◆ Underline the vague phrase in each sentence.

1. We stayed friends through thick and thin.

2. Baseball is as American as Mom's apple pie.

3. The stamps are selling like hotcakes.

4. "This is a tried and true cure," the doctor said.

5. It's raining cats and dogs out today.

6. "I am sick and tired of your lateness," the boss said.

7. The old gum was as hard as nails.

8. The light breeze is as gentle as a lamb.

9. If you want to do well, you have to take the bull by the horns.

Guided Writing ◆ Replace each of the vague underlined phrases with more specific words.

1. **Vague:** I've had my ups and downs today.

   Specific: _____

2. **Vague:** "Now it's time to face the music," Mr. Wright said.

   Specific: _____

3. **Vague:** If you eat well, get enough rest, and have a good outlook, you will live to a ripe old age.

   Specific: _____

4. **Vague:** A summer cold is no tea party.

   Specific: _____

5. **Vague:** The fly was dead as a doornail.

   Specific: _____

Journal Writing ◆ Write a persuasive paragraph on one of the topics below. Use specific words to help convince your reader of your point.

Topic choices: Cigarettes should (should not) be declared illegal.

   The space program should (should not) be ended.

   There should (should not) be speed limits on American highways.

Check your answers on page 226.

Grammar: Subject-Verb Agreement

For sentences to be correct, subjects must match verbs. This means subjects and verbs must be in the same form. A singular subject must have a singular verb, and a plural subject must have a plural verb. To make subjects and verbs match or agree, follow these steps.

1. Find the subject in the sentence. The subject tells <u>who</u> or <u>what</u>.
2. See if the subject is singular (one) or plural (more than one).
3. If the subject is singular, add -s or -es to most verbs.
4. If the subject is plural, use the base form of most verbs.
5. *I* and *you* use the base form of the verb: *I think* (not *thinks*), *I eat* (not *eats*), *you think* (not *thinks*), *you eat* (not *eats*).

Example

| **singular subject:** | The <u>moon glows</u>. | <u>She is</u> busy. (verb: <u>to be</u>) |
| | <u>I want</u> to leave now. | <u>You laugh</u> a lot. |

| **plural subject:** | The <u>planets glow</u>. | <u>They were</u> busy. (verb: <u>to be</u>) |
| | My <u>friends want</u> to leave now. | <u>They laugh</u> a lot. |

Exercise A Circle the correct verb form in each sentence.

1. I (hope/hopes) the store will be open late.

2. We will (takes/take) the gift to the party later.

3. The egg (has/have) a strange taste.

4. She (works/work) hard at her new job.

Words Between the Subject and Verb

Words that come between the subject and the verb do not affect agreement.

Example

The box of gifts contains food, clothing, and books.

The subject is *box*, not *gifts*. The verb is *contains*. The words *of gifts* that come between the subject and the verb do not change agreement.

Exercise B First circle the subject in each sentence. Then underline the correct verb. Cross out any words that come between the subject and the verb.

1. A salad with extra carrots (is/are) my usual lunch.

2. The people in the back of the crowd (needs/need) to be heard.

3. Ned, with his three dogs, (run/runs) around the block after work.

4. The leader of the unions (say/says) profits are down this year.

For more practice on subject-verb agreement, turn to page 186.

Check your answers on pages 226–227.

Grammar: And/Or

A **compound subject** has two parts joined by *and*, *or*, or *nor*. A compound subject joined by *and* needs a plural verb. For a compound subject joined by *or* or *nor*, the verb must agree with the subject that is closer to the verb.

◆ Example

Plural verb:	A hot dog <u>and</u> a soda <u>cost</u> $2.
Singular verb:	A hot dog <u>or</u> a soda <u>costs</u> $1.
Plural verb:	The bus <u>and</u> subway <u>stop</u> here.
Singular verb:	<u>Neither</u> the bus <u>nor</u> the subway <u>stops</u> here.

Exercise A ◆ Write the correct form of the verb in each sentence.

1. The roof and the window _____ when it rains. (leak)

2. Marie or Juan _____ me a ride to work on Thursdays. (give)

3. My boss and I _____ lunch to work every day. (bring)

Singular and Plural Words

When groups of people act as one unit, the noun that refers to the unit is singular. Examples: *class, team, staff, crew, troop, jury, public, group.*

Pronoun subjects are a different case. Some are always singular, some are always plural, and some can be either. Refer to this chart:

Singular	Plural	Singular or Plural	
words with *one*: someone, no one	several	all	any
words with *other*: another, other	few	some	part
words with *body*: somebody, nobody	both	none	half
words with *thing*: nothing, something	most		
other words: each, either, much, neither			

◆ Example

Singular	Plural
<u>No one</u> <u>gives</u> a better haircut.	<u>Few</u> people here <u>drive</u> to work.
<u>Some</u> of the cake <u>is</u> eaten.	<u>Some</u> of the guests <u>have</u> <u>left</u>.

Exercise B ◆ Decide if the verb used in each of the following sentences is correct. If so, write *C* in the blank. If not, write the correct form of the verb.

_____1. Americans spends more than $30 billion a year on fast food.

_____2. Many people eats burgers and fries nearly every night.

_____3. The public love fast food.

_____4. We takes it home at least once a week, as a matter of fact.

For more practice on subject-verb agreement, turn to page 186.

Check your answers on page 227.

Supporting the Main Idea

Persuasive essays try to make a reader agree with the writer's point of view on a topic that can be argued. To support your main idea, give your reader facts, opinions, and reasons.

Facts. A fact is a statement that is true. Facts can be proved by testing or observing. Good writers use facts to support the main idea of their essays. Here is how one writer used facts in a letter to the editor.

Example

Today, as I was walking to work, I saw a newspaper in the street. It caught my eye, and I bent down to pick it up. I lifted a corner of the paper and found a thin cat mewing with hunger. I could not leave the cat on the street, so I took it to an animal shelter for care. The man in charge told me that was the tenth animal that had been dropped off that day. In fact, more than five hundred cats and one thousand dogs are dropped off every year at animal shelters in our town alone. The shelter does not have the money to feed and treat this many animals, so more than half must be killed. I hope that the cat I left there today will live and that others like it will not suffer from lack of care. Please give what you can to the local animal shelter.

Opinions. An opinion is a point of view or belief that cannot be proved. Writers use opinions as well as facts to support their main ideas. Good writers back up their opinions with reasons. The next passage begins with the opinion that all child-care workers must be licensed by the state. As you read, look for the reasons the writer uses.

Example

Taking care of children is more difficult than many people realize. That is why all child-care workers should be licensed by the state. People who mind children in day-care centers or in their homes must be trained to watch for possible dangers and know how to prevent accidents. They also need to know how to get help fast. Specific courses should be given in how to feed and handle infants and small children. Child-care workers must also know how to choose safe toys and games for children, and how to help children get along with others.

Exercise Write *O* if the sentence is an opinion or *F* if the sentence is a fact.

_____1. Main Street is ten blocks long.

_____2. Main Street has the best shopping around.

_____3. Cigarette smoking is America's worst health problem.

_____4. Men have shorter hair than women.

_____5. Juan's sister has three children.

_____6. The federal government of the United States consists of three branches.

Reasons. You know that supporting the main idea with reasons will help convince your reader of your point of view. Writers must be sure that the reasons they give make sense. Avoid the following three ways that writers may confuse their reasons.

<u>Jumping to Conclusions</u>. Reasons fall apart when writers reach a decision without having supplied enough facts. This is called *jumping to a conclusion*. Where is the error in the following example?

> Our union will not support the new overtime rules. I know this because I spoke to Mike at lunch.

By speaking to Mike, the writer draws the conclusion that the entire union will not support the new overtime rules. Just speaking to one union member is not enough reason to reach this conclusion.

<u>Quoting False Experts</u>. Reasons are also weak when writers rely on false experts. Make sure the person you quote as an expert truly is an expert in that field and that he or she can be fair. Read the example below.

> Dr. O. Malhot, an eye doctor, says that no one should eat more than five ounces of fat per day.

Dr. Malhot is an expert on eyes, not diet. Quote a person who works in the study of diet to make this point.

<u>Switching Cause and Effect</u>. **Causes** are the reasons things happen, and **effects** are the results. Writing is also weak when writers switch cause and effect. Here is an example.

> When parents do not keep their teenage kids at home at night, crimes such as theft and arson increase.

This is an error in cause and effect, because letting teenagers go out at night does not cause a rise in theft and arson.

Exercise ◗ For each item, name the kind of false reasoning: jumping to conclusions, quoting false experts, or switching cause and effect.

_____ 1. The local radio station never plays good records. There is nothing good on the radio at all.

_____ 2. Shaun says that Flair makes the best slacks. He knows this because he saw a hockey star wear this brand.

_____ 3. Marc used to be a good worker. Since he started to dating Lucy, his work has been poor. If he were to stop dating her, his work would improve.

_____ 4. I eat bran and fruit every day. That is why I never get colds.

Check your answers on page 227.

Application

Write a Letter to the Editor

Put together all you have learned about persuasive writing. Apply what you have learned by writing a letter to the editor of the newspaper on this topic:

Taxes should (or should not) be raised on liquor, cigarettes, and luxury items.

As you write, make sure you follow the **Writing Process**. The steps are reviewed below.

Prewriting

Define Your Topic. The subject of your letter is whether taxes should be raised on some items. Your topic is the side you chose to argue.

1. First, list the pros and cons of raising taxes on these items. You can make two lists side by side, or put your ideas in chart form. List as many ideas as you can.

2. Read your list. Think about both sides of your argument. Which side makes more sense to you?

3. Think about which side of the topic you support. Why do you feel this way about the issue? Look at your list to see which side has more facts, opinions, and reasons to support.

4. Pick the side you feel strongly about, the one for which you have more facts, opinions, and reasons to use in your letter.

Identify Your Audience and Purpose. You are writing to the editor of the newspaper and to the people who read the newspaper. Your purpose is to persuade the newspaper editor and readers to support your side of the issue. After they read your letter, they may change their minds about the issue, or at least think more about it.

Develop Main Ideas. List the main ideas you want to cover in your letter.

Organize Your Ideas. Arrange your ideas in a way that will help you best make your point. Do not ignore the side of the issue that you do not support. Instead, you can put all the points against your topic first. Write about each of these points one at a time to show how they are not valid. Then present the points that support your side.

Writing the First Draft

Write the Topic Sentence. Write several topic sentences to find the one that will grab your reader's eye and state your topic best.

Develop Supporting Details. Use facts, opinions, and reasons to persuade your reader of your point. Be sure that your writing does not jump to conclusions, quote false experts, or switch cause and effect.

Write the Conclusion. Write a strong ending that ties up all the points you argued. Do not bring up any new issues here. Try to save one very strong point for the end.

Editing/Revising

Review. Read the entire letter to make sure you did what you set out to do. Ask yourself: "If I were reading this letter in a newspaper, would my ideas change?"

Edit/Revise. Read each paragraph carefully, and revise your work using the Editing Checklist on page 24. In addition to the items on the checklist, be sure you followed the guidelines for persuasive writing that you just learned:

- ☐ Did you write compare and contrast sentences?
- ☐ Did you use specific, not vague, language?
- ☐ Did you replace overused words and phrases with fresh language?
- ☐ Do all your subjects and verbs agree?
- ☐ Did you use connecting words to link your ideas?
- ☐ Did you support your ideas with facts, opinions, and reasons?

Writing the Final Draft

Proofread. When you have finished your revisions, reread your letter. Check for correct spelling, punctuation, and neatness. Use the proofreader's marks on page 26 to correct any errors you find. Rewrite or retype your work if necessary.

Sharing Your Final Draft

Publish. Read to a partner or have someone read your letter. Ask this person if your point was clear. Discuss what the person sees as the letter's weak and strong points. Then ask someone else to read the letter just for pleasure. You may wish to send it to a newspaper.

File. Save the essay in your notebook or portfolio for your future reference.

Apply

For further practice in writing persuasive essays, go to your Personal Writing Notebook. Each day write a paragraph that convinces your reader to agree with your point of view. Possible topics include:

1. The drug laws should (should not) be changed.
2. Local taxes should (should not) be raised.

Letter Writing

Personal Letters and Business Letters

People make phone calls far more often than they write letters. Still, at times it is necessary to write letters. There are two main types of letters: personal letters and business letters.

A **personal letter** is written to someone you know. The purpose may be to keep in touch with a friend or relative in another city. It may be to say thank you for a gift or a favor, or to invite someone to visit. Other reasons for writing personal letters are to ask someone to do something or to give someone information.

Example

> 140 W. 116 St., Apt. 10
> New York, NY 10026
> July 25, 1992
>
> Dear Toni,
>
> How are you? I hope you're enjoying the summer. The weather here has been miserable. I would love to leave the city for a few days to visit you and Vernon. I will be able to take some time off in a couple of weeks. Please write or call to let me know if that would be a good time for me to visit. I would have called you, but my phone bill last month was high. See you soon.
>
> Love,
> Yolanda

Journal Writing 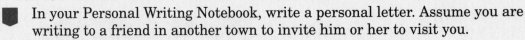 In your Personal Writing Notebook, write a personal letter. Assume you are writing to a friend in another town to invite him or her to visit you.

Check your answer on page 227.

Writing personal letters is a matter of choice. You can choose to make a phone call rather than write. Business letters are a different matter. A **business letter** is usually written to a company or to a person who works for some type of organization. You may or may not know the person to whom you are writing.

The purpose of a business letter is to communicate a specific message and to have a written record of the message. In some cases a business letter is written after a phone conversation to confirm a spoken agreement. Four common types of business letters are listed below:

Letter of Request. To ask that something be done, to get information, to place an order, to issue an invitation. See the example below.

Letter of Reply or Confirmation. To respond to a message (written or oral) or request, or to create a written record of a spoken agreement

Follow-up Letter. To remind someone of something, to thank someone, or to provide additional information

Letter to Conduct Business. In a business, writing letters or memos may be a part of the job.

 Example

Letter of Request:

> Overland Medical Center
> 39000 South Oak Drive, Overland Park, MA 00990
> 404-555-3200
>
>   October 6, 1992
>
> Mr. Antonio Torres
> 201 Lowell Avenue
> Overland Park, MA 00910
>
> Dear Mr. Torres:
>
> Thank you for your letter inquiring about our medical technician training program at Overland Medical Center. We will be accepting applications for our winter program as of November 1. Please send me a copy of your resume and a cover letter stating your reason for wanting to join the program. We will review your application and get back to you as soon as possible.
>
>   Sincerely,
>
>   *Joyce Hawkins*
>
>   Joyce Hawkins
>   Human Resources Dept.

Journal Writing ■ Practice writing a business letter by replying to Ms. Hawkins. State that your resume is enclosed, and give a couple of reasons why you would like to be admitted to the training program for medical technicians at Overland Medical Center. Write the letter in your Personal Writing Notebook.

Formal and Informal Styles

Personal letters are written in an **informal style.** They may be handwritten instead of typed. Writing in an informal style also means that the writing may sound very much like the way you speak. Business writing requires a **formal style.** Since you may not know the person to whom you are writing, do not address him or her in a familiar way. A business letter should directly state the information in a pleasant but reserved way.

■ **Example**

Informal Style:	Dear John, I've been calling you for two weeks and you haven't called me back.
Formal Style:	Dear Mr. Smith: I have called your office several times, but I have not been able to reach you.
Informal Style:	Mary, I'm busy on Friday, so we'll have to change our lunch plans. Can you make it on Monday instead? Call me.
Formal Style:	Dear Mrs. Yazzie: Thank you for your invitation to the Community Center luncheon on Friday. I am sorry that I will not be able to attend. Please send me the date of the next luncheon, and I will be sure to put it on my calendar.

Guided Writing ■ Practice informal and formal writing styles by writing a few sentences for each situation described below.

1. **Informal:** Write a note to your friend Kareem, asking him to return the $5.00 you loaned him.

_____

_____

_____

2. **Formal:** Ask your boss, Ms. Chen, for approval to take five days of vacation.

_____

_____

_____

_____

Formatting Letters

Personal letters are written on plain paper, note paper, or stationery. Business letters are usually written on plain paper or letterhead. **Letterhead** is stationery that is printed with a company name and address at the top. For example, see the letterhead on page 78.

All personal and business letters must conform to a specific format. **Format** refers to the way the parts of the letter are set up on the page. Setting up letter parts is called **formatting.** Below is a list of the parts.

1. **Return address.** The writer's address is placed at the top above the date on plain paper or stationery.
2. **Date line.** Date on which the letter is written
3. **Inside address.** Address of the person to whom the letter is written
4. **Salutation.** Opening greeting such as *Dear Mr. Morales,*
5. **Message.** Contents or body of the letter
6. **Closing.** A parting phrase such as *Sincerely,* or *Very truly yours,* and the name of the writer. In a typewritten letter, the name is typed but is always signed by hand as well.

Example

Personal Letter:

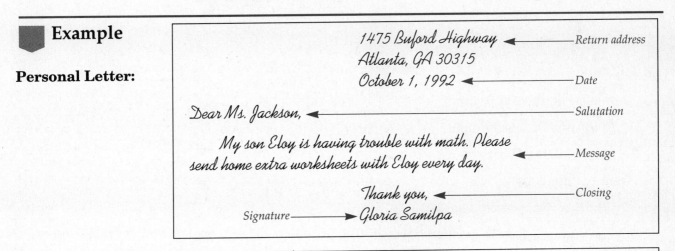

1475 Buford Highway ← Return address
Atlanta, GA 30315
October 1, 1992 ← Date

Dear Ms. Jackson, ← Salutation

My son Eloy is having trouble with math. Please send home extra worksheets with Eloy every day. ← Message

Thank you, ← Closing
Signature → Gloria Samilpa

Business Letter:

14201 Mendota ← Return address
Detroit, MI 48236
May 6, 1992 ← Date

Harper Hospital
Accounting Dept.
1100 Woodward Ave. ← Inside address
Detroit, MI 48230

Dear Mr. Zamora: ← Salutation

This letter will confirm our telephone conversation of May 5, 1992, concerning an error on the bill for my outpatient surgery on April 12. The hospital room charge of $225.50 should be taken off my bill, since I did not stay in the hospital overnight. ← Message

Sincerely,
Ben Davidson ← Closing with signature
Ben Davidson

Exercise ▇ Below are two unformatted letters: 1) a personal letter and 2) a business letter. For each letter, put a ring around the message. Then rewrite the remaining parts in their proper format.

1. P.O. Box 32 Eden Prairie, MN 55344 October 20, 1992 Dear Aunt Frances, Thanks for the beautiful sweaters! It gets really cold up here this time of year, so your timing was perfect. After living in Florida for so long, I had forgotten what cold weather feels like. Give my love to Uncle Harold. Tell him I'll visit soon. Your nephew, Danny

_____

_____

_____

_____

_____

2. 222 East 24th St. Philadelphia, PA 20035 June 14, 1992 Mr. Bernard Adams, Travelworld, 901 Harrison Avenue, Philadelphia, PA 20039 Dear Mr. Adams: Thank you for talking to me about the position in your word-processing unit. I learned a lot about the company. I think my skills would fit your needs. Our meeting made me eager to work at Travelworld. I look forward to hearing from you about the job. Sincerely, Elaine Evans

_____

_____

_____

_____

_____

_____

_____

_____

Check your answers on pages 227–228.

Grammar: Capitalization and Punctuation

Correct capitalization and punctuation are important in everything you write. Making sure that your writing is free of errors is most important in business writing. Your business letters create an impression of you in the mind of the reader. Because the reader may not know you, mistakes create a bad first impression, such as that you are careless or unskilled. However, very neat, error-free letters create a good first impression. Here are some rules of capitalization that will help you write error-free letters.

Example

Rule 1. Always capitalize the first word of a sentence.

Please send me a copy of your latest catalog.

Rule 2. Capitalize each part of a person's name.

Louise **G**uccione   Samuel **C.** **J**ohnston

Rule 3. Capitalize titles and abbreviations that come before and after people's names.

Mr. Zell D. Moore, **Jr.**   **Mrs.** Barbara Westmass   **Dr.** Katherine Lord

Rule 4. Capitalize words showing family relationships when they are used as a title or in place of a name.

Capital: **Aunt J**ane will not be able to go.
No Capital: My aunt will not be able to go.

Rule 5. Capitalize names of cities, states, and sections of the country.

City and state: **C**hicago, **I**llinois   Section: **M**idwest

Rule 6. Capitalize names of countries, languages, nationalities, religions, and regions of the world.

Country: **S**audi **A**rabia   Religion: **M**uslim   Nationality: **F**rench
Language: **A**rabic   Region: **M**iddle **E**ast

Rule 7. Capitalize names of streets, highways, bodies of water, buildings, monuments, and bridges.

Street: **M**ain **S**treet   Building: **E**mpire **S**tate **B**uilding
Highway: **N**ew **J**ersey **T**urnpike   Monument: **S**tatue of **L**iberty

Rule 8. Capitalize months, days, and holidays.

September   **W**ednesday   **T**hanksgiving

Rule 9. Capitalize names of companies and organizations.

Company: **A**dams-**C**larke **A**ssociates   Organization: **V**eterans **S**ociety

Exercise A ■ Rewrite each sentence with correct capital letters. Refer to the rules on page 77 when you need help.

1. last year I worked on senator smith's campaign.

_____

2. The campaign office was on fifth avenue in the chrysler building.

_____

3. The victory party was sponsored by the independent voters of america.

_____

4. The party was held at their building on the hudson river.

_____

5. laura washington, vice president of the organization, made a speech.

_____

Exercise B ■ Use proofreader's marks to correct each capitalization error in the letter below. The proofreader's mark to capitalize is: <u>a</u> = A.

> **Bradley Advertising Agency**
> **45 Capital Street**
> **Columbus, OH 30725**
>
> may 20, 1992
>
> supreme computer, inc.
> 958 alexander street
> river tower bldg.
> columbus, oh 30921
>
> dear mr. potter:
>
> my supervisor, doris healy, director of sales here at bradley associates, asked me to send you the enclosed brochure. the brochure gives details on the services our company provides to computer stores like yours. if you are interested in our services, please call me within the next ten days to take advantage of our free trial offer. the offer ends on may 31. we are closed next monday, due to the memorial day weekend.
>
> sincerely,
>
> *James Hobson*
>
> james hobson
> sales assistant

For more practice on capitalization, see pages 158–161.

Check your answers on page 228.

Grammar: Punctuation

Here are some helpful rules of punctuation.

Example

Rule 1. End a sentence with a period, question mark, or exclamation point.

The party was over too soon. How did you like the party?
The party was terrific!

Rule 2. Use a period after an abbreviation or an initial.

Sharon A. Kaufman   Co. (Company)   Inc. (Incorporated)

Rule 3. Use a comma after each item in a list of three or more items.

We need a new supply of red, green, and white labels.

Rule 4. Use a comma between the name of a city and state, and between the day and year in a date.

New Orleans, Louisiana   June 2, 1992

Rule 5. Use a comma after the salutation in a personal letter and after the closing of a personal or business letter. Use a colon after the salutation of a business letter.

Dear Toni,   Sincerely,   Dear Ms. Thomas:

Exercise Place correct punctuation marks in the letter below.

1670 Evergreen Road
Houston TX 80023
January 25 1992

Ms. Vanessa Lewis
Lewis and Evans Assoc
Houston TX 80025

Dear Ms Lewis
I attended your career planning workshop at the Valley College Library on December 15 1991
Your presentation was just what I needed to organize myself Would it be possible for you to send
me a resume writing worksheet Unfortunately, you ran out of handouts before you got to me

Sincerely
Joseph Wallach
Joseph Wallach

For more practice on punctuation, see pages 150–157.

Check your answers on page 228.

Organizing Business Letters

Paragraphs in business letters are organized the same as any other kind of writing. Each paragraph has a topic sentence followed by supporting details. However, there are a few tips that make business writing easier.

1. A business letter should not be more than one page unless absolutely necessary. Two to four paragraphs is usually long enough.

2. The topic sentence should directly state the point of the paragraph.

3. Paragraphs should be short, usually no more than three or four sentences. A paragraph with only one sentence is acceptable.

4. Supporting details do not always have to be written in paragraph form. If the information will be more clear, it is acceptable to list details.

5. The concluding paragraph should state what you expect to happen next and offer a polite thank-you.

Example

Universal Computer Company
509 Union Square
Lexington, KY 40027

March 1, 1992

Ms. Irma Salinas
Meeting Planner
Crown Plaza Hotel
1 City Plaza
Lexington, KY 40027

Dear Ms. Salinas:

Universal Computers would like to rent a meeting room in your hotel to hold a computer training program. The dates we would like to reserve are April 2–4 or April 9–11. We will need the room from 9:00 A.M. to 4:00 P.M. Below is a list of our specific needs.

Topic sentence directly states a request.

1. A room that will hold approximately twenty people.
2. Table space for ten computers.
3. Electrical wiring and outlets that will accommodate the equipment.
4. Refreshments for a morning and an afternoon break.

Details are listed in brief statements, not complete sentences.

Please let me know the cost of the items listed and the dates you can best serve our group. After I receive this information, I will call you to finalize the plans. Thank you for your help.

Conclusion states what will happen next and thanks the reader.

Sincerely,

Janice Adams

Janice Adams
Administrative Assistant

Write a reply to the following letter. Use the tips on page 80. Write the message only.

Family Day-Care Center
3300 North Beach Drive
Los Angeles, CA 90033
212-555-8899

September 23, 1992

Mr. Calvin Simpson
304 West End Blvd.
Los Angeles, CA 90011

Dear Mr. Simpson:

We are seriously considering your application for the position of administrative assistant at the Family Day-Care Center.

It is our policy to screen all applicants by checking their references. Would you please send me the names of two people we can contact regarding your past work experience and personal background? I need the name, address, telephone number, and a brief description of your relationship with each person.

As soon as we have this information, we can complete the processing of your application.

Sincerely,

George Walker

George Walker
Director, Human Resources

Your Reply (message only)

_____

_____

_____

_____

_____

_____

Application 1

Write a Letter Requesting Information

Apply what you have learned about writing a business letter. Write a letter requesting information. Follow the **Writing Process.** Assume that you are planning to take a vacation. You saw the following advertisement in a newspaper.

> Take a Trip to Paradise!
> Save $$$. Group rates available.
> Write for details of a once-in-a-lifetime
> VACATION DEAL!
> Address inquiries to Vacation Deal,
> P.O. Box 25, Grand Central Station,
> NY, NY 10021.

Prewriting

Write the topic, purpose, and audience of your letter.

Topic _____

Purpose _____

Audience _____

Develop Main Ideas. List or map the main ideas you will put in your letter. What information will you need about this vacation offer to decide if you are interested or not?

_____

_____

Organize Your Ideas. Write an outline or draw an idea map of your main ideas in your Personal Writing Notebook.

Writing the First Draft

In your Personal Writing Notebook, write a draft of your letter.

Format the Letter. Write your return address, the date, your inside address, and the salutation.

Write the Message. Follow the outline or map you wrote. Write the appropriate conclusion. Then write your closing, leaving space for your signature.

Editing/Revising

Review. Read the letter. Does it say what you want?

Edit/Revise. Use the Editing Checklist on page 24 to edit your first draft. In addition to the items on this list, check the formatting of your letter. Did you include the following letter parts?

- ☐ Return address
- ☐ Date line
- ☐ Inside address
- ☐ Salutation
- ☐ Message
- ☐ Closing

Did you have a problem with the salutation because you did not know the name of a particular person to address? Here are three ways to write the salutation:

> Dear Vacation Deal:
> Dear Sir or Madam:
> Dear Gentlepeople:

You may have seen the salutation To Whom It May Concern used on some letters. This salutation is outdated.

Writing the Final Draft

After correcting all the mistakes you found, write your final draft.

Proofread. Reread your final draft using the Proofreading Checklist on page 26 and the rules for capitalization and punctuation on page 77.

Sharing Your Final Draft

Publish. Share the final draft with a friend or someone whose opinion you value. Be sure to show this person the ad, so he or she can judge if you requested all the information you need.

File. Place the final draft and your notes in your notebook or portfolio for future reference.

Apply

Apply what you have learned about writing personal letters by writing a letter to a friend or relative. Use the **Writing Process** to prepare a draft of your letter. Write the draft in your Personal Writing Notebook. Write the final draft on stationery or notebook paper and mail it.

Write Letters for a Job Interview

Follow the **Writing Process** to write two letters in your Personal Writing Notebook. These letters can be used as models for specific letters you will write the next time you are job hunting.

Letter A: Letter of Request for a Job Interview

You may write a letter to apply for one of the jobs in the want ads below, or if you wish, bring in an ad for a job you want and write a letter of application for that job.

<table>
<tr><td>

Want Ad 1:

Security guards for warehouse

Day or night positions available. No experience required. Will train. Send letter of application to Mike Anderson, XYZ Packing Company, 655 Landers Avenue, Chicago, IL 60612.

</td><td>

Want Ad 2:

Retail Sales Clothing Store

Some experience preferred, but will train. Must be willing to work long hours & weekends. Send letter of application to Antonia Lucci, Rave Wear, Box 130, Sears Tower Bldg., Chicago, IL 60620.

</td></tr>
</table>

Prewriting

Define Your Topic. Decide which ad you want to answer. Think about the working hours, the amount of experience wanted, the neighborhood, and transportation requirements. The job in Want Ad 2 is downtown. The warehouse job in Want Ad 1 is in an industrial area. You cannot consider the salary for either of these jobs since neither ad mentions the pay.

Identify Your Audience and Purpose. Check the ad to see if the letter is to go to a specific person. If not, use the salutation *Dear Sir* or *Madam:* and assume you are writing to a director of personnel. Your purpose is to get the job you want.

Develop the Main Ideas. Write the ideas you want to put in your letter. Why are you interested in applying for the job? What qualifications do you have for the job? What do you want the person reading the letter to do after he or she receives your application?

Organize Your Ideas. Write an outline or idea map to organize your ideas in the space below.

Writing the First Draft

Format the Letter. Write your return address, the date, the inside address, and the salutation.

Write the Message. Follow the idea map or outline you wrote. Then write an appropriate conclusion. Write your closing, leaving room for your signature.

Editing/Revising

Review. Read the first draft of your letter. Does it say what you want?

Edit/Revise. Check the format of your letter using the model on page 75. Then revise the letter using the Editing Checklist on page 24.

Writing the Final Draft

Proofread. Reread your letter using the Proofreading Checklist on page 26 and the rules for capitalization and punctuation on page 77.

Sharing Your Final Draft

Publish. Share the final draft of your letter with someone whose opinion you value. Ask this person if your message was clear.

File. Save the letter in your notebook or portfolio for your future reference.

Letter B: Follow-up Letter After a Job Interview

Assume that your request for an interview was granted. The interview took place and went well. You are now waiting to hear if you got the job. Write a follow-up letter to the person who interviewed you.

Prewriting

Define Your Topic, Audience, and Purpose. Your topic is the job opening. Your purpose is to reinforce your qualifications and interest in the job. Your audience is the interviewer.

Develop Main Ideas. Make notes on the points you want to cover in your letter. Organize your ideas in an outline or idea map.

Follow the remaining steps in the **Writing Process.** Refer to the steps above.

Apply

For further practice in letter writing, go to your Personal Writing Notebook. Assume you got the job. Your new employer told you that you got an excellent reference from each of the two people whose names you submitted. Write a thank-you letter to each of the people who gave you the good references.

Report Writing

Elements of Report Writing

A **report** is an organized summary of facts and information on a topic. A report usually includes an analysis of the information. An **analysis** is the writer's conclusions about the meaning of the information in the report.

Types of reports include book reports, research reports, and business reports. In a **book report**, the writer summarizes the contents of a book he or she has read. For a **research report**, the writer gathers information from many sources. The writer then presents an analysis of the information. Both of these types of reports are used in school courses. For a **business report**, the writer gathers and analyzes information from sources on the job. The writer then presents the report to others who need it to make business decisions.

In this section, you will learn some basic skills of report writing. These skills can be applied to any type of report you may have to write.

To prepare to write a report, you will need to gather information. Here are several methods you can use:

- **Conduct a survey.** Identify a group of people and ask each person the same set of questions. The questions may be oral or written.

- **Do research.** Read books, magazine and newspaper articles, or other reference materials. A library is a good source for these materials.

- **Collect firsthand information.** Interview people, attend meetings, or visit places to observe something you want to write about.

Here is an example of a report that a government employee wrote after conducting a survey of businesspeople to find out what skills they look for when they hire new employees.

 Example

The Skills Employers Want

Many employers say that the most important skills for any employee are the basic skills — reading, writing, and math. Employers are saying, "Give me people who can read, write, and do simple math, and I'll train them for the jobs I have available."

But checking further, one finds that employers want good basic skills and much more. Employers want employees who have the ability to learn new job skills quickly. They need people who can think on their feet. This means being able to solve problems, make decisions, and come up with new ways of doing things.

Employers want employees who are good listeners and who can make a good impression on their customers. They want employees who can get along well with others and who are willing to take on responsibility.

Guided Writing ▪ Answer the following questions about the report.

1. Do you think that employers in your area would agree that the skills in the article on page 86 are the most important? Below, list some methods you could use to gather information from employers in your area on the topic "The Skills Employers Want."

_____

_____

_____

2. List two library sources that you could use.

_____

_____

3. List the questions you would ask if you were going to conduct a survey of employers.

_____

_____

_____

Summarizing Information

A report sums up information. **Summarizing** is a way to take a large amount of material and trim it down to a few major points. To summarize, read the material and pick out the facts that support the information you want to include in your report. A **summary** may be a phrase, several sentences, or several paragraphs in length.

Example   The following list summarizes the first paragraph of the article "The Skills Employers Want" on page 86.

■ Basic skills are most important — reading, writing, and math.

■ Employers say, "Give me people who can read, write, and do simple math, and I'll train them for the jobs I have."

Here are some guidelines to help you summarize information.

1. Look first at the title, subtitle, and captions under pictures and graphics. These items often summarize key points.

2. Look at any other material that is set apart from the main text. This might be quotations, headings, or subheadings. These are often set in _italic_ type or **boldface** type to emphasize key points.

3. Look for key points in topic sentences, concluding sentences, lists, and words in italics and boldface.

Paraphrasing

When you write a summary, put the information into your own words. This is called **paraphrasing.** If you copy the information word for word, enclose it in quotation marks. Only a small amount of information can be quoted without the permission of the author or publisher of the material. Quoting material without permission is called **plagiarism** and is illegal.

Example

Original paragraph:

Many job applicants do not look at want ads or go to an employment agency. They go directly to a company and request employment. If you choose this method of job hunting, make sure you find out something about the company's business and the kinds of jobs available before you go. Employers are more favorably impressed by applicants who know what kind of job they want to apply for and who can explain how their skills match the job.

Paraphrased paragraph:

One way to find a job is to go to a company and ask. This is not a good idea unless you first get some information about the company and the job you want to apply for. Employers look for people who know the kind of job they want and how their skills fit the job.

Guided Writing Paraphrase each of the following sentences.

1. There is no substitute for correct grammar and a good vocabulary in the business world.

_____

_____

2. Be very aware of your sentence structure, including correct subject-verb agreement, parts of speech, tone, and tense.

_____

_____

3. Dressing appropriately will make you feel confident when you speak.

_____

_____

4. Much of your success in the business world will depend on the image that you project through the way you look and speak.

_____

_____

Guided Writing Underline the main points in the two paragraphs below. Then write a paraphrased summary of each paragraph in your Personal Writing Notebook.

Paragraph 1

Learning is now a fact of life in the workplace. Even routine jobs are changing as the demands of businesses change. Often employees are moved from one job to another. They must be able to absorb information quickly. They must be able to move to another task with little supervision. The first step in adapting to this demand is losing the fear of the unknown. Most new situations are not as different as they seem at first. Learn to look at the big picture. Then you can apply what you already know to the new situation.

Paragraph 2

When you are faced with a problem on the job, your first reaction should be to think about it. Thinking about the problem means trying to figure out *why* something is going wrong. Knowing why will usually help you come up with a solution. Most problems have more than one solution. Don't always think that you have to have the *right* answer. Most bosses are grateful for an employee who suggests a way to solve a problem, even if they don't always think the employee's way is the best way.

Taking Notes

The best way to summarize information for your report is to take notes in a notebook or on index cards. **Index cards** are 3" x 5" lined cards. Using index cards makes it easy to take notes at random and organize them later. In addition to listing the summarized information, list the sources used to get the information.

Here are some tips for taking notes.

1. At the top of the notebook page or index card, write a phrase or a key word that identifies the subject.

2. Next, list the source on the first note card. Include the author's name, the title of the publication, the name of the article, and the date of publication. If the source is a book, also note the publisher's location and name.

3. Finally, summarize the information that you want to use in your report.

Example

> *Employment Skills*
> *U.S. Dept. of Labor, "What Do Employers Want," page 22.*
> *Employers want more than basic skills — they also want:*
> *ability to learn new skills, quick thinkers, problem solvers,*
> *good listeners, people who can get along with others.*

Check your answers on page 229.

Suppose that you found the following article. It was published on page 35 of *Careers* magazine in April, 1992. Use the space below to summarize the three key points in the article. Set up each summary as if it were on an index card.

Communication Skills: A Key to Success
by Dorothy Warren

Getting along with others is a key to success on any job. No other skill is more important to good human relations than knowing how to communicate. What you say to visitors in the office or what you say to coworkers makes an impression that is difficult to change. The saying "We never get a second chance to make a good first impression" is very true.

Informal and Formal Language

One major factor in the impression you make in the business world is your *use of language*. Do you ever use slang expressions or incorrect grammar? This use of informal language is all right when you are with your family and friends. For example, when a friend introduces you to someone, you may say "Hi" or "What's happening?" to greet your new acquaintance. In a business setting, this type of greeting would not be appropriate. In a business setting, you would use a more formal expression by saying something like "How do you do?" or "I'm pleased to meet you."

Correct English

There is no substitute for *correct grammar* and a *good vocabulary* in the business world. Using correct English creates an image of authority and intelligence. Be very aware of your sentence structure, including correct subject-verb agreement, parts of speech, tone, and tense.

Notes

1. _____

_____

_____

2. _____

_____

_____

3. _____

_____

_____

                    Check your answers on page 229.

Classifying Information

After you have finished your index cards, organize them. Do this before you write an outline. One way to organize your notes is to classify them. **Classifying** means sorting into groups. For example, for a report on new ways to do your job, you might classify your notes according to "old" ways and "new" ways. For a report on books that your reader may not be familiar with, you might sort the notes another way. You might group information as "alike" or "different" from other books that your reader would know about.

Suppose you have gathered information on skills that businesses in your area would like their employees to have. Your report could compare and contrast what employers in your area said about job skills to what the article said. You could group your notes according to things that employers said that were similar to the article, and things that were different. You could organize your facts in one of these two ways:

1. **Point by point.** Discuss each point in the article. Show the similarities and differences between employers' information and the facts in the article.

2. **One side at a time.** Another way to present your facts is to list first all the things that the local employers said that were similar to the statements in the article. Then list all the things that were different.

Example

Point by point. According to a government survey, employers place reading, writing, and math skills at the top of their list of skills they want employees to have. In the East River business district, most employers agree with this. But they would add one item to the list. Most employers in this area want employees who speak Spanish as well as English.

One side at a time. When asked what they wanted from employees, employers in the East River district placed getting to work on time, not being absent, and being willing to work hard as the top three traits on their list. They think these traits matter the most because without them nothing gets done. It doesn't matter how well people can read, write, or do math if they are not on the job, on time, and ready to do the work. Surprisingly, employers said that many qualified people lack these traits.

Journal Writing

Interview two or three employers or people who work in your area. Ask them to list the most important traits or skills that employers want in their employees. Take notes in your notebook or on index cards. Then in your Personal Writing Notebook, write a short report on what you found out. Classify the information according to similarities to and differences from the government report. You may want to ask the people you interview to talk about the specific points in the report.

Grammar: Irregular Verbs

A report is usually written for a teacher or a supervisor. It is important to present your best possible work. Correct use of verbs will help you achieve this goal. Read the rules below.

Irregular Verbs

The basic forms of verbs are called their **principal parts**. Verbs have four principal parts:

Present	**Past**	**Past Participle**	**Present Participle**
walk	walked	walked	walking

Most verbs are **regular verbs**. The past and the past participle are formed by adding -*ed*. The present participle is formed by adding -*ing*. The principal parts of **irregular verbs** do not follow this pattern. Become familiar with the different ways that irregular verbs form their principal parts, so that you can use verbs correctly. Below are some guidelines.

The past participle and present participle of verbs are used with a **helping verb**. The helping verb for the past participle is a form of the verb *have*. The helping verb for the present participle is a form of the verb *be*.

Helping Verbs

Past Participle: have, has, had   (have walked)
Present Participle: be, am, is, are, was, were   (am walking)

Patterns of Irregular Verbs

1. Some irregular verbs form the past participle by adding -*n* or -*en* to the present or past. In some irregular verbs, the last consonant is doubled.

Present	**Past**	**Past Participle**	**Present Participle**
speak	spoke	spoken	~~spoken~~ Speaking
know	knew	known	knowing

2. Some irregular verbs have the same past and past participle.

bring	brought	brought	bringing
find	found	found	finding

3. Some irregular verbs change their spelling to form the past participle and add -*ing* to the present to form the present participle. Notice that the final consonant is doubled to form the present participle of some verbs.

drink	drank	drunk	drinking
begin	began	begun	beginning

4. Some irregular verbs have the same present, past, and past participle.

cost	cost	cost	costing
shut	shut	shut	shutting

Exercise A   Underline the correct form of the irregular verb in each sentence.

1. Many employers have (spoke, spoken) about what they need.

2. Writers have (wrote, written) articles on the subject as well.

3. The question is whether schools have (teach, taught) people what they need to know to get good jobs.

4. Too many students have (fell, fallen) behind in their education.

5. Most schools have (began, begun) to look for new ways of doing things.

Exercise B   Fill in the blank with the correct form of the verb in parentheses.

1. (see) We _____ some great scenery on our vacation last summer.

2. (go) We _____ on a fishing trip to the mountains.

3. (drive) We _____ two hundred miles to a camping area.

4. (sleep) It was the first time I had _____ in a tent.

5. (eat) My son was almost _____ alive by mosquitoes.

6. (catch) The first day he _____ a large fish.

7. (freeze) We _____ it in the cooler.

8. (fry) Later we _____ the fish over an open fire.

9. (swim) After a nap we _____ in the river.

10. (take) We _____ pictures of the sunset over the water.

Guided Writing   Write sentences using the principal part of the irregular verbs listed.

1. buy (past participle)

   _____

2. do (past participle)

   _____

3. come (past)

   _____

4. drop (present participle)

   _____

For more practice on irregular verbs, turn to pages 183 and 185.

Check your answers on page 230.

The Parts of a Report

All reports have three main parts: an **introduction,** a **body,** and a **conclusion.** An **informal report,** such as a paper you would write for a class or a short report for your boss, might have only these three parts. A **formal report,** such as a research paper, may have more parts: a title page and a bibliography. Below is a description and an example of each of the five parts of a report.

1. **Title page.** This includes the title, the name of the writer, the person the report is being submitted to, and the date.

Example

> Technical Skills for the 1990s:
> A New Age for Workers
>
> Prepared by
> Sean A. Young
>
> Submitted to
> Beverly Johnson
>
> April 30, 1992

2. **Introduction.** This briefly states the subject and the main idea of the report.

Example

In the 1990s, many people will have to learn new skills or risk losing their jobs. Bank tellers, telephone operators, and factory workers are among those whose jobs have been taken over by computers.

3. **Body.** This presents facts and conclusions that support the main topic.

Example

When computers take over jobs, workers must be retrained. In auto factories where robots now work on the assembly line, workers are needed to repair robots when they break down. This work requires different skills from those needed to place bolts on car parts.

4. **Conclusion.** This restates and summarizes the main point.

Example

People who are entering the workforce in the 1990s must be prepared with technical skills. They should also seek out companies that provide retraining when the need arises.

5. **Bibliography.** This is a list of the sources that were used to gather information for the report.

Example

Book: Ortego, Daniel. *The Computer Society*. New York: Dolphin Press, 1992.

Magazine: Warren, Dorothy. "Technology and Work." *Computers Today*, May 1992, pages 25–27.

Newspaper: Walker, Dorothy. "Jobs for the 1990s." *USA Today*, Jan. 23, 1991.

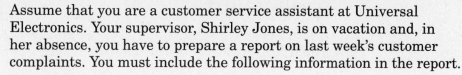

Journal Writing A 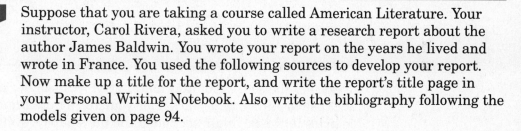 Assume that you are a customer service assistant at Universal Electronics. Your supervisor, Shirley Jones, is on vacation and, in her absence, you have to prepare a report on last week's customer complaints. You must include the following information in the report.

1. How many calls were received?
2. How many calls involved equipment problems? What kind?
3. How many calls involved problems with repairers?
4. Report any additional kinds of problems.

Using the following notes left by your supervisor, write the introduction, body, and conclusion of the report. Remember to summarize the information and classify it in a way that will make the report easy to organize. Write the report in your Personal Writing Notebook.

Notes

April 4. A. Berry called — the VCR repairer did not show up.
         B. Simpson called — the channel selector on his VCR is broken.

April 5. L. Rossi returned a CD player — it was making a funny noise.

April 6. G. Jones called — the remote control for his new TV was not included in the delivery.
         L. Holloway called — the repairer was three hours late.
         S. Herrera returned a tape player — the record button was defective.

April 7. J. Fallon returned a CD player — Q-Mart sells the same brand for less.

April 8. R. Weiss called — repairer did not show up.

Journal Writing B Suppose that you are taking a course called American Literature. Your instructor, Carol Rivera, asked you to write a research report about the author James Baldwin. You wrote your report on the years he lived and wrote in France. You used the following sources to develop your report. Now make up a title for the report, and write the report's title page in your Personal Writing Notebook. Also write the bibliography following the models given on page 94.

1. A book by Leon J. Goldberg, entitled *The Life of James Baldwin*, published in New York by Random House in 1988.

2. A magazine article in *Look* magazine, on pages 24–27, entitled "Mr. Baldwin: An Interview," published in March 1970, written by William McMillan.

3. A magazine article by James Baldwin, entitled "No Man's Land," published in *Esquire* magazine in January 1980, on pages 15–17 and 89–92.

4. A newspaper article by Alice Williams, entitled "A Native Son Returns," published in *The New York Times* on March 25, 1980, on page 35.

Application

Write a Report

Now you will write a report to share with your instructor. The subject of your report is employment opportunities in the area in which you live. You may define the word *area* as your neighborhood, or as the entire town, city, or region in which you live. The purpose of the report is to get information on jobs that you might want to apply for. You can use the information for yourself, and you can share it with others. The report should provide the following information:

1. What types of businesses are hiring people at the job level and type of employment that you are interested in?
2. What types of jobs do they have available?
3. What past experience is required for the available jobs?
4. What education and training are needed to be able to do these jobs?
5. What is the salary range for the type of work that is available?
6. Include any additional information that would be helpful to you or to the reader.

Prewriting

Decide what types of jobs you will explore for the report. In the space below, list your **purpose**, **audience**, and **topic**.

Purpose _____

Audience _____

Topic _____

Next, list the sources of information you will look for and the methods you will use to gather information for your report. Examples of sources include articles in the business section of the newspaper, want ads, people you know who work in different businesses, and businesses that you can call or visit. Review the information on page 86 if you need help deciding on methods to use to get the information you need.

Sources

_____

_____

Methods

_____

_____

Now you are ready to collect your information. Take notes on index cards or in your notebook. Review the information on pages 87–89 before you take notes.

After gathering your information, organize and classify your notes. In your Personal Writing Notebook, write an outline or draw an idea map that organizes the ideas you want to cover in your report.

Writing the First Draft

Write the Introduction. Tell the subject of the report. Write a strong topic sentence that states the main idea.

Write the Body of the Report. Make sure each main point starts a new paragraph. Use your index cards and outline as a guide. Present facts that support the main topic.

Write the Conclusion. Restate and summarize the main point of the report.

Editing/Revising

Review. Read the whole report to see if it is well-organized. Does the report follow your outline?

Edit/Revise. Read each paragraph carefully, and revise your work using the Editing Checklist on page 24. In addition to the items on the general editing checklist, check to see that you did the following:

☐ Did you use the correct form of regular verbs?

☐ Did you use the correct form of any irregular verbs?

☐ Did you use a businesslike tone?

If you want to write a formal report, also write a title page and bibliography.

Writing the Final Draft

Proofread. Complete the necessary revisions, and then reread the report. Check for correct spelling, punctuation, and neatness. Use the proofreader's marks on page 26 to correct any errors you find. Rewrite or retype your report if necessary.

Sharing Your Final Draft

Publish. Share the report with your instructor and others who can use the information.

File. Keep the report and your note cards in your notebook or portfolio for future reference.

Section 8

Expository Writing

Elements of Expository Writing

Expository writing shows, tells, or proves. Filling out forms and writing bills are examples of this type of writing. Since expository writing gives facts, using precise words is very important.

Example

Vague: My sister works hard.
Precise: My sister works full-time and is taking a night course.

One of the most common types of expository writing deals with using precise facts and words to tell <u>why</u>. Through this method, writers define a word or idea to tell about it. Here is how one writer defined _warranty_.

Example

How can you be sure that something you buy will do what it promises? You can protect yourself with a warranty. A warranty is a guarantee put into writing. It says that the item you have bought will do what the maker promises. It may promise that the maker will repair or replace the item if something is wrong with the way the item was made. Beware — some warranties are "limited warranties." They are good for only a short time.

Here are three ways to define:

1. Name the pieces or parts that make up the whole.

Example

<u>Ketchup</u> is a sauce made of tomatoes, sugar, vinegar, salt, and onions.

2. Define a word by tracing its past. Look in a dictionary.

A <u>bootlegger</u> breaks the law to make or sell alcoholic drinks. The first bootleggers smuggled liquor in the tops of their tall boots.

3. Give other words that describe the word or idea.

A <u>kiwi fruit</u> can also be called a berry.

Guided Writing Use a dictionary to define each of these words.

1. Give other words to define _freedom_: _____

1. Define _macadam_ by tracing its history: _____

_____

Connecting Words and Phrases

Good writing flows smoothly as the ideas lead from one to another in a way that makes sense to the reader. If writing flows smoothly, readers do not have to back up and reread a passage to figure out what you mean. One of the best ways to make your writing flow is to use connecting words and phrases. Read these two samples.

Example

I had three reasons for not going to work today. I tripped over a branch in the backyard last night and injured my foot. I cannot wear my shoe. My son is not going to school. He has a bad case of the flu. The power is off at work. I would not be able to get much work done there anyway.

I had three reasons for not going to work today. First, I tripped over a branch in the backyard last night. As a result, I hurt my foot and cannot wear my shoe. Also, my son is not going to school because he has a bad case of the flu. Further, the power is off at work, so I would not be able to get much work done there anyway.

What does the second sample have that the first one does not? Notice the words and phrases *first, as a result, and, also, because, further,* and *so.* These words link the ideas. There are many words that link ideas. Use the word that joins your ideas the best.

Exercise A   Write several different connecting words and phrases to link the ideas in each sentence.

1. I am not going out today. I have a cold coming on; _____ , it is raining.

    _____   _____   _____

2. Pete made dinner; _____ , he washed the dishes.

    _____   _____   _____

3. Frances studied hard for the GED; _____ , she passed the exam.

    _____   _____   _____

Exercise B   Insert a connecting word or phrase in each sentence. Add any commas or semicolons you think are needed.

1. Julio put an ad in the paper _____ he put signs on the bulletin board at work.

2. The storm damaged the roof _____ the harm could have been a lot worse.

3. Hong's mother is ill _____ he is flying to visit her.

4. Mei Lee worked hard _____ she got a raise.

Check your answers on page 230.

Connecting Words for Style

There is no one "right" connecting word or phrase to use. Pick the one that best makes your point and joins your ideas. The words you pick help create your writing style, your own special way of putting your ideas on paper. Here is the same idea joined three ways:

Example

I like living in this building; <u>as a result</u>, I renewed my lease.

I like living in this building; <u>thus</u>, I renewed my lease.

I like living in this building; <u>so</u> I renewed my lease.

Below is a list of common connecting words and phrases:

Connecting Words and Phrases			
also	as a result	later	but
and	still	after a while	next
besides	what is more	for example	for instance
first, second			

Guided Writing

Rewrite this paragraph to make the ideas flow more smoothly. You can add, take away, or replace words and phrases.

People who win big prizes in the lottery often find that the money does not make them happy. Therefore, they have to deal with lots of people trying to get a piece of the pie. Winners find that their friends expect them to hand over some of the winnings. But they have to be on guard all the time. Lottery winners find that they cannot trust anyone. All this pressure takes the fun out of winning. They can no longer relax and enjoy life. I am willing to give it a try!

_____

_____

_____

_____

_____

_____

Journal Writing

Someone once said, "There is only one success — to be able to spend your life in your own way." In your Personal Writing Notebook, write a paragraph to define success. Use connecting words and phrases to link your ideas.

Expanding Your Vocabulary with Synonyms

Words are the building blocks of thought, the means by which you express yourself. Being able to use many words makes anyone a better writer, speaker, and reader. A research study showed that having a good vocabulary, more than any other factor, was what people with good jobs had in common.

There are many ways to learn new words. Reading a newspaper every day helps you learn new words. Another good way to add new words to your writing is to use a book called a **thesaurus.**

The word *thesaurus* comes from a Latin word meaning "storehouse of knowledge." Unlike a dictionary, a thesaurus does not give meanings or trace a word's past. Instead, it has lists of **synonyms** and **antonyms,** words that mean the same and the opposite. For example, look up the word *big* in a thesaurus. Here are just a few of the words you will find under *big*.

Example

Synonyms for *big*			Antonyms for *big*		
large	huge	grown	little	small	meek
immense	ample	adult	minute	bantam	cheap
vast	great	head	minor	unknown	young
vital	prime	mature	modest	humble	little

Since a thesaurus has lists of words to choose from, it can help you find new words as well as words whose meanings you may not recall. These words add spice and flair to your writing style.

Exercise Use a thesaurus. Write four synonyms for each word.

1. red   _____   _____   _____   _____

2. win   _____   _____   _____   _____

3. walk   _____   _____   _____   _____

4. money   _____   _____   _____   _____

Guided Writing Practice using a thesaurus. Write a sentence that has two or more vivid words to tell about each item below.

   1. a nice day   2. a good meal   3. a newborn baby   4. a sunburn

1. _____

2. _____

3. _____

4. _____

Choosing the Best Synonym

Words have varied shades of meaning. For instance, there are many words that mean "to hit." Although *bump* and *smash* both mean "to hit," *smash* suggests a harder action that may be more painful. So, use the word that says exactly what you want to say.

Exercise A ◼ Each line has four words. Three are synonyms; one word does not belong. Write the word that is not a synonym for the others.

_____1.   careless   hasty   rushed   neat

_____2.   still   racket   hushed   quiet

_____3.   mansion   cabin   hut   cottage

_____4.   decrease   explore   survey   probe

_____5.   stony   rigid   steely   gentle

_____6.   yearn   crave   scorn   wish

Exercise B ◼ Select the best synonym for the underlined word in each sentence. Write the letter for that word in the blank.

_____1.   The belligerent dog bit the mail carrier again.
    (A)   hostile   (B)   unfriendly   (C)   warlike

_____2.   That gentleman is a brilliant research scientist.
    (A)   glorious   (B)   colorful   (C)   distinguished

_____3.   The family was upset when the power went out during the championship game.
    (A)   baseball game   (B)   Super Bowl   (C)   match

_____4.   The ad states that the new cereal is good for you.
    (A)   nutritious   (B)   sufficient   (C)   benign

_____5.   The redhead was made the person in charge of the bowling team.
    (A)   moderator   (B)   ruler   (C)   captain

Journal Writing ◼ In your Personal Writing Notebook, write a paragraph to agree or disagree with this quote: "A friend is a person with whom I may be sincere. Before him or her, I may think aloud."

Grammar: Active and Passive Voice

Verbs show time through tense. Verbs also show if the subject is doing the action or if the action is done to the subject. In English, there are two voices of verbs to show how an action is done: active and passive. In the **active voice,** the subject does the action. In the **passive voice,** the action is done to the subject.

Example	**Active Voice**	**Passive Voice**
	He hit the ball.	The ball was hit by him.
	Rain helps crops to grow.	Crops are helped to grow by rain.
	Jen opened the book.	The book was opened by Jen.

Exercise A Find the verb in each sentence. On the line, write *active* if the verb is in the active voice or *passive* if the verb is in the passive voice.

_____1. The pill was taken by my wife.

_____2. We bought a few extra hot dogs for later.

_____3. The bad news was given to Sal by the doctor.

_____4. I read the newspaper every night after supper.

_____5. New York was reached by the Mexican tourists in a day.

In most cases, use the active voice in your writing. It helps you write crisp, clear sentences. The active voice is also more direct than the passive voice. There are two good reasons to use the passive voice, though. Use the passive voice when you do not know a person's name and when you want to take the focus off the person.

Example	**Name unknown:**	A woman has been charged with theft.
	Name left out on purpose:	A mistake has been made.

Exercise B Pick the reason why each sentence is in the passive voice. Write *(A)* or *(B)* on each line below.

(A) The person's name is unknown.   (B) The name was left out on purpose.

_____1. My friend was struck by a car.

_____2. A bad check was passed in the food store.

_____3. The weird phone call was made at 2:00 A.M.

_____4. At 10:00 A.M. the doors to the store were unlocked.

For more practice on the active and passive voice, see pages 188–189.

Grammar: Changing Voice

To recast a sentence in the active voice, start with the subject.
To recast a sentence in the passive voice, end with the subject.

Example   **Active Voice ——→ to ——→ Passive Voice**

The players wore new hats.   New hats were worn by the players.

Passive Voice ——→ to ——→ Active Voice

The soda was sold by them.   They sold the soda.

Exercise A ◢ Rewrite each of these passive sentences in the active voice.

1. passive voice: After four o'clock, the lock was broken by the thief.

   active voice: _____

2. passive voice: The moon was landed on by the crew of *Apollo 11*.

   active voice: _____

3. passive voice: A plaque was left on the moon by them.

   active voice: _____

Exercise B ◢ Pick the best way to rewrite the underlined phrase or sentence. Write the letter of your answer in the blank.

_____1. <u>A creature has been seen by those who visit Loch Ness</u>.
   - (A) Visitors to Loch Ness have seen a creature.
   - (B) A creature, by those who visit Loch Ness, has been seen.
   - (C) No change is needed.

_____2. <u>These sightings have been doubted by many</u>.
   - (A) These sightings were doubted by many.
   - (B) Many have doubted these sightings.
   - (C) No change is needed.

_____3. <u>Tests were done by experts</u> to see if a monster is in the lake.
   - (A) Experts did tests
   - (B) Tests have been done
   - (C) No change is needed.

_____4. <u>Many photos were taken by scientists</u> to see if the lake's cold water is a factor.
   - (A) Photos, many by scientists, were taken
   - (B) Scientists took many photos
   - (C) No change is needed.

For more practice on active and passive voice, see pages 188–189.

Check your answers on page 231.

Grammar: Revising Sentences — Wordiness

There are many reasons why writers take the time to go back over their work. Revising sentences helps writers more clearly state what they mean. Revising helps get rid of excess words that make it harder for readers to get the point. When you revise, sometimes you can just take out extra words; in other cases, you will have to rewrite all or part of a sentence.

Example	**Too Wordy:**	The hikers saw the big, massive, dark, black cloud covering over the sun.
	Revised:	The hikers saw the big, black cloud covering the sun.
	Too Wordy:	Mike is of the belief that the death penalty should be allowed.
	Revised:	Mike believes the death penalty should be allowed.

Exercise ▪ For each pair of sentences, underline the sentence that is clearer.

1. (A) At the same time that he was driving a taxi, he was also working at a lawn-care type of business.
   (B) While he was driving a taxi, he was also doing lawn care.

2. (A) Today, many people do not vote.
   (B) In this day and age, many people do not vote.

3. (A) The large dog growled fiercely when anyone walked by.
   (B) The dog was very large in size and gave a nasty and fierce growling sound when anyone walked by the yard.

4. (A) Because of the fact that it took a really very long time to get to his work, Sam quit his job.
   (B) Because it took a long time to get to work, Sam quit his job.

Guided Writing ▪ Revise each sentence to get rid of extra words.

1. Far away in the distance, we could see the little, small ships.

_____

2. Modern cars of today can be driven faster than the old cars of the past.

_____

3. I asked the speaker to repeat again what he had said.

_____

4. The dead wilted plant was laying on the floor.

_____

For more practice on revising sentences, see page 202.

Check your answers on page 231.

Point of View

Another reason to revise your writing is to use the same point of view in all your sentences. The **point of view** is the way the writer tells a story. This chart shows some of the ways you can use point of view:

Point of View	
If the writer...	**he or she would use...**
speaks as himself or herself	I went to the store.
speaks to someone	You went to the store.
speaks about someone	He (or She or They) went to the store.
speaks as a member of a group	We went to the store.

The best point of view for a piece of writing depends on the purpose and audience for the work. "You," for example, makes the writing sound personal. Pick the point of view that best suits your needs. Be careful not to change your point of view in the middle of a sentence or passage.

Example

Change in point of view: Today, people want to watch your health.
No change: Today, <u>people</u> want to watch <u>their</u> health.

Change in point of view: They like to work hard, but when a job is hard, you sometimes get upset.
No change: <u>They</u> like to work hard, but when a job is hard, <u>they</u> sometimes get upset.

Guided Writing 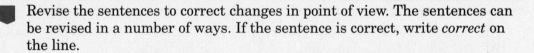 Revise the sentences to correct changes in point of view. The sentences can be revised in a number of ways. If the sentence is correct, write *correct* on the line.

1. I like to read forecasts of the future, but you have to wonder if any of them are true.

_____

2. When a person is treated with respect at work, you feel better about your work.

_____

3. This morning I could not find my keys, so I left the back door unlocked when I left.

_____

4. When one looks for a loan, you find who has the best rate.

_____

Journal Writing In your Personal Writing Notebook, write a letter to your boss explaining a problem at work. Be sure to use the same point of view in the whole letter.

Polishing Your Work

Your writing reflects on you. Take the time to add the final shine to your efforts. To polish your work, check it over before you hand it to anyone. Make sure your writing is clear. Check for correct spelling and punctuation. Be sure no letters or words were left out. Ask yourself:

- 1. Does each sentence begin with a capital letter?
- 2. Does each proper noun begin with a capital letter?
- 3. Does each sentence end with a period or question mark?
- 4. Is each word spelled correctly?

Exercise ◆ Read the paragraph below. Then circle the best answer to each item. Items 1–3 refer to the paragraph.

(1) When I was in school, the teachers did not try to erase our backrounds. (2) they tried to say our real names, even though they did not speak our language. (3) We were never punished for speaking our native langauge in class.

1. Sentence 1: **When I was in school, the teachers did not try to erase our backrounds.** What correction should be made to this sentence?

   (1) Change *backrounds* to *backgrounds*.

   (2) Insert a comma after *teachers*.

   (3) Change *teachers* to *Teachers*.

   (4) Put a question mark at the end of the sentence.

   (5) No correction is necessary.

2. Sentence 2: **they tried to say our real names, even though they did not speak our language.** What correction should be made to this sentence?

   (1) Remove the comma after *names*.

   (2) Insert a comma after *tried*.

   (3) Change *they* to *They*.

   (4) Change *language* to *langauge*.

   (5) No correction is necessary.

3. Sentence 3: **We were never punished for speaking our native langauge in class.** What correction should be made to this sentence?

   (1) Change *were* to *are*.

   (2) Put a question mark at the end of the sentence.

   (3) Change *langauge* to *language*.

   (4) Add a comma after *langauge*.

   (5) No correction is necessary.

Check your answers on page 231.

Application

Write an Expository Essay

Draw together all you have learned about expository writing. Apply what you have learned by writing an essay on one of these two topics:

Should gambling be legalized?
The best show on TV is . . .

As you write, make sure you follow the **Writing Process.** The steps are reviewed below.

Prewriting

Define Your Topic. Before you pick a topic, read both choices. The subject of your essay depends on which topic you choose. If you pick whether gambling should be legalized, your topic is the side you choose to argue. If you pick the best show on TV, your topic is the TV show you want to write about in your essay.

1. To pick a topic, first make a list for both choices. Start by making a list of the pros and cons of making gambling legal. Jot down your ideas or make a chart. Try to write as many ideas as you can. Then make a list of all the TV shows that you like.

2. Read over both your lists. Decide which topic you know more about.

3. If you want to write about gambling, think about which side of the issue you support. Why do you feel this way about the issue? Look at your list to see on which side you have the most supporting facts, opinions, and reasons. If you want to write about a TV show, make sure you can think of at least three things about each show. If you cannot write three things about a show, cross it off your list.

4. Pick the topic you feel more strongly about, the one for which you have more facts, opinions, and reasons to use in your essay.

Identify Your Audience and Purpose. You are writing for your friends. Your purpose is to convince your friends to support your side of the gambling issue or to watch a TV show that you think is the best.

Develop Main Ideas. List or make an idea map of the main ideas you want to cover in your essay.

Organize Your Ideas. Arrange your ideas in a way that will help you best make your point. If you are writing about legalizing gambling, do not ignore the side of the issue you do not support. Instead, put all the points <u>against</u> your topic first. Write about each of these points one at a time to show how they are not valid. Then, present the points that support your stance. If you are writing about the best TV show, list your ideas in order from the strongest to the least strong.

Writing the First Draft

Write the Topic Sentence. Write several topic sentences until you have one that will grab your reader's interest and state your topic best.

Develop Supporting Details. Make sure that each main point starts a new paragraph. Each paragraph should start with a topic sentence. Use facts, details, and examples to persuade your reader of your point. Be sure that your writing uses connecting words to link your points. Find vivid synonyms to make your point clear. Use the active voice. Check to make sure you have revised your sentences and cut all extra words.

Write the Conclusion. Write a strong ending that ties up all the points you made. Do not bring up any new issues here.

Editing/Revising

Review. After you have finished writing, read the entire essay to make sure you did what you set out to do. Ask yourself: "If I were reading this essay, would my ideas change?"

Edit/Revise. Read your essay carefully, and revise your work using the Editing Checklist on page 24. In addition to the items on the general editing checklist, check to see that you followed these specific guidelines:

- ☐ Did you use connecting words and phrases?
- ☐ Did you use a thesaurus to find good synonyms for overused words?
- ☐ Did you replace the passive voice with the active voice?
- ☐ Did you revise your work to cut extra words?
- ☐ Did you revise your work so there are no changes in point of view?
- ☐ Did you polish your work?

Writing the Final Draft

Proofread. After you have completed all the necessary revisions, reread the essay. Check for correct spelling, punctuation, and neatness. Use the proofreader's marks on page 26 to correct any errors you find.

Sharing Your Final Draft

Publish. Read your essay to a partner or have someone read it. Ask this person if your message is clear. Discuss what the person sees as the essay's weak and strong points. Make notes on the feedback.

File. Save the essay and your notes in your notebook or portfolio.

Apply

For further practice writing expository essays, go to your Personal Writing Notebook. Each day write a paragraph that shows, tells, or proves a point to your reader. Possible topics include:

1. You do (do not) learn more from life than you do in school.
2. It should be easier (harder) to get a divorce.

Section 9

Creative Writing

Variety Is the Spice of Life!

Creative writing uses words in new ways to express feelings and ideas. Unlike other types of writing you have read about in this book, creative writing is not so tightly tied to a certain form. Rather, creative writing includes poems as well as paragraphs, songs as well as essays.

Creative writers vary their words and sentence patterns to create an interesting style. They include both long and short sentences and use questions and exclamations as well. Read the two brief paragraphs below. Which one do you like better?

Example

Strawberries! I love the deep red ones with little greenish seeds all over them. When I was a child, every June we trekked to a farm at the end of Long Island. There, we plucked the lush ruby berries from their prickly green leaves. What could be sweeter than juicy strawberries on a hot summer's day?

Strawberries are my favorite fruit. I love the dark red ones. They have little green seeds all over them. When I was a child, every June we went to a farm at the end of Long Island. We picked strawberries there. The berries were ruby red. They were very sweet because the days were very hot.

The first paragraph has a mixture of long and short sentences to keep you interested in reading. It also contains an exclamation and a question. The opening sentence catches your eye because it has only one word — *strawberries* — and ends with an exclamation point. This short sentence is followed by a longer one, and then a still longer one. Note how the fourth sentence starts with the single word *there* to grab your eye. The whole passage ends with a question, another kind of sentence.

Journal Writing

Practice creative writing. In your Personal Writing Notebook revise this paragraph to make it more creative. Make some of the sentences long, others short. Use questions and exclamations as well.

Pet owners must keep their animals safe. This is not as crucial if you live on a farm or other open land. If not, you should not let your pet run loose. Pets can run onto roads and be struck by passing cars. Pets should also not be left alone in cars. This is very true on hot days. Cars can heat up inside very quickly with all the windows closed. Animals can suffocate in a matter of minutes.

Language as Expression

"See you later!" you shout to a friend, thinking you will meet at the coffee shop in half an hour. Suppose that an hour later you are standing in front of the coffee shop, tapping your foot with anger because your friend has just arrived. Whose fault is it? Is your friend wrong for thinking that *later* means "in an hour"? Are you wrong for thinking *later* means "in half an hour"?

As with spoken language, written words also help you express precise, exact ideas. With speech, the volume and tone of your voice help you express your ideas. With writing, you have only the words on the page. Thus, the words must be as precise and expressive as you can make them.

Exercise ◤ For each sentence, replace the underlined word with a more precise word or phrase to make your meaning clear. Write the word on the line by the sentence.

_____ 1. She threw down her towel and <u>sat</u> on the sand.

_____ 2. <u>Feeling</u> shot across his face after the shocking news.

_____ 3. With the engine <u>going</u>, the truck began to speed up.

_____ 4. Paul <u>walked</u> out the door after the fight.

_____ 5. For his overtime hours, Mike got <u>money</u> at the end of the week.

_____ 6. We heard the sleet <u>hitting</u> the new metal roof of the garage.

_____ 7. When someone <u>said</u> there was a fire in the building, everyone ran through the doors.

_____ 8. Jill was <u>happy</u> to hear that she would not have to pay the late fee on her income tax.

_____ 9. After working an extra shift to help his friend, Juan was <u>tired</u>.

_____ 10. Because she was late for the bus, Marie <u>ate</u> her food and dashed out the door.

Journal Writing ◤ In your Personal Writing Notebook, write six goals you have for the next year. Under each goal, write a sentence that tells how you are going to make your goal come true. Pick words that make your goals clear and exact. Then share one goal with a partner. For example:

Goal: To be on time for work
I will be at the bus stop fifteen minutes early each morning.

Formal Language

As you have seen, language can help you express exact shades of meaning. The words you pick depend on your audience and your purpose. <u>Slang</u> words, for example, are often used in talks with friends or in everyday notes, but slang is not suited for a letter to your boss. Slang words vary with the time and place. In the 1950s, people used the slang words *beatnik*, *daddy-o*, and *hepcat*. Today people laugh at those words, which shows that slang becomes out-of-date.

Example

Slang	My boss <u>gave me grief</u> for coming in late.
Formal Language	My boss <u>scolded</u> me for coming in late.
Slang	It's a <u>bummer</u> when it rains on your day off.
Formal Language	It's a <u>shame</u> when it rains on your day off.

Exercise ◢ Replace each of the underlined slang words or phrases with formal language. Write the formal language on the lines.

1. The movie was <u>a real bomb</u>. _____

2. Older cars <u>were gas guzzlers</u>, but the newer models get much better mileage. _____

_____

3. By the end of each week, I am <u>flat broke</u>. _____

4. They <u>goofed off</u> on the job. _____

5. I keep my wallet in my front pocket, so it cannot be <u>ripped off</u>. _____

6. If you work too hard, you may <u>burn out</u>. _____

7. With his new leather jacket, Hector is really <u>macho</u>. _____

8. I am really <u>into</u> plants. _____

9. That's a <u>foxy</u> outfit. _____

10. Don't <u>jive me</u>! _____

Journal Writing ◢ Replace the slang in this note with formal language. Then revise the sentences to make them smoother. Write in your Personal Writing Notebook.

You really ticked me off when you yelled at me about the wood that was swiped. I'm not the one who waltzed off with the stuff. This whole thing stinks to high heaven! You have been treating me lousy all week over this. I know I am not the most dynamite worker in the plant, but I don't goof off. Don't hassle me about it anymore.

Choosing Your Words

If every word had only one meaning, choosing words would be fairly simple — and boring! However, English is a rich language, with many words that have varying shades of meaning. To express your precise meaning, be aware of the different meanings a word may have. The dictionary can help you with shades of meaning.

A word's **denotation** is the meaning given in the dictionary. All words have a meaning, or denotation. Some words also carry a feeling or impression different from the denotation. This is a **connotation.** The words *man* and *gentleman,* for example, have the same meaning: a fully grown male. But the words do not carry the same feelings. The word *man* suggests (connotes) a mature, able person. The word *gentleman* suggests a proper way of acting as well.

Exercise ▉ Write the denotations for each of these words. Use a dictionary to look up any words you do not know.

1. latent _____

2. gaudy _____

3. feign _____

4. somber _____

5. agile _____

6. caustic _____

7. rigid _____

8. fluster _____

9. purge _____

10. compress _____

Guided Writing ▉ Practice choosing words. Both words in each of these pairs have the same denotation but not the same connotation. Pick the word you want to use from each pair and use it in a sentence.

1. spying/looking

_____

2. closed/slammed

_____

3. car/limo

_____

4. commented/criticized

_____

5. grabbed/pulled

_____

Good and Bad Connotations

Since a word can carry good or bad connotations, the word you choose can sharply change the meaning of your writing. Think about *thrifty* and *cheap,* for example. Both words describe someone who does not spend a lot of money. We think of *thrifty* as "a good value." If we talk about people being thrifty, we mean they can handle money well. If we talk about people being cheap, in contrast, we mean they are stingy or tightfisted. Look at these examples.

Example

Good Connotation	Bad Connotation
loyal	stubborn
trusting	childish
thrifty	stingy
brave	reckless

Exercise Each of these sentences has two words with the same meaning but different connotations. Circle the word that you think best fits the meaning of the sentence.

1. Rest was (important, vital) for the patient to improve.

2. My feelings were so (hurt, warped) that I could not even think of a thing to say.

3. Since she has little to do all day, my sister is always (prying, looking) into my business.

4. The (slender, skinny) model showed the latest styles for the next season.

5. The (noise, uproar) from the party next door woke me up and made further sleep impossible.

6. My boss refused to (budge, move) on the issue, even though we talked about it for a week.

7. Hank posted the new work (list, schedule) with our hours for the coming month.

8. I call my roommates the "Odd Couple"; one is very neat and the other is (untidy, a slob).

9. The month-old baby was cute, cuddly, and (chubby, fat).

10. Matt is so (pushy, ambitious) that he sticks his nose where it does not belong.

Journal Writing Your friends said you picked a bad place for a vacation. After going there, you decided they were right, but you do not want them to know. In your Personal Writing Notebook write a postcard to your friends making the awful vacation sound great. Choose words that carry good connotations to tell about your trip.

Grammar: Homonyms

A **synonym** is a word that means the same as another word. Use synonyms when you want to restate the same idea.

A **homonym** is a word that sounds like another word. But the two words have different meanings and often different spellings. Here is a chart of common homonyms.

Word	Meaning	Example
bare **bear**	not dressed an animal; to carry	Bare feet are not allowed here. The bear was huge. I can't bear the pain.
board **bored**	a piece of wood not interested	Make a shelf from the board. The movie bored us.
buy **by**	purchase next to	I will buy new shoes. The shoes are by the boots.
hear **here**	to listen to in this place	I hear you. Put it here.
hour **our**	sixty minutes belonging to us	The meter runs for an hour. This is our parking space.
its **it's**	possessive form of it contraction of it is	The dog hurt its paw. It's too late to go out.
meet **meat**	come together animal flesh	Let's meet at 3:00. I like my meat well done.
pane **pain**	window glass hurt	The pane of glass is broken. I have a pain in my arm.
piece **peace**	a part not war	Take a piece of pie. The cities were at peace.
no **know**	the opposite of *yes* to be sure	No, you can't have the pie. I know I ate it all.
red **read**	a color past tense of *to read*	The red towel is clean. I read the book last night.

Exercise ◢ Underline the correct word to complete each sentence below.

(1) Before you go camping, you should (buy/by) the right equipment. (2) I (here/hear) that you need to buy bug spray, a tent, and food. (3) You might want to take along a (board/bored) to go under the tent. (4) You will also need at least one (piece/peace) of plastic to use as a tent liner. (5) If not, you could wake up with a (pain/pane) in your back. (6) Some people try to hunt their own (meet/meat), but take along some food just in case you don't succeed. (7) In frontier days people used to like to eat (bare/bear), but now deer is preferred. (8) I (red/read) that squirrel is tasty, but I have never tried it.

For more practice with homonyms, turn to page 168.

Check your answers on page 232.

Generating Ideas

There are a number of ways to generate ideas before you begin your first draft. These methods can help you check how much you know about a topic before you begin to write. Here are two of the most useful methods you can use to help you begin the writing process: **Brainstorming** and **The Six Questions.**

Brainstorming

Brainstorming means making a list of all the ideas that you can think of for your topic. You can draw an idea map or list the ideas as words. Brainstorming works best if you let your mind flow freely. Don't worry about spelling, commas, or writing the same idea twice. Just try to keep on writing for five to ten minutes or until you have a list of ideas. Here is how one writer brainstormed ideas for the topic "Should people be allowed to smoke when and where they want?"

Example

lung disease	*headaches*	*smell*	*causes litter*
rights of others	*cancer*	*stroke*	*foul odors*
danger of burning ash	*food*	*freedom*	*stroke*
dirty habit	*expensive*	*danger of secondhand smoke*	

Some words can be crossed off the list right away. *Expensive* and *food* are off the topic. *Stroke* is on the topic, but the word is written twice. *Smell* and *foul odors* mean the same thing, so delete one. Now try to find ways that some of the items on the list fit with each other. See if you can put the items into groups. The groups with the most items are likely to be the ones you can write about the best. Here are some groups of similar ideas:

Example

lung disease	*smell*	*rights of others*
headaches	*dirty habit*	*freedom*
cancer	*causes litter*	
stroke		

Exercise Here is a brainstormed list for the topic "The pros and cons of divorce." Cross off any items that are off the topic.

costs a lot	fights	being alone	children hurt
no money	children better off	pressure from parents	
people judge you badly	no more fights	money problems	

Journal Writing Choose one of these two topics: "Junk food can be good for you" or "The best place to live." Brainstorm a list of ideas. Write your ideas in your Personal Writing Notebook. Then group the ideas.

The Six Questions

The second method of beginning the writing process is **The Six Questions.** This method uses questions to help you look at the topic from a number of angles. Here are the six questions: Who? What? Where? When? Why? How? Apply the questions to your topic.

Example

Topic: Living alone

Who lives alone?

people who never married   divorced people   widowed people

What do people living alone have to do?

find a place to live	buy things they need	make friends
clean and cook	deal with being alone	buy food

Where do people live alone?

cities	country	apartments
suburbs	houses	rented rooms

When do people have a problem living alone?

when they become ill	when they don't know what to expect
when they lose their jobs	when they can't take care of themselves

Why do people live alone?

they like the quiet   they have no choice

How do people learn to live alone?

they meet new people	they learn from their mistakes
someone helps them	they stay busy

Exercise   Write two short answers to each of these questions. The topic is "Looking for a new job."

1. Where do people look for a job?

     _____   _____

2. Why do people look for a new job?

     _____   _____

3. When do people look for a new job?

     _____   _____

4. What will help you get a new job?

     _____   _____

Journal Writing   Choose one of these two topics: "Day-care Centers" or "Buying a Used Car." Then generate ideas using The Six Questions. Write your ideas in your Personal Writing Notebook.

Application

Write a Creative Essay

Draw together all you have learned about creative writing. Apply what you have learned by writing a creative essay on the following topic:

My Ideal Vacation

As you write, make sure you follow the **Writing Process.** The steps are reviewed below.

Prewriting

Define Your Topic. The subject of your essay is your ideal vacation. Your specific topic is the place you select to visit.

1. To help you pick a place, first make a list of places that you think might make ideal vacation spots. List as many as you can.

2. Think about each place on your list. Get a clear picture of each place in your mind. Which place do you know the most about?

3. Jot down three things to discuss about each place on your list. You might want to answer these six questions: **Where** is this place? **What** makes this an ideal vacation? **Who** (if anyone) would be there with me? **When** would I like to have this vacation? **Why** is this an ideal vacation? **How** is this vacation different from others? If you cannot write three things about a vacation idea, cross it off your list.

4. Pick the place you feel most strongly about, the one for which you have the most details and reasons to use in your essay.

Identify Your Audience and Purpose. You are writing for your friends, so they are your audience. Your purpose is to describe your ideal vacation to your friends. After they read your essay, they may get their own ideas.

Generate Main Ideas. Use brainstorming or The Six Questions to help you generate ideas. Recall that brainstorming is listing as many ideas as you can. As you write, don't worry about spelling, commas, or listing ideas twice. If you use The Six Questions to generate ideas, answer as many as you can. Whichever way you use to generate ideas, list the main ideas you want to cover in your essay. Make your list as complete as possible.

Organize Your Ideas. Arrange your ideas in a way that will help you best make your point. If you are brainstorming, make groups of like ideas after you finish your list. If you are using The Six Questions, see which questions you would like to answer first. No matter which method you use, organize the details you want to cover under your main ideas. You can organize ideas into an idea map or an outline.

Writing the First Draft

Write the Topic Sentence. Write several topic sentences to find the one that will grab your reader's eye and state your topic best. You might want to start your essay with a question to capture your reader's interest.

Develop Supporting Details. Make sure that each main point starts a new paragraph. Each new paragraph should start with a topic sentence. Then give details to back up your point. Use expressive language and precise words to tell your reader about your ideal vacation. Be sure that your writing is free of slang and that you have picked words with the connotations that persuade readers of your point of view. Find vivid synonyms to make your writing clear and creative.

Write the Conclusion. Write a strong ending that ties up all the points you made. Do not bring up any new main points about your ideal vacation here. You can save one very creative detail for the end.

Editing/Revising

Review. After you have finished writing, read the entire essay to make sure you did what you set out to do. Ask yourself: "If I were reading this essay, why would I think this describes an ideal vacation?"

Edit/Revise. Read each paragraph carefully, and revise your work using the Editing Checklist on page 24. In addition to the items on the editing checklist, check to see that you followed the guidelines for creative writing that you just learned:

- ☐ Did you use precise words and phrases to express your exact meaning?
- ☐ Did you replace slang with formal language?
- ☐ Did you pick words with correct denotations?
- ☐ Did you choose words with the connotations you prefer to get your point across?
- ☐ Did you use vivid synonyms to replace tired words and phrases?
- ☐ Did you generate ideas using brainstorming or The Six Questions?

Writing the Final Draft

Proofread. When you are finished with your revisions, reread the essay. Check for correct spelling, punctuation, and neatness. Look for missing letters in words, too. Use the proofreader's marks on page 26 to correct any errors you find. Rewrite or retype your work if necessary.

Sharing Your Final Draft

Publish. Read to a partner or have someone read your essay. Ask this person if your point was clear. Discuss what the person sees as the essay's weak and strong points. Make notes on the feedback. Then ask someone else to read the essay just for pleasure.

File. Save the essay and your notes in your notebook or portfolio.

Apply

For further practice writing creative essays, go to your Personal Writing Notebook. Each day write a paragraph that uses expressive language in a creative way.

Section 10

Special Writing Situations

Resumes and Job Applications

When you are looking for a job, there are a number of ways to use your writing skills. For example, you have already practiced writing a letter of application and a follow-up letter to a job interview. Now you will use your writing skills to prepare a resume and fill out a job application form.

Resumes

A **resume** is a written summary of your qualifications for work. It provides an employer with personal data. It also gives a summary of your job experience and skills. A resume represents you to an employer. In some cases, employers will see your resume before they meet you. Many employers use the resume to decide whether to grant an interview. You can see why a resume should be carefully written to *sell* you to the employer.

Write your resume to present the best possible picture of yourself. There are probably many things about you that will help you sell yourself to an employer. Always be honest about your background, but use whatever you can to make yourself look good. What you say about yourself and how you present facts on the resume can make the difference.

A resume usually includes the following parts:

1. **Personal data:** Your name, address, and telephone number
2. **Objective:** The position you wish to apply for
3. **Work experience:** Your employment record or employment skills
4. **Education:** Schools attended and courses taken
5. **Other skills/activities:** Skills that you acquired through experience other than paid work
6. **References:** A list of people who will recommend you for the job

Information you should not include in a resume includes:

1. Your age
2. Your race or ethnic origin
3. Your marital status
4. Your height or weight
5. Your health status

This personal information is not relevant to whether you can do most jobs. An employer's request for information in some of these personal areas is not legal. Certain jobs, such as police officer or firefighter, may have special physical requirements. Find this out before you go to apply for the job, and be prepared to provide the necessary information.

Judith D'Angelo
1225 Pharr Road South
Los Angeles, CA 94111
213-555-3509

OBJECTIVE:

Sales position with potential for career growth

WORK EXPERIENCE:

January 1991–Present

Stock Clerk, Baldwin's Department Store, Los Angeles, CA

- Recorded merchandise inventory of incoming stock.
- Stocked shelves and assisted sales clerks in keeping merchandise in order.
- Assisted in maintaining inventory records.
- Handled return of damaged merchandise to manufacturers.

June 1990–December 1990

Sales Clerk, Power Video, Los Angeles, CA

- Processed sales and rentals of videotapes.
- Assisted customers in finding merchandise.
- Trained new sales clerks to use computer system.

EDUCATION:

Attended Dover High School, 1987–1989
High School Diploma Received from Southview Learning Center,
January 1990

SKILLS:

Computer operations, word processing
Fluent in Spanish, Italian, and English

REFERENCES:

Marlon Jackson, Instructor
Southview Learning Center
1635 North Jefferson Ave.
Los Angeles, CA 94100

Alfreda Zavala, Manager
Power Video
North Center Mall
Los Angeles, CA 94309

Personal Data Sheet

Before writing your resume, gather and organize the information for it. One way to gather and organize the data is to complete a **personal data sheet.** It may also help you discover things about yourself that you would not have thought of putting on your resume. Even if you do not use all the information on the data sheet, completing it will help you make sure you didn't leave anything out. It will also help you think about questions you will be asked when you have a job interview.

Personal Data Sheet

Personal Data

Name _____

Address _____

City, State, Zip Code _____

Telephone _____

Objective

An objective is something you are seeking to achieve. Right now your objective may be just to get a job. Or perhaps you already have a job, but would like a better one. Think about what type of work you want to do — is it sales, computer work, health care? Write a statement that summarizes your objective.

_____

_____

_____

_____

_____

_____

Work Experience

Company _____ Telephone _____

Address_____

Dates of Employment _____

Type of Business _____

Name and Title of Supervisor_____

Your Title_____

Your Job Duties _____

    Did you receive any special training on the job, such as using equipment, handling customer problems, or anything not described in your job duties?

_____

_____

_____

_____

What did you like best about this job? _____

_____

What did you like least?_____

_____

Why did you leave?_____

_____

What was your salary when you started the job? _____

What was your salary when you left?_____

Other Experience/Skills

    List your personal strengths that are related to your objective. For instance, if you want to be a salesperson, do you enjoy working with people? Are you good at solving problems, making decisions, and organizing things? Do you have good writing skills? Can you draw? Can you fix things? You may want to ask someone who knows you well to help you identify your strengths.

_____

_____

_____

_____

What are your interests, hobbies, or accomplishments? Are you an athlete? A singer? A dancer? An artist? Have you done volunteer work?

_____

_____

Do you have training in any technical skills, or do you know how to operate any kind of equipment used on the kind of job you want?

_____

_____

References

Ask three people if they are willing to recommend you for a job.

1. Name _____ Telephone _____

   Title _____

   Company _____

   Address _____

2. Name _____ Telephone _____

   Title _____

   Company _____

   Address _____

3. Name _____ Telephone _____

   Title _____

   Company _____

   Address _____

Grammar: Action Verbs and Phrases

Resumes should be short and to the point. Businesspeople are very busy, and some of them read hundreds of resumes. Long sentences and paragraphs are likely to lose the attention of the person reading the resume. When stating your job objective, use short phrases rather than complete sentences.

Example   Objective

    Phrase: Sales position with growth potential

    Sentence: I would like a position as a sales clerk and eventually hope to become a supervisor.

When describing your work experience and skills, use phrases with action verbs rather than sentences that explain.

Example   **Phrase with action verb:** Planned fund-raising drive for the homeless.

    Sentence that explains: My church had a fund-raising drive for the homeless, and I helped plan the bake sale.

Certain action verbs are commonly used to describe work experience and skills. Using the verbs listed below helps create a professional impression about you and what you have done or can do.

Action Verbs

accomplished	created	led	processed	taught
achieved	designed	managed	repaired	trained
answered	developed	operated	scheduled	typed
approved	directed	organized	sold	used
assisted	handled	performed	solved	won
completed	input	planned	supervised	

Exercise   Write the best action verb to complete each phrase.

1. _____ letters and memos for department staff.
   Typed   Solved   Coordinated

2. _____ telephone calls for two executives.
   Completed   Trained   Handled

3. _____ weekly reports on service calls.
   Taught   Accomplished   Completed

4. _____ computer equipment and a fax machine.
   Operated   Developed   Processed

For more practice with action verbs, turn to pages 188–189.

Exercise ◤ Rewrite the sentences below to change them into phrases with action verbs.

1. When the copier broke down, I was able to repair it.

   _____

2. I drew all the signs we used in the window of the hardware store.

   _____

3. I made up schedules for covering the reception desk.

   _____

4. When the newsstand owner was out or on vacation, I took over.

   _____

5. I got awards for running track when I was in high school.

   _____

Guided Writing ◤ Practice using action verbs by writing phrases that summarize your work experience and skills. Use the information on your personal data sheet. If the verbs listed on page 125 do not fit, think of other action verbs to use.

Job Duties

_____

_____

_____

Skills

_____

_____

_____

Other Experience

_____

_____

Skills

_____

_____

Special Training/Equipment

_____

_____

_____

Skills

_____

_____

_____

For more practice with action verbs, turn to pages 188–189.

                    Check your answers on page 233.

Application 1

Writing a Resume

Now you are ready to write your resume. Before you begin, study the example below and the one on page 121. You can use either or both as models for setting up and wording your resume. The resume below shows how a person with very little work experience presented his skills and background.

Jonathan Sowell
26047 Birch Road
Detroit, MI 48234
313-555-2310

OBJECTIVE

Entry-level position in data entry or computer operations

WORK EXPERIENCE

Messenger, Reed Printing Company, 19000 Jefferson Ave., Detroit, MI 48232. July 1990 to October 1992

EDUCATION

Attended Northern High School 1986–1990.
Attended night school at J. P. Alexander Adult Learning Center.
Received high school diploma April 1990.

SKILLS

- Keyboarding and computer literacy
- Ability to listen, follow instructions, and learn quickly
- Dependable and able to work with little supervision

OTHER EXPERIENCE/ACTIVITIES

- Operate photocopy and fax machines
- Courses in record keeping and accounting
- Group leader in summer day camp program

REFERENCES

Mary Lee, Recreation Program Coordinator, City of Detroit, County Building, Detroit, MI 48232

Alvin Reed, President, Reed Printing Company, 19000 Jefferson Ave., Detroit, MI 48232

The writer of this resume does not have work experience that is related to the job he is seeking. So the resume emphasizes skills that tell the employer that this person is a hard worker, mature, and willing to learn. The resume also lists courses taken that are related to the use of organizational and math skills and experiences that are needed by a data-entry operator. It mentions a leadership role, which could have been at any point in the past. This item supports the image of maturity and initiative that the writer is trying to create.

Write Your Own Resume

Prewriting

Your prewriting work was filling in the personal data sheet on pages 122–124. To prepare your resume on a separate sheet of paper, use the information from your personal data sheet and revise your writing as necessary to create a first draft.

Writing the First Draft

Objective. Are you satisfied with the way you stated your objective? Is it specific to one type of job? If so, you may want to rewrite it to make it more general, so you can use it for several job openings. Or you may prefer to create more than one version of your resume with different objectives.

Work Experience. Review the work experience section of your personal data sheet, and copy the information on each job. Organize the information in the following order:

1. Name and address of company
2. Your job title
3. Dates of your employment
4. Job duties
5. Additional experience/skills you acquired on the job

Remember to list your most recent job first on your resume. If you have held a lot of jobs, you do not need to put the earliest ones on the resume, unless they are strongly related to the job you are currently seeking.

Write the first draft of the work experience section. Refer to the list of job duties and skills on page 126. Use action verbs that tell what you did on the job.

Education. List all your past education, starting with the most recent. Do not go back beyond your high school years. If you had a good grade point average, you can mention this under education. If you did well in any courses that are related to the job you are seeking, you can list them too.

Other Experience/Skills. List the other experience and skills that you outlined on page 126.

References. Include only two of the three people listed on your personal data sheet. Make sure that you check with them to get their approval before using their names on your resume.

Another way to handle references is to state: "References available upon request." Most companies do not check references unless they have decided that they want to hire you. If the names are not on your resume, they will call and ask you for them. Employers usually do not contact your present employer until after they have offered you the job and you have accepted it.

Editing/Revising

Carefully edit your first draft. Be particularly careful that all words are spelled correctly and that the information is accurate. Have someone read your first draft before you prepare the final draft. Use the advice to polish what you have written.

Writing the Final Draft

Your final draft must be typed. If you are unable to type, find someone who can do it for you or go to a resume preparation service. Make sure the type is arranged attractively on the page. There should be enough space between items to make it easy for the reader to skim over the page and find things. If possible, the resume should all fit on one page. Below is another example of a resume with a different format.

Binh Do
2041 Wyndam Road
Marietta, GA 30375
404-555-8997

Position Sought	Administrative assistant in accounting or management
Work Experience	Office Temp Services, Atlanta, GA June 1992–Present Temporary secretary • Performed routine secretarial duties — typing, filing, answering telephones. Marietta Power Company, Marietta, GA January 1992–June 1992 Accounting assistant in high school internship program • Prepared weekly payroll reports. • Updated employee records on a computer. • Handled telephone requests for information.
Education	Marietta High School, June 1992 Business Education Curriculum
Other Experience	Courses in word processing, spreadsheet software, accounting, and record keeping

References Available upon Request

Application 2

Complete a Job Application Form

The information on a job application form is mostly the same as the data on your resume. A job application form usually asks for the following categories of information:

1. **Name, address, telephone.**

2. **Position you are applying for.** If you are not applying for a specific job opening, list a general job category such as secretary, trainee, supervisor. You can also just write, "entry-level position."

3. **Salary required.** If you are not sure, you can leave this blank. However, the interviewer is likely to ask you for an answer. You can state the salary you are honestly hoping to make, given your qualifications. If you are not sure what certain kinds of jobs pay, you should learn this before you apply. Check the want ads, talk with people who do similar kinds of work, or check with the company personnel office.

4. **Social Security Number.** If you don't have a Social Security number, you can apply for one at a local Social Security office. You must have a Social Security number in order to be employed.

5. **U.S. citizenship.** If you are not a U.S. citizen, the company will inform you of their requirements for hiring noncitizens.

6. **Other personal data.** Examples include listing relatives who are employed in the same company; how you found out about the company or open position; whom to contact in case of an emergency.

7. **Educational data.** Formal schooling and any additional courses.

8. **Skills.** Although you may be applying for a particular position, there may be other jobs in the company that you are unaware of. It is important that you list all your skills here, whether they are relevant to the specific job you are applying for.

9. **Employment history:**

   - Names and addresses of companies you worked for in the past.
   - Name and title of supervisor. If the person you worked for is no longer with the company, you should still give his or her name.
   - The reason you left, if you are no longer working there. If you were fired or left a job without giving notice, you may not want to include this work experience on your resume. Some other common reasons can be stated as follows: to return to school, to seek a better position, staff reduction or layoffs, assignment was temporary. Do not state personal reasons for leaving a job, such as not having anyone to care for your children or not getting along with the boss. The phrase "to seek a better position" covers these kinds of reasons.
   - Your starting and ending salary. Although you may consider this confidential, it is routine, and employers expect an answer.

Use the information from your personal data sheet and resume to fill in the following job application form for openings as an orderly, nurse's aide, and receptionist at a hospital.

BELVEDERE HOSPITAL

Employment Application

An Equal Opportunity Employer

Belvedere policy and federal law forbid discrimination because of race, religion, age, sex, marital status, disability, or national origin.

Date _____

Personal Data

Applying for position as _____ Salary required _____

Name _____
            (Last)   (First)   (Middle)

Address _____
       (Street)   (City)   (State)   (Zip)

Telephone _____ Social Security Number _____

Are you a U.S. citizen? _____ Yes _____ No

If noncitizen, give Alien Registration Number _____

Person to notify in case of emergency:

Name _____ Telephone _____

Address _____

Have you ever been employed by Belvedere? _____ Yes _____ No

If yes, list department _____ Dates _____

Have you previously applied for employment with Belvedere? _____ Yes _____ No

If yes, give date _____

How were you referred to Belvedere? _____ Agency _____ School

_____ Advertisement _____ Belvedere Employee Other _____

Name of referral source above _____

Military Data

Have you served in the military service of the United States? _____ Yes _____ No

If yes, branch of service _____ From _____ To _____

Rank _____ Service duties that apply to civilian jobs _____

_____

Educational Data

School Name and Address Date Type Course/Major Graduated? Degree Received

_____

High School _____

_____

College _____

_____

Trade, Business _____

_____

Other _____

_____

Grade Point Average: High School _____ College _____

Skills

List any special skills _____

_____

Business machines you can operate _____

_____

Typing speed _____ Equipment _____

Steno speed _____ Method _____

Computer skills _____

_____

Employment Data

List all full-time, part-time, temporary, or self-employment. Begin with current or most recent employer.

Company Name	Employed From/To
Street Address	Salary or Earnings
City	State	Zip	Telephone

_____

Name/Title of Supervisor

_____

Your Title and Duties

_____

Reason for Leaving _____

Company Name   Employed From/To

_____

Street Address   Salary or Earnings

_____

City   State   Zip   Telephone

_____

Name/Title of Supervisor

_____

Your Title and Duties

_____

Reason for Leaving _____

This employment application is not a contract and is not meant to impose any legal obligation on either you or the Belvedere Hospital.

Belvedere Hospital does not require or administer a lie detector test or a drug test as a condition of employment.

I confirm that all my answers to the questions in this employment application are accurate and complete. I understand that my employment will be contingent upon the accuracy, completeness, and acceptability of the information furnished to you. Permission is granted to Belvedere Hospital to verify all statements in this employment application. I understand that my present employer will not be contacted until after I accept an offer of employment with Belvedere Hospital.

I further understand that after employment, I may be required to take a complete physical exam.

I have read the above statement and accept the same as a condition of my employment with Belvedere Hospital.

_____   _____

Date   Signature of Applicant

PART A REVIEW

Write pronouns in the blanks to take the place of the underlined nouns.
Choose from these pronouns: *he, she, they, her, him, them, his,* **and** *their.*

1. <u>Mike and Sonia</u> are planning a vacation. _____

2. <u>Mike</u> wants to go to Florida. _____

3. <u>Sonia's</u> brother Mario lives in Miami. _____

4. Mike and Sonia decide to stay with <u>Mario</u>. _____

Choose the correct pronoun to complete each sentence.

5. Those car keys belong to _____.
   I   me

6. Lilly and _____ parked on the street.
   he   him

7. Oscar gave Otis and _____ a ride.
   she   her

8. Rick and _____ want to buy a used car.
   I   me

For more practice with pronouns, see pages 172–174.

Put one line under each complete subject and two lines under each complete predicate.

9. Diana started her new job on Friday.

10. Bob and she work at the baseball stadium.

11. They sell peanuts and ice-cream sandwiches.

12. Bob's friends attend most of the games.

13. The employees can buy tickets for half-price.

For more practice on subjects and predicates, see pages 186–187.

Put an *S* in the blank next to each complete sentence. Put an *F* next to each fragment.

_____ 14. The groceries in the car.

_____ 15. Ms. Valdez wrote a check.

_____ 16. The clerk opened another line.

_____ 17. Before the end of the day.

_____ 18. Lost the shopping list in the parking lot.

_____ 19. Mr. Nio wants change for a dollar.

For more practice correcting sentence fragments, see pages 190–191.

Fill in the blank with one of the connecting words listed below.

so	and	because	unless	but
if	although	even	when	since

20. I can't give you a refund _____ you have a receipt.

21. Ana saw Rudy, _____ he didn't see her.

22. Carlos gave the file to Ms. Webb, _____ she gave it to me.

23. Mr. Smith will get the message _____ he returns from lunch.

Correct each of the following run-on sentences by separating it into two complete sentences.

24. George completed the form, he gave it to Ms. Golov.

_____

25. She liked his resume it was neat and well-organized.

_____

26. Ms. Golov offered George a job, he would have to work Saturdays.

_____

27. The job pays well the company offers good benefits.

_____

For more practice with run-on sentences, see pages 192–193.

Check your answers on page 233.

Choose the correct adjective or adverb to complete each of the following sentences.

28. Huntington Gardens has a _____ library and museum.
    large (adj.)   **largely** (adv.)

29. The museum has many _____ paintings and sculptures.
    fine (adj.)   **finely** (adv.)

30. Old books are _____ displayed in glass cases.
    careful (adj.)   **carefully** (adv.)

31. The rose garden is _____ year round.
    beautiful (adj.)   **beautifully** (adv.)

32. You can get to the museum _____ from the Foothill Freeway.
    easy (adj.)   **easily** (adv.)

33. The museum employees will _____ give you directions.
    glad (adj.)   **gladly** (adv.)

Choose the correct form of the adjective or adverb to complete each sentence.

34. Of all our employees, Monica is the _____ typist.
    fast   **faster**   **fastest**

35. She also writes _____.
    well   **better**   **good**

36. Of our two new employees, Jesse works _____ than Carolyn.
    hard   **harder**   **hardest**

37. Monica and Jesse will be promoted _____.
    quickly   **more quickly**   **most quickly**

38. Of the three employees, Monica has the _____ salary.
    high   **higher**   **highest**

For more practice with adjectives and adverbs, see pages 177–181.

Identify the tense of each of the underlined verbs in the sentences below.
Write *past*, *present*, or *future* in each blank.

_____ 39. Gina <u>started</u> her own business last year.

_____ 40. Her business <u>will earn</u> a large profit this year.

_____ 41. She <u>makes</u> custom picture frames.

_____ 42. Last week, the bank <u>gave</u> her a loan.

_____ 43. Gina <u>wants</u> to rent a bigger workshop.

_____ 44. She <u>will call</u> a realtor next week.

Choose the correct verb to complete each sentence.

45. I _____ before you called.
    will cook   cooking   had been cooking

46. Hector _____ a new job last week.
    starts   started   has started

47. Doug _____ a file clerk for the last two years.
    will be   has been   is being

48. By next Friday, Lucy _____ eight hours of overtime.
    works   has worked   will have worked

49. Katrina _____ the news before Issiah arrived at work.
    has told   had told   will have told

For more practice with verbs, see pages 182–185.

Rewrite each sentence with correct capital letters.

50. bob and angela went to the kentucky derby last year.

_____

51. they stayed at the middletown hotel on main street.

_____

52. on wednesday they crossed the ohio river and visited bob's aunt in indiana.

_____

53. aunt mary works as a travel agent for american travel incorporated.

_____

54. on friday angela wanted to go to the louisville zoo.

_____

55. afterward, they ate dinner at clarke's cafe on south fork road.

_____

For more practice with capitalization rules, see pages 158–161.

Place punctuation marks correctly in the following sentences.

56. Is Stan coming to Nita's Halloween party

57. She is serving hot dogs potato salad and baked beans

58. Sheila was born on May 25 1965

59. Kham's boss Charles H Garrett is from Boise Idaho

60. Do you want red blue or gold ribbon

61. Discount Photo Company put an ad in the newspaper

62. The last conference was held in Denver Colorado

63. Jesse Lupe Rita and Anna are Dodgers fans

For more practice with punctuation rules, see pages 150–155.

Choose the correct verb form to complete each sentence.

64. Mei Lee had _____ the memo before she left.
    wrote   written

65. Mr. Lucas has _____ learning Spanish.
    began   begun

66. The TV had _____ $350 before the sale.
    cost   costed

67. Laura _____ the results of the test yesterday.
    knew   known

68. He will have _____ the phone number by this time.
    finded   found

Write the correct form of each verb in parentheses.

69. (go) We _____ to a football game last Saturday.

70. (take) I _____ my binoculars to see the action.

71. (see) I haven't _____ many games as good as this one.

72. (buy) During the half time, we _____ hamburgers.

73. (eat) I had _____ only half of mine when snow began to fall.

For more practice with irregular verbs, see page 185.

Find the verb in each sentence. On the line, write *A* if the verb is in active voice or *P* if the verb is in passive voice.

_____74.   Gordon locked his keys in the car.

_____75.   The copy machine was broken by someone.

_____76.   A wallet was found near the candy machine.

_____77.   Tonya sprained her ankle yesterday.

_____78.   A computer error was made on your bill.

These sentences are in the passive voice. Rewrite each sentence in the active voice.

79.   The chicken soup was made by Aretha.

_____

80.   The letter was written by Mr. Kington.

_____

81.   The pennant was won by the Chicago Cubs.

_____

82.   Early this morning, the pay phone was broken by someone.

_____

For more practice with active and passive voice, see pages 188–189.

Choose the correct word to complete each sentence.

83.   _____ a beautiful day.
      It's   Its

84.   Your notebook is _____ on my desk.
      hear   here

85.   We can have the cookout at _____ house.
      are   our

86.   _____ is my boss, Ms. Goldhammer.
      Their   There

87.   I do not _____ if the office will be open after 5:00 P.M.
      know   no

For more practice with homonyms, turn to page 168.

Check your answers on page 234.

Part B

HANDBOOK

Clear writing is essential in business and personal situations.

The Handbook gives you more instruction and practice with grammar skills. Most of these grammar skills are first presented in Sections 2–10 of Part A. If you need more practce with a certain skill, you can refer to the appropriate page in this Handbook. Once you have completed the grammar page in Part B, return to the section you were working on in Part A.

The four sections of this Handbook are described below. A complete table of contents follows on page 141.

The Writing Process. This section presents writing models for each of the five steps of the Writing Process. Study the models to be sure you can follow the five steps in your own writing.

Mechanics. This section covers end punctuation, commas, semicolons, colons, quotation marks, dashes, parentheses, capitalization, and spelling.

Usage. This section covers how to use each of the main parts of speech: nouns, pronouns, adjectives, adverbs, and verbs.

Sentence Structure. This section explains run-on sentences, sentence fragments, sentence combining, sentence revision, compound and complex sentences, subordinate clauses, parallel structure, and misplaced modifiers.

Handbook Contents

The Writing Process

Models

Prewriting

Plan your writing by following these prewriting steps:

A. Define your topic. Is your topic too broad or too narrow? Do you already have information about the topic? What information do you need to gather about the topic?

B. Identify your purpose. To narrate; to describe; to persuade; to explain; to entertain; to inform

C. Identify your audience. The general public; an instructor; classmates; family; friends; your boss; co-workers; potential employers

D. Generate ideas. Explore your thoughts and feelings about the topic. Brainstorm — ask Who? What? Why? When? How? Where? Talk to others to exchange opinions; ask experts. Read/research — consult magazines, newspapers, TV.

Model

A. Purpose: To convince or persuade people

B. Audience: Classmates

C. Topic: A low-cholesterol diet is good for the heart.

D. Generate Ideas: Read articles on foods, cholesterol, and fat. Brainstorm — What foods are low in cholesterol?

Notes: Foods high in cholesterol/fat include:
eggs, red meat — especially organ meats and fatty meats —
pork, poultry skin, shortening, butter
Foods low in cholesterol include: fish, beans, soybean products, vegetables, fruit
Different types of fat—butter, oil, margarine

E. Outline or Map Your Ideas

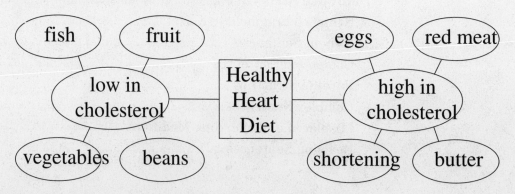

Outline Format	**Outline Model**

Outline Format

I. Main idea
   A. Subtopic
      1. Supporting detail
      2. Supporting detail
      3. Supporting detail
   B. Subtopic
      1. Supporting detail
      2. Supporting detail
      3. Supporting detail

II. Conclusion
   A. Concluding statement
      1. Supporting detail
      2. Supporting detail

Outline Model

I. Healthy heart diet
   A. High-cholesterol foods
      1. Red meat
      2. Egg yolks
      3. Saturated fat
   B. Low-cholesterol foods
      1. Fish
      2. Beans
      3. Fruits and vegetables
      4. Polyunsaturated fat

II. Conclusion
   A. Benefits of a healthy diet
      1. Helps the heart
      2. Controls weight

Writing the First Draft

Write the first draft. Write a good topic sentence for each paragraph and include supporting details that relate to each main idea. Include details that state facts or reasons, give examples, compare and contrast, show time order, show order of importance, or show cause and effect. End with a concluding paragraph.

Foods for a Healthy Heart

Paragraph 1
Topic Sentence
Supporting Detail
Cause/Effect

When it comes to heart disease, eating a low-fat, low-cholesterol diet is the key to staying healthy. In the past, if people were killing themselves with a poor diet they didn't know it. Today, unless you live in a cave, you cannot ignore that the choice of eating healthy foods or unhealthy foods is yours.

Paragraph 2
Topic Sentence
Supporting Detail
Examples
Supporting Detail
Facts/Reasons

The biggest problem in avoiding cholesterol is to avoid eating fatty red mean and egg yolks. Unless ate in very small amounts, red meat is harmful to a diet for a healthy heart. That means avoid too much meat — especially organ meats such as liver. Other meats that are high in fat should also be avoided, such as bacon, ham hocks, and chicken skin. A large egg contains about 274 milligrams of cholesterol and saturated fat. egg whites, on the other hand, have protein, but don't add cholesterol or saturated fat to the diet.

Paragraph 3
Supporting Detail
Facts/Reasons

Cause/Effect

It is also important to be aware of the different types of fat. Even without eating meat, the body creates cholesterol from foods that contain saturated fats. Coconut and palm oils are sourses of saturated fats. These types of fat are found in many prepared and processed foods. Avoid shortening and butter, because they also have high levels of saturated fat. Instead, eat soft margarine that has liquid oil, or use vegetable oils that contain little saturated fat.

Paragraph 4
Topic Sentence
Supporting Detail
Facts / Reasons
Examples

Eat plenty of loow-fat foods. Fish is low in fat and provides protein for the diet. Beans are an excellent source of protein, because they are completely free of saturated fat and cholesterol. Some authorities also consider them the cheapest source. They also provide iron, B vitamins, and vitamin A. Fresh fruit and and vegetables are another delicious source of low-fat foods. Use soft margarine or liquid oil — soybean or corn oil are the best.

Conclusion
Summary and
Final Thought

In addition to being fit and healthy, you will look your best. One of the best things about a low-fat, low-cholesterol diet is that while helping your heart, it will also regulate your weight. All you have to is choose the right foods. Remember, you can't say you didn't know.

Editing / Revising

Use the Editing Checklist below to edit and revise your first draft.

Editing Checklist

Content	YES	NO
Does the content reflect your original purpose?	☑	☐
Is the content right for your intended audience?	☑	☐
Is the main idea stated clearly?	☑	☐
Does each paragraph have a topic sentence?	☑	☐
Are topic sentences supported by details?	☑	☐
Are details written in a logical order?	☐	☑
Is the right amount of information included?	☐	☑

(Check for details that are not needed and
for details that are missing.)

Style	YES	NO
Will the writing hold the reader's interest?	☑	☐
Are thoughts and ideas expressed clearly?	☐	☑
Are any ideas repeated?	☑	☐
Are some words used too many times?	☐	☑

Grammar	YES	NO
Are all sentences complete sentences?	☑	☐
Are any sentences too long and hard to understand?	☐	☑
Are any sentences too short and choppy?	☐	☑
Are nouns and pronouns used correctly?	☐	☑
Are verbs used correctly?	☐	☑
Are adjectives and adverbs used correctly?	☑	☐
Are there any other obvious errors?	☐	☑

Paragraph 1

When it comes to heart disease, eating a low-fat, low-cholesterol diet is the key to staying healthy. In the past, if people were killing themselves with a poor diet they didn't know

Idea not clear

it. Today, ~~unless you live in a cave~~ *with all the data available*, you cannot ignore that the choice of eating healthy foods or unhealthy foods is yours.

Paragraph 2
Incorrect verb form
Incorrect verb tense

The biggest problem in avoiding cholesterol is to avoid *having* eating fatty red mean and egg yolks. Unless ~~ate~~ *eaten* in very small amounts, red meat is harmful to a diet for a healthy heart. ~~That~~ *It is necessary to*

Language not clear

~~means~~ avoid too much meat — especially organ meats such as liver. Other meats that are high in fat should also be avoided,

Detail missing

such as bacon, ham hocks, and ~~chicken skin.~~ *sausage. Poultry can be eaten in large amounts but the skin should be removed.* A large egg *yolk*

Not clear

contains about 274 milligrams of cholesterol and saturated fat. egg whites, on the other hand, have protein, but don't add cholesterol or saturated fat to the diet.

Paragraph 3
Detail missing

Cholesterol is a fat that is found in the human body and in animal fat. It is also important to be aware of the different types of fat. Even without eating meat, the body creates cholesterol from

Detail missing

foods that contain saturated *(solid)* fats. Coconut and palm oils are sourses of saturated fats. These types of fat are found in many prepared and processed foods. Avoid shortening and butter, because they also have high levels of saturated fat. Instead, eat

Detail missing

soft margarine that has liquid oil, or use vegetable oils *such as soybean or corn oils,* that contain little saturated fat.

Paragraph 4   Eat plenty of loow-fat foods. Fish is low in fat and provides protein

for the diet. Beans are an excellent source of protein, because they are

Unnecessary detail   completely free of saturated fat and cholesterol. ~~Some authorities also~~

~~consider them the cheapest source.~~ They also provide iron, B vitamins,

and vitamin A. Fresh fruit and and vegetables are another delicious

Detail repeated   source of low-fat foods. ~~Use soft margarine or liquid oil — soybean or~~

~~corn oil are the best.~~

Conclusion   In addition to being fit and healthy, you will look your best. One
Detail out of order

of the best things about a low-fat, low-cholesterol diet is that while

helping your heart, it will also regulate your weight. All you have to is

choose the right foods. Remember, you can't say you didn't know.

Writing the Final Draft

Proofread and correct any errors in spelling, punctuation, or paragraph
indentation. Use the proofreader's marks shown on page 147.

Proofreading Checklist	YES	NO
Is correct punctuation used in every sentence?	☐	☑
Is correct capitalization used in every sentence?	☐	☑
Are all words spelled correctly?	☐	☑
Are new paragraphs clearly shown?	☑	☐
If handwritten, is handwriting as neat as possible?	☐	☐
If typed, is typing neat and without errors?	☑	☐
Is there enough space between words and lines?	☑	☐
Are the margins too wide or too narrow?	☐	☑

Proofreader's Marks

<u>a</u>	capital letter
A̸	lowercase letter
⊙ / ∧	insert period
∧,	insert comma
word ∧	insert punctuation or word
(Sp) (thiir)	check spelling
¶	paragraph
no ¶	no new paragraph
ℓ	delete a letter, word, group of words
ℓ	delete and close up space

Paragraph 1

Punctuation missing

When it comes to heart disease, eating a low-fat, low-cholesterol diet is the key to staying healthy. In the past, if people were killing themselves with a poor diet, they didn't know it. Today, with all the data available, you cannot ignore that the choice of eating healthy foods or unhealthy foods is yours.

Paragraph 2

Spelling error

The biggest problem in avoiding cholesterol is having to avoid eating fatty red *meat* (mean) and egg yolks. Unless eaten in very small amounts, red meat is harmful to a diet for a healthy heart. It is necessary to avoid too much meat — especially organ meats such as liver. Other meats that are high in fat should also be avoided, such as bacon, ham hocks, and sausage. Poultry can be eaten in large

Punctuation missing

Capital letter missing

amounts, but the skin should be removed. A large egg yolk contains about 274 milligrams of cholesterol and saturated fat. egg whites, on the other hand, have protein, but don't add cholesterol or saturated fat to the diet.

Paragraph 3

It is also important to be aware of the different types of fat. Cholesterol is a fat that is found in the human body and in animal fat. Even without eating meat, the body creates cholesterol from foods that contain saturated (solid) fats. Coconut and palm oils are

Spelling error

sources (sourses) of saturated fats. These types of fat are found in many prepared and processed foods. Avoid shortening and butter, because they also have high levels of saturated fat. Instead, eat soft margarine that has liquid oil, or use vegetable oils such as soybean or corn oils that contain little saturated fat.

Paragraph 4
Extra letter

Eat plenty of low-fat foods. Fish is low in fat and provides protein for the diet. Beans are an excellent source of protein, because they are completely free of saturated fat and cholesterol. They also provide iron,

Extra word

B vitamins, and vitamin A. Fresh fruit and ~~and~~ vegetables are another source of low-fat foods.

Conclusion

One of the best things about a low-fat, low-cholesterol diet is that while helping your heart, it will also regulate your weight. In addition to

Word missing

being fit and healthy, you will look your best. All you have to do is choose the right foods. Remember, you can't say you didn't know.

Publishing (Sharing the Final Draft)

Make the final corrections, and share your work with the intended audience.

Mechanics

End Punctuation

Just as road signs direct drivers, so punctuation in a sentence directs readers. **Punctuation** is the set of symbols used in writing to guide the reader. A sentence always ends with one of three types of punctuation. The three end punctuation marks are the period, the question mark, and the exclamation point. Which end mark you use will depend on your purpose, because each end mark has a different use.

Period

Use a period to show the end of a sentence that states information or gives facts. Also use a period to show the end of a command.

Example

A circle has 360 degrees.   Don't eat that cake.

Question Mark

Use a question mark to show the end of a direct question. A direct question is one that needs an answer.

Example

When are you planning to move?   Are you hungry now?

Exclamation Point

Use an exclamation point to end a sentence that shows strong emotion.

Example

That's great!   Watch out for broken glass!

Exercise

Complete each of the following sentences with the correct end punctuation.

1. When do you think the first soap opera was broadcast on TV

2. The first TV soap opera was aired on October 2, 1946

3. Called *Faraway Hill,* it was the only network show on Wednesday nights

4. It's amazing that the show was done live — on a budget of less than $300 a week

Check your answers on page 234.

Commas

Commas are used within sentences to tell readers where to pause and take a breath. Commas also help make long sentences easier to read. Commas are used in lists, to add facts and information, and to set off parts of a sentence.

Use commas in lists. A list is a group of items that come one after the other. Lists can be made up of single words or groups of words. **Use commas to separate three or more items in a list.**

Example

> Juan, Paul, Hector, and Luis are going camping.
> They plan to go fishing, take walks, and sleep late.

Use commas to add facts and information. Use commas to add details that help make your writing clearer and more exciting. Separate two or more adjectives that describe the same thing.

Example

> The camping area has a new, well-built lodge.
> The tall, old trees shade the grounds on even the hottest day.

Do not use a comma to separate adjectives that have to stay in a specific order.

Example

> It took <u>many long</u> days to get to the woods.
> (*Long* must come after *many*. No comma is needed.)

Use commas with facts that show to whom the writer is speaking. Also use commas to set off common phrases that show contrast.

Example

> Hector, we will clean up after dinner if you cook.
> That was a great meal, Juan.   You forgot the beans, however.

Exercise

Correct each of the following sentences by adding commas where needed.

1. The cute cuddly Teddy Bear is a popular toy.

2. Reader do you know how the Teddy Bear was named?

3. Well-liked athletic Theodore Roosevelt loved to hunt.

4. However while hunting in 1902 he would not shoot a bear that had been tied to a tree.

5. The man who drew a picture of the tense exciting scene started a fad: the Teddy Bear.

Check your answers on page 234.

Use commas to separate two complete thoughts. Use a comma to set off the two complete parts of a compound sentence. Join the complete parts with *and, but, for, nor, or, so,* or *yet*. Put the comma before the connecting word.

Example

> They saw a lot of rabbits while camping, but they saw no deer.
> The weather was bad the first day, so everyone stayed inside.

Use a comma to set off the opening part of a sentence. This opening can be a word or a group of words and can be short or long.

Example

> Well, maybe you should bring rain gear.
> Over the green hills, we saw a flock of birds.
> After they left the camp, they put all their trash in bins.
> As soon as we get everything packed in the car, we'll head off.

Use a comma to set off words or phrases that can be removed from a sentence. Many times, these details are adjectives or phrases that start with *who* or *which*. Make sure that the words are really not needed. **Words that must be included are <u>not</u> set off by commas.**

Example

> **Can be removed:**   Juan, <u>my cousin</u>, is a fine cook.
>   Hector, <u>who is just back from a trip</u>, had
>   never been camping before.
> **Cannot be removed:**   My <u>cousin</u> Juan is a fine cook.
>   The tent <u>on the left</u> cost a fortune.

Exercise

Correct each of the following sentences by adding commas where needed.

1. Born in Texas in 1905 billionaire Howard Hughes led a sad life.

2. His mother who kept him from playing with other children died when Howard was sixteen.

3. His father died two years later and Howard took charge of the family business.

4. Howard was a great businessman but he soon became restless.

5. Lured by the movies Howard went to Hollywood.

6. Over the next few years he produced many famous movies.

7. Hughes who loved flying formed the Hughes Aircraft Company.

8. By 1938 he was a hero having set three world speed records.

9. Not a happy man he spent the rest of his life alone in a hotel.

                                    Check your answers on pages 234–235.

Use commas with dates. Dates are often made up of several parts, such as days, months, and years. Use commas to help your reader avoid confusion with dates. When a date has two or more parts, use a comma after each part. However, do not use a comma between the month and the number of the day.

Example

> The first person walked on the moon on July 20, 1969.
> Thursday, March 16, is the day we have set for the party.
> Starting on Friday, June 15, 1992, all workers will get an extra break.

Use commas with place names. Names of places also may have a number of parts. You may want to use the name of a town, the name of a county, and the name of a state one after the other, for example. In these cases, use commas to make your writing clear.

Example

> Is it true that your parents came from Dublin, County Cork, Ireland?
> He went to the town where he was born, Red Cloud, New York.

Use commas with titles. Many people sign their names with their title. Doctors use *M.D.* after their names, and registered nurses use *R.N.* Some men add *Jr.* for *junior* or *Sr.* for *senior* after their names. Use a comma between the name and title to keep your writing clear. Do not use a comma when the title comes before a person's name.

Example

> Are Bob White, Sr., and Bob White, Jr., working for the same firm?
> My dentist is Delfina Chapa, DDS.
> Dr. Nguyen practices dentistry in San Francisco.

Exercise

Correct each of the following sentences by adding commas where needed.

1. Martin Luther King Jr. was a very famous leader.

2. After he earned his last degree, people called him Martin Luther King Ph.D. or Dr. King.

3. He worked in Montgomery Alabama to improve civil rights.

4. On April 3 1968 he gave his last public speech.

5. He was shot and killed April 4 1968 in Memphis Tennessee.

6. On June 8 1968 his killer was arrested in London England.

7. More than 150,000 people were at his funeral in the Ebenezer Baptist Church in Atlanta Georgia.

8. On May 2 1968 a poor people's march began to honor Dr. King.

9. The march ended on June 24 1968.

Check your answers on page 235.

Semicolons and Colons

Semicolon

The **semicolon** is made up of a comma and a period (;). The semicolon, then is a cross between a comma and a period. It breaks apart two sentences, but it lets the writer show that the ideas are connected.

Use a semicolon to connect two complete sentences that are not joined by the words *and, or, nor, for, so, but,* or *yet.*

Example

> She liked to eat meat once a day; he wanted to eat only fish.
> We have tried three times to reach you by phone; you have not
>   returned a single call.

Colon

A **colon** is made up of two periods (:). Like an arrow, it points the reader to information to come.

Use a colon to start a list of items. Also use a colon after the greeting in a business letter.

Example

> My friend told me to go to the store and buy these items: milk, bread,
>   cheese, and eggs.
> Dear Mr. Chang:

Exercise

Correct each of the following sentences by adding semicolons or colons where needed.

1. Many Americans like the British Royal Family this is shown by the number of people who view royal events.

2. People like to watch royal weddings the best they also watch shows about royal birthdays.

3. Over 750 million people watched the wedding of Prince Charles and Lady Diana this was the most popular royal event ever.

4. The wedding took place July 29, 1981 it was held at 4:30 P.M.

5. There were TV shows on the following topics parties, cost, and guests.

6. The bride went to the church in a glass coach it is part of the family's custom.

7. Diana was nervous she said Charles' names in the wrong order.

Check your answers on page 235.

Quotation Marks

Use quotation marks to show a person's exact speech. If the quotation is a complete thought, it begins with a capital letter and ends with an end punctuation mark. Quotations that give facts or commands end with a period. Quotations that ask questions end with a question mark. Quotations that show strong feeling end with an exclamation point. Put the end mark before the last quotation mark.

Example

Fact:	Lupe said, "I will be late tonight."
Question:	Maria asked, "How late do you think you will be?"
Strong feeling:	Lupe said, "I hate to work late on Friday!"

Use a comma before the last set of quotation marks if you are quoting a statement.

Example

"We have to go shopping for the party," Maria said.
"You know I will try to finish early," Lupe replied.

Sometimes you do not write the speaker's exact words. Instead, you give the general meaning of what the person said. **If you do not quote the speaker's exact words, do not use quotation marks.**

Example

He thought she was joking.
The man asked where the store was.

Exercise

Add quotation marks where needed. Not every sentence needs quotation marks.

1. On June 3, 1965, astronaut Ed White left the space capsule to go on a twelve-minute space walk.

2. When the twelve minutes passed, White's partner said, It's time to come in.

3. I'm not coming in because I am having fun, said White.

4. Come in! McDivitt ordered.

5. Get back in here before it gets dark, McDivitt pleaded.

6. White said that it would make him sad to come back in.

7. Get him back in now! ground crew workers ordered.

8. McDivitt answered, He's in his seat now.

Check your answers on page 235.

Dashes and Parentheses

Dash

A **dash** is made up of two hyphens and looks like this: —. Use a dash to set off words that interrupt the main thought of a sentence or to show a sudden change of thought. A dash creates a more dramatic pause than a comma. The dash is most often used to stress some part of a sentence, because it makes a sentence look different. You can use one dash or a pair of dashes.

Use a dash to show a sudden change in thought. In this case, use one dash.

Example

> My day was very dull—but you don't want to hear all about it.
> Food, clothing, housing—all these things are getting so much harder to afford.

Use a dash to set off ideas that break into the main thought. In this case, use a pair of dashes.

Example

> The new seats—Mr. Harris claims—will make my back less tired.
> One job above all others—the cleaning—is usually ignored.

Exercise

For each sentence, add one or two dashes where needed.

1. Sunburn, snakebite, and arrow wounds people going west in the 1800s faced all these dangers.

2. There were some cures if you could call them that.

3. Women already working very hard made up most of the potions.

4. Salt, goose grease, and skunk oil these were the main parts of many salves and creams.

5. Toasted onion skins and raw chicken if you can believe it were used to treat snakebite.

6. People put salt pork in their ears to cure an earache I can't stand it!

7. Wild herbs, seeds, and plants these were the key to healers.

8. Some cures were more harmful than the sickness that's no surprise.

9. Records show that ammonia and paint cleaner of all things were used to cure aches and pains.

Parentheses

Like the dash, **parentheses** set off facts and details. These facts and details add something extra to a sentence. Unlike the dash, parentheses do not stress the part of the sentence they set off. Parentheses are always used in pairs.

Use parentheses to set off words and phrases only when they are not essential to the meaning of the sentence.

Example

The shoe sale (held only once a year) has some great deals.
My second job brings in money that we need (but staying up late every night is very hard).

Use parentheses to set off the dates of a person's birth and death or any other facts that use numbers.

Example

My father (1925–1980) saw many changes in his life.
Add two cans of sauce (8-ounce size).

Use parentheses around letters or numbers in a list.

Example

We caught these fish: (a) carp, (b) tuna, (c) flounder.
The job calls for the following tools: (1) a wrench, (2) a hammer, and (3) a screwdriver.

Exercise

For each sentence, add parentheses where needed.

1. Being an actor calls for 1 talent, 2 a thick skin, and 3 luck.

2. Actor Edward James Olmos famous for his role in *Miami Vice* surely has talent.

3. Olmos is also well known for his role as Jaime Escalante a teacher.

4. Pedro Olmos Edward's father left Mexico to marry Eleanor Huizar.

5. Mr. Olmos 1925–1988 couldn't speak English when he arrived in the United States.

6. As a result, he tried many different jobs at least a dozen.

7. Mr. Olmos had these skills: a dancing, b singing, c playing music.

8. Edward learned how to jitterbug and cha-cha old-time dances.

9. Olmos sang and danced at clubs on Sunset Strip located in Hollywood.

Check your answers on page 235.

Capital Letters

Use a capital letter for the first word in a sentence.

Example

> This plant needs more light.
> Do you want to put it on the table?
> It is doing great here!
> I'm not sure we want to move it.

Use a capital letter for the first word in a quotation if the quotation is a complete sentence. Do not use a capital letter for the second half of a quotation.

Example

> "The soil is dry," she said.
> He said, "Look at these brown leaves."
> "The plant is dry," she said, "because we did not water it."
> "The leaves are falling off," he said, "but I think we can save it."

Exercise

In each sentence, show where capital letters are needed. Use the proofreader's mark for a capital letter ($\equiv$).

1. many people stay up late at night to watch talk shows.

2. the first talk show was the *Tonight Show*.

3. it started on September 27, 1954.

4. the first host, Steve Allen, said, "this is sort of a mild little show."

5. on the show, Steve Allen played music, talked to people, and did funny skits.

6. three years later, *The Jack Parr Show* took over in the same time slot.

7. "this is an hour and forty-five minutes a night," Parr said, "and I can't figure it out."

8. in 1962, Parr stepped down, and Johnny Carson was made the host.

9. this show became one of NBC's biggest moneymakers.

10. many people think the show is such a success because of Carson's great skits and jokes.

Check your answers on page 236.

Use a capital letter for proper nouns. A proper noun names a certain person, place, or thing. **Do not use a capital letter for common nouns.**

	proper nouns	common nouns
person	Mark Walsh	man
	Tina Crill	woman
	Broncos	team
place	Kenya	country
	Smith Street	street
	New York	state
thing	White House	building
	Star Wars	movie
	USS Bounty	ship

Use a capital letter for proper adjectives. A proper adjective is an adjective that is made from a proper noun.

Example

> the French language   British tourists
> German food   Canadian bacon

Exercise

Correct the following sentences. Use the proofreader's mark (≡) under letters that should be capitalized, and put a slash (/) through any letters that should not be capitalized.

1. harriet quimby was the first Woman to earn a pilot's license.

2. She was a writer in new york city before she became a Flyer.

3. She fell in love with Airplanes in 1910 when she saw her first Flying meet.

4. harriet became a pilot and toured in mexico with a troupe of Pilots.

5. She decided she would be the first Woman to cross the english channel.

6. She took off on april 16, 1912, sitting on a wicker Basket in the cockpit.

7. After a scary flight, she landed on a french Beach.

8. The *new york times* was not on her side; a writer said that her flight did not prove anything at all.

Check your answers on page 236.

Use a capital letter for each part of a person's name. Notice that when a last name begins with Mc or O', the next letter is also a capital.

Example

Chang S. Hong	Dick Mack	Jon McDuff
M. L. Peron	Liz Fink	Dave O'Leary

Use a capital letter for titles.

Example

Dr. Jones   Mr. Adams   Ms. Smith   Miss Henry

Use a capital letter for any place that can be found on a map.

Example

streets:	Broadway	Park Place	Main Street
towns:	Taylor	Islip	St.George
cities:	Sioux Falls	Berlin	Baghdad
states:	Texas	Kansas	Georgia
nations:	Spain	Chad	France
islands:	Guam	Puerto Rico	Prince Edward Island
bodies of water:	Dead Sea	Great Salt Lake	North Sea
tourist attractions:	Six Flags	Grand Canyon	Disneyland

Exercise

In each sentence, use the proofreader's mark (≡) to show where capital letters are needed.

1. ed j. smith reports people are taking cheaper trips in the summer.

2. mr. and mrs. jenks got a room in orlando, florida, and went camping.

3. Last year, the jenkses would have gone to sea world instead.

4. This year, dr. Perez and his family went hiking instead of going to mt. rushmore in south dakota.

5. ms. Wills went to see her friend rather than flying to the island of st. kitts.

6. miss e.k. link from new town, long island, spent two days in maine.

7. She went to lake meade last year.

8. busch gardens in tampa, florida, is still very busy, though.

9. mr. hunt wants to go to the middle east and see the dead sea.

                    Check your answers on page 236.

Use a capital letter for holidays.

Example

> New Year's Eve comes on December 31.
> On the Fourth of July, we hold a big picnic.
> Labor Day is considered the end of summer.

Use a capital letter for the months of the year. Do not capitalize the names of the seasons.

Example

> My birthday is in March.
> His son was born in June.
> The first day of fall is in September.

Use a capital letter for the days of the week.

Example

> It is hard to get out of bed on Monday.
> Tom has to go to the dentist on Wednesday.
> I enjoy my days off, Saturday and Sunday.

Exercise

In each sentence, use the proofreader's mark (≡) to show where capital letters are needed.

1. As of friday, april 16, martin luther king's birthday will be a holiday.

2. This holiday is in the place of columbus day, which we took as a day off on october 10.

3. The plant will, of course, still be closed on the fourth of july, labor day, and new year's eve.

4. But if any of these holidays falls on a monday or a friday, you will have a long weekend.

5. This year the company's fourth of july picnic will be on sunday, july 7.

6. I will be back at work on Tuesday, september 6, the day after labor day.

7. Some people want to have the party on flag day, june 14, instead.

8. There has also been talk of a halloween party for october 31, which is a thursday this year.

9. We could hold the party on friday, november 1, if that is a better time.

Check your answers on page 236.

Spelling

One good way to spell better is to study a few spelling rules. While some words must be memorized, many others follow these six spelling rules.

Rule 1: *ie*. There is a rhyme to help you learn the *ie* rule: Use *i* before *e* except after *c* or when sounded as *a* as in *neighbor* and *weigh*.

Example

i **before** *e:*	achieve	believe
ei **after** *c:*	receive	conceive
ei **when sounded as** *a:*	weight	reign

The following words do not fit this rule. Memorize them.

Example

either	neither	heir	seize
weird	sheik	their	height
forfeit	foreign	ancient	conscience

Rule 2: *-ceed/-cede*. Only three English verbs end in *-ceed*. All the other verbs with that long *e* vowel sound end in *-cede*. There is one exception: the verb *supersede,* which ends in *-sede*.

Example

-ceed:	succeed	proceed	exceed
-cede:	secede	recede	concede

Rule 3: *-ful*. The sound /*full*/ at the end of a word is spelled with one *l*. The one exception is the word *full* itself.

Example

graceful   careful   helpful

Exercise

Circle the correct spelling of each word.

1. Sitting Bull was (chief/cheif) of the Hunkpapa tribe of Sioux.

2. This very (anceint/ancient) tribe was settled near the Grand River.

3. As leader of the Sioux, Sitting Bull felt he had to (succede/succeed) against efforts to (sieze/seize) his tribe's land.

4. After all, he was the (hier/heir) to a great nation.

5. (Their/Thier) culture reached back hundreds of years.

6. Sitting Bull was (hopefull/hopeful) that the Sioux would be a powerful nation again.

 Check your answers on page 237.

Rule 4: Adding prefixes. Do not change the spelling of a word when you add a prefix to it. Keep all the letters of the prefix and of the word.

Example

| pleased | displeased | spell | misspelled |

Rule 5: Adding suffixes to words ending in *y*. If a word ends in a consonant and *y*, change the *y* to *i* before adding the suffix. Do not change the *y* to *i* when adding *-ing*.

Example

| hurry | hurried | happy | happier |

If a word ends in a vowel and *y*, do not change the spelling to add a suffix.

Example

| joy | joyous | play | playing |

Rule 6: Adding suffixes to words ending in silent *e*. If a word ends in silent *e* and the suffix with a vowel, drop the final *e*. If the suffix begins with a consonant, do not drop the final *e*.

Example

| fascinate | fascinating | nice | niceness |

There are some exceptions to rule 5, such as *shyly, babyish, laid, paid,* and *truly.*

Exercise

Circle the correct spelling of each word.

1. I have not yet (receiveed/received) my check for this week's work.

2. None of my checks has been (delayed/delaied) before.

3. This means that I have not been (payed/paid) for the last week.

4. That is why I am (writing/writting) to you.

5. This is a very (worrisome/worrysome) problem for me.

Check your answers on page 237.

Plurals

Plural means "more than one."

To form the plural of most nouns, add *-s* or *-es*. Add *-es* to nouns that end in *ch, s, sh, x,* or *z*.

Example

friend	friends
box	boxes
church	churches

Many nouns ending in *f* or *fe* form the plural by changing the *f* to *v* and adding *-es*.

Example

leaf	leaves
thief	thieves
knife	knives

Nouns that end in a consonant followed by *y* form the plural by changing the *y* to *i* and adding *-es*.

Example

city	cities
fly	flies

For other irregular plurals, look in dictionary. Here are some irregular plurals.

Example

ox	oxen	crisis	crises
tooth	teeth	woman	women
deer	deer	mouse	mice

Exercise

Circle the correct spelling of each word.

1. Today all the (businesses/businesses) in town are closing for a week-long vacation.

2. Many of my friends are going on (holidies/holidays).

3. My (nieces/niecies) and (nephews/nephewes) are coming for a visit.

4. I like to watch them play hide-and-seek in the (bushes/bushs).

5. They also like to pick (peachs/peaches) from the trees.

6. My niece Sammi lost her two front (teeth/teeths) and looks cute.

7. Their visits always leave me with great (memory/memories).

                                    Check your answers on page 237.

Possessives

The **possessive** form of a noun shows that something is owned and to whom it belongs.

Form the possessive of singular nouns and plural nouns (that don't end with an s) by adding an apostrophe (') and s.

Example

> Troy drove his *wife's* car to work yesterday.
> I had to stay up last night to put away the *children's* toys.

To form the possessive of plural nouns and other nouns ending in s, add only an apostrophe (').

Example

> Both of my *sisters'* houses are quite large.
> The *workers'* goggles were hanging by the door.

To form the possessive of proper nouns, add an apostrophe (') and s to singular forms. Add an apostrophe (') alone to a plural form.

Example

> I saw him yesterday at *Juan's* house.
> We were invited to the *Meads'* house for dinner last night.

Exercise

Circle the correct spelling of each word.

1. (Trans/Tran's) workday begins very early.

2. He gets up at six o'clock to make his (childrens'/children's) breakfast.

3. At seven o'clock, he drives by his (friend's/friends') houses to take them to work.

4. By eight o'clock, Tran and his friends are at work on the (factories/factory's) main floor.

5. Tran enjoys his work painting car (body's/bodies).

6. All of the (worker's/workers') clothing is protected from the paint by coveralls.

7. The supervisor is there to make sure that (everyones'/everyone's) work is up to the highest standards.

8. At five o'clock, everyone changes clothes in the (workers/workers') locker room.

9. Tonight Tran and his wife will go over to a (friend's/friends) house to play cards.

Check your answers on page 237.

Contractions

A **contraction** is a word formed by joining two other words. An apostrophe (') shows where a letter or letters have been left out. Many people use contractions when they speak and write informal letters. Do not use contractions, however, in formal writing.

Common Contractions

Contraction	Words It Replaces
I'm	I am
he's, she's, it's	he is, she is, it is
you're, we're, they're	you are, we are, they are
isn't, aren't, wasn't	is not, are not, was not
he'll, she'll, you'll	he will, she will, you will
I'll, we'll, they'll	I will, we will, they will
won't	will not
didn't	did not
I'd	I would
I've, we've	I have, we have
you've, they've	you have, they have
who's	who is
there's	there is
let's	let us
can't	cannot

Exercise

Write the words that each underlined contraction replaces.

_____ 1. I've read about the first pro baseball player.

_____ 2. I didn't know it was a second baseman named Al Reach.

_____ 3. There's not much information about his career.

_____ 4. He wasn't cheered when he left Brooklyn to take a job with the Phillies.

_____ 5. Fans weren't pleased that a player wanted a salary.

_____ 6. You won't be surprised to hear that players took bribes.

_____ 7. Let's admit that Reach changed baseball into a real sport.

_____ 8. By the end of 1865, players didn't need bribes— they were making good money openly for playing the sport they loved.

Check your answers on page 237.

Contractions or Possessive Pronouns?

Be careful not to confuse contractions with possessive pronouns. Pronouns with apostrophes (') are contractions. Pronouns that show ownership do not have an apostrophe.

Pronoun	Contraction	Possessive Pronoun
he	he's (he is)	his
she	she's (she is)	hers
it	it's (it is)	its
you	you're (you are)	your
they	they're (they are)	their
who	who's (who is)	whose

Therefore, these words are misspelled: *its', his', hers', yours', theirs', whos'*. Always correct them.

Example

> The airplane lost power to one if *its* engines.
>
> *It's* possible that we'll make an emergency landing.

Exercise

Circle the correct word to complete each sentence.

1. People have a lot to say about (their/they're) jobs.

2. "(Its / It's / Its') hectic!" says a thirty-year-old nurses' aide.

3. "My patients are so ill that (they're / their) always asking for me."

4. "(You're / Your) always up and down helping someone."

5. "(Who's/Whose) going to do the job with as much care?"

6. "I know one thing about this job: (it's /its'/its) never dull."

7. A bartender said, "What I really like is helping people solve (their/they're) problems."

8. A cook said, "(They're / Their) never going to come back for seconds if I don't put in the time!"

9. "I'm happy when (your/you're) at the counter at 6:00 A.M.," he said.

10. "(Who's / Whose) unhappy when the bacon is crisp and the coffee is hot?"

Check your answers on page 237.

Homonyms

Homonyms are words that sound alike but are spelled differently and have different meanings. Study this list of common homonyms to help you use each word correctly.

	Word	Meaning		Word	Meaning
1.	accept	to receive	7.	forth	forward
	except	to exclude		fourth	number four
2.	aisle	a space between rows	8.	hole	opening
	isle	an island		whole	complete
3.	brake	to stop	9.	know	to understand
	break	to destroy		no	not at all
4.	capital	center city of government	10.	lessen	decrease
	capitol	building in which a legislative body meets		lesson	something taught
5.	clothes	things to wear	11.	loose	not tight
	close	to shut		lose	misplace
6.	fair	even, just	12.	weak	not strong
	fare	money for transportation		week	seven days

Exercise

Circle the correct word to complete each sentence.

1. Last (week/weak), our city council passed a new law.

2. The law says the town can (except/accept) more new dumps.

3. The council thinks the law is (fair/fare), but some people don't agree.

4. The meeting was so crowded that all the (isles/aisles) were full.

5. This is the (forth/fourth) meeting this month!

6. I (no/know) we have to work out a way to deal with this problem.

7. We don't want to (brake/break) the law, but we don't want dumps.

8. We need to (lessen/lesson) our need for new dumps.

9. The government should be trying to (clothes/close) old dumps, not open new ones.

10. We need a (hole/whole) new plan for taking better care of our environment.

Check your answers on page 237.

Words Often Confused

Here are some more words that are often misused.

Word	Use	Example
fewer	separate pieces	I have fewer books than you.
less	can't be counted	I have less patience than you.
good	an adjective	This is a good job!
well	an adverb	You are looking well.
among	three or more	The three fought among themselves.
between	two	The choice was between the two of them.
bring	carry to the speaker	She will bring the pen to me.
take	carry from the speaker	She took the pen away.
can	ability	Can you give me the pen?
may	permission	May I leave the room?
that	use with animals or things	That is my dog. Here is the pen that you need.
who/whom	use with people	He is a person who works hard. He is the one to whom I spoke.

Exercise

Circle the correct word to complete each sentence.

1. Michael Cullen, (who/that) opened the first "warehouse grocery" store, did not know that he was making history.

2. People were looking for (good/well) prices in the middle of the 1930s, because many people were out of work.

3. Almost at once, his store was doing (good/well) because it was self-service, cash-and-carry, and one-stop shopping.

4. There was a lot of competition (among/between) all of the different grocery stores.

5. Small grocers tried to convince shoppers to (bring/take) their business back to the neighborhood stores.

6. But since high sales volume allowed these huge stores to cut prices by 25 percent, the small grocers (that/who) fought had little chance of success.

Check your answers on page 237.

Usage

Nouns

The word *noun* comes from the Latin word *nomen,* which means "name." **A noun is the name of a person, place, or thing.** All nouns belong to one of two groups: common and proper nouns.

Common Nouns

A common noun names a person, place, or thing.

Example

person		place		thing	
writer	athlete	street	country	movie	book
singer	actor	city	sea	test	car

Proper Nouns

A proper noun names a specific person, place, or thing. A proper noun always begins with a capital letter.

Example

	person	place	thing
Common noun:	writer	street	movie
Proper noun:	Stephen King	Front Street	Band Aids

Exercise

Draw one line under the common nouns in each sentence. Put two lines under the proper nouns.

1. The television program *Gunsmoke* went on the air on September 10, 1955, and history was made.

2. *Gunsmoke* was shown until the fall of 1975.

3. The show was the first and most popular adult Western.

4. The program started on the radio in the spring of 1952 with William Conrad.

5. Conrad played Marshal Matt Dillon of Dodge City, Kansas, "the first man they look for and the last they want to see."

Collective Nouns

Collective nouns are nouns that name groups of people, places, or things.

Example

family	team	jury
company	committee	race

A collective noun usually takes a singular verb.

Example

The team begins the tournament on Tuesday.

Mass Nouns

Mass nouns are nouns that name qualities and things that cannot be counted.

Example

water	chaos	strength	anger
time	courage	hair	silver

Mass nouns do not have plural forms. This is because the things they name cannot be counted.

Example

The swimmers ate a good breakfast to give them <u>strength</u> for the race. We didn't have much <u>time</u> to enjoy our vacation.

Exercise

Underline all the collective nouns. Circle all the mass nouns.

1. Even though the water was cold, the team was ready.

2. The committee had picked relay partners two weeks ago.

3. The runners had spirit and strength.

4. The race began, and the swimmers felt their power surge.

5. The gravel crunched as the audience ran to the water.

6. Time was running out.

7. Families cheered; this was for the gold!

8. The jury ruled that the red team won.

9. The crowd was furious!

10. It took courage to race in the cold.

Check your answers on page 237.

Pronouns

A pronoun is a word used to take the place of a noun. A pronoun may also take the place of a group of words acting as a noun.

Example

> When the <u>Johnsons</u> moved, <u>they</u> gave <u>their</u> fish to friends.
> (The pronouns *they* and *their* take the place of the noun *Johnsons*.)

Personal Pronouns

There are different kinds of pronouns. The pronouns used most often are called *personal pronouns* because they refer to you, to other people, and to things. Personal pronouns that refer to the person speaking are called *first-person pronouns*. Those that refer to the person spoken to are called *second-person pronouns*. Those that refer to the person, place, or thing spoken about are called *third-person pronouns*.

Personal Pronouns

	Singular	Plural
first-person:	I, me, my, mine	we, us, our, ours
second-person:	you, your, yours	you, your, yours
third-person:	he, him, his, she, her, hers, it, its	they, them, their, theirs

Personal Pronouns in the Nominative Case

Case refers to the different forms that pronouns take. The case of a pronoun shows how that word is used in a sentence. Personal pronouns have three cases: nominative, objective, and possessive.

Personal pronouns in the nominative case act as the subject of a sentence. *I, we, you, he, she, it,* and *they* are the nominative pronouns.

Example

> <u>We</u> are going to get married. (*We* is the subject.)
> <u>I</u> need to rent a hall. (*I* is the subject.)

Exercise

Write a nominative pronoun in each blank to take the place of the underlined word or words.

_____ 1. <u>Mike and I</u> also have to find a band. (Us, We, They)

_____ 2. <u>Mike</u> wants a band to play the hits. (You, Him, He)

_____ 3. <u>He and I</u> can't agree on a band at all. (They, We, Me)

_____ 4. <u>My mother</u> does not know much about music. (Her, You, She)

                            Check your answers on page 238.

Personal Pronouns in the Objective Case

A personal pronoun is in the **objective case** when it is the direct or indirect object of a verb or the object of a preposition. *Me, us, you, her, him, it,* and *them* are the objective pronouns.

Use an objective case pronoun as a direct object. A direct object tells who or what receives the action of the verb.

Example

> I met my new boss today. I liked her.
> Take the glass and put it in the sink.

Use an objective case pronoun as an indirect object. An indirect object tells to whom or for whom an action is done.

Example

> My sister sent me a gift for my birthday.
> The mail carrier gave us a wave when he saw the party.
> "Give them some help with all the gifts," he joked.

Use the objective case as the object of a preposition. The object of a preposition is the noun or pronoun that follows the preposition.

A preposition is a word that relates the noun or pronoun following it to another word in the sentence. Here are some common prepositions: *about, above, across, in, off, on, by, to, until, at, before, inside, into, near, over, past, up, with, without.*

Example

> Sit down by me.
> You know I will not speak to him.
> I still can't understand why he went without her.

Exercise

The following sentences are written from the first-person point of view. Circle the correct pronoun to complete each sentence.

1. My friend gave (us/we) four tickets to a big play-off game at Mitchell Field.

2. My mother lent (I/me) her umbrella, but I was sure we would have good weather.

3. Between the two of (we/us), we put together a list of people with whom to share the tickets.

4. I wanted to include Gino and Angie, so I gave (them/they) tickets.

5. Among the three of (they/us), we decided to give Carlos the fourth ticket.

Check your answers on page 238.

Personal Pronouns in the Possessive Case

A personal pronoun is in the **possessive case** when it shows ownership. *My, mine, your, yours, his, her, hers, its, our, ours, you, yours, their, theirs* are the possessive pronouns.

Use the possessive case pronouns *my, his, her, its, our, your,* and *their* before nouns to show ownership.

Example

> Nick left <u>his</u> glove on the bus.   <u>Their</u> dog buried <u>its</u> bone.
> <u>His</u> sister needs <u>our</u> help.

Use a possessive case pronoun before a gerund. A **gerund** is the *-ing* form of a verb. A gerund acts as a noun.

Example

> <u>Their</u> driving to Nashville was my idea.
> He did not agree with <u>my</u> changing jobs.
> <u>Your</u> walking home in the snow could make your cold worse.

Use the possessive case pronouns *mine, yours, his, hers, its, ours,* and *theirs* alone to show ownership.

Example

> Is this coat <u>his</u>?   No, they are <u>theirs</u>.
> Are those papers <u>ours</u>?

A possessive pronoun is <u>never</u> written with an apostrophe. Spellings such as *their's, your's,* and *our's* are incorrect.

Exercise

Circle the correct pronoun to complete each sentence.

1. Hank, who works with me, left (his/he's) glasses at home today.

2. I took the chance to speak to Hank about (him/his) getting an eye exam.

3. (His/He) squinting has become apparent to us.

4. "Do you mind (me/my) giving you some advice?" I asked.

5. "My eyes are (mine/me), not (yours/your's)," he growled.

6. I thought he would understand (our/us) concern.

7. "We are really worried about (you/your) vision," I told him.

8. We found out the next day that Hank had left (his/him) name with the eye doctor's office to set up an eye exam.

Pronoun Antecedents

A pronoun gets its meaning from the noun to which it refers. This noun is called the *antecedent*. Pronouns usually have specific antecedents.

An antecedent is the word to which a pronoun refers. The antecedent often comes before the pronoun.

Example

Louisa forgot to buy her weekly bus ticket.
(*Louisa* is the antecedent for the pronoun *her*.)

Every cat in the shelter received its shots.
(*Cat* is the antecedent for the pronoun *its*.)

Carolyn and I left our books on the desk.
(*Carolyn and I* is the antecedent for the pronoun *our*.)

Sometimes the antecedent comes after the pronoun.

Example

Since they moved, Donna and Jim have not called us.
(*Donna and Jim* is the antecedent for the pronoun *they*.)

Because of its climate, San Diego is my favorite city.
(*San Diego* is the antecedent for the pronoun *its*.)

Exercise

Circle the antecedent for each underlined pronoun in these sentences.

1. Although Diego can swim now, he once had a fear of the water.

2. Della told me it was not the shirt she had ordered.

3. Annette asked Peter to help her repair a leak in the pipe.

4. The workers loaded the new machine into its casing.

5. The Fitzpatricks enjoyed their summer vacation.

6. The horse we saw had red silks; it came in last.

7. The women asked for diet soda to drink with their meal.

8. Sharon and Danielle have to weed their flower garden before lunch.

9. I helped my neighbor carry his sofa into the living room.

10. Having received their light bill, the newly-married couple worried about paying it.

Pronoun Agreement

Pronouns and antecedents must match. Parts of sentences that match are said to agree with one another.

A personal pronoun must agree with its antecedent in number, person, and gender. *Number* means that the words are either singular or plural. *Person* refers to the first person, second person, or third person. *Gender* refers to whether words are used to refer to men, women, or objects. *Him* and *he* are masculine; *she* and *her* are feminine; *it* and *its* are neuter (neither masculine nor feminine).

Example

> <u>Jill</u> gave <u>her</u> bill to the clerk.
> (Both the antecedent *Jill* and the pronoun *her* are singular, in the third person, and feminine.)

Use a plural personal pronoun with two or more antecedents joined by *and*.

Example

> My roommates <u>and</u> I cannot match <u>our</u> schedules.

Use a singular personal pronoun with two or more singular antecedents joined by *or* or *nor*.

Example

> Either Steve <u>or</u> Ricardo should give up <u>his</u> seat on the bus.

Avoid shifts in person and gender. A personal pronoun and its antecedent will not agree if there is a change in person or gender.

Example

> **Correct:**   Rich is studying for the GED, a test <u>he</u> wants to take.
>
> **Shift in person:**   Rich is studying for the GED, a test <u>you</u> wants to take.

Exercise

Circle the correct personal pronoun to complete each sentence.

1. Most of us have (you/our) own views on professional ball players.

2. Athletes push (his/their) bodies to the limit in every game.

3. Bo Jackson works out a lot, which (he/you) must do to stay on top.

4. Some athletes even risk (their/his) health by training too hard.

5. Bo Jackson injured (their/his) hip playing two sports.

 Check your answers on page 238.

Adjectives

An **adjective** is a word that describes a noun or pronoun. Adjectives describe by answering one of these questions:

How much?	more tea	little time	some luck
How many?	few fish	many bills	ten cards
Which one?	first hit	this box	any choice
What kind?	red light	good dog	hot shower

An adjective often comes before the noun or pronoun it describes.

Example
> The sick dog lay by the door.   I saw a green tree.

An adjective can also come after the word it describes.

Example
> The dog, sick from the heat, lay by the door.
>
> The tree is green with new leaves.

Proper adjectives are proper nouns used as adjectives. Capitalize proper adjectives.

Example
> Eric sent his friend a can of Florida sunshine.

A compound adjective is made up of more than one word. Some compound adjectives are joined by a hyphen; others are made into one word.

Example
> I saw a movie about a far-off land.
> Many of the workers think they are underpaid.

Exercise

Underline all the adjectives in these sentences.

1. Dogs first served people as skilled hunters.

2. Irish setters and Russian wolfhounds come from early hunting dogs.

3. Work dogs have a long history as well.

4. German shepherds and English collies are part of this big group.

5. Dogs make good workers because many of their senses are strong.

Check your answers on page 238.

Adverbs

An adverb is a word that describes a verb, an adjective, or other adverb. Adverbs describe by answering one of these four questions:

Where?	flew <u>above</u>	moves <u>aside</u>	climbs <u>up</u>
When?	left <u>today</u>	start <u>now</u>	arrived <u>early</u>
How?	walked <u>slowly</u>	ate <u>well</u>	worked <u>carefully</u>
To what extent?	<u>almost</u> done	<u>fully</u> healed	<u>barely</u> open

Adverbs describe verbs. Adverbs can come before or after the words they describe.

Example

> **Adverb before verb:**   We <u>often eat</u> chicken.
>
> **Adverb after verb:**   Chicken must be <u>cooked well</u>.

Adverbs describe adjectives. Adverbs often come right before the adjectives they describe.

Example

> I was <u>very happy</u> to hear about your success.
>
> Helene is <u>never ready</u> on time.

Adverbs describe other adverbs. Adverbs often come right before the adverbs they describe.

Example

> Helene moves <u>very slowly</u>, even after she has had her coffee.
>
> She <u>just barely</u> catches her bus on time.

Exercise

Underline all the adverbs in these sentences.

1. Are people ever really happy with their appearance?

2. They must not be, judging by how warmly they greet each new diet.

3. Many smart people often take new diets quite seriously.

4. They must want to lose weight very badly.

5. Some people barely finish one diet before they begin another.

6. My friend had almost finished his powdered diet drink when he quickly started another type of diet.

7. He is completely hopeful for the success of this diet.

    Check your answers on page 238.

Adjective or Adverb?

Some words can be either adjectives or adverbs, depending on how they are used in a sentence.

Example

Adjective	Adverb
I had a hard day.	I work hard.
He has a late meeting.	She fell asleep late.

Usually, however, adjectives and adverbs have different forms. **Many adverbs are formed by adding -ly to the end of an adjective.**

Example

Adjective	Adverb
bright light	lit brightly
poor work	works poorly

Some adverbs do not end in -ly.

Example

My boss lives far from work.   The bee flew past my arm.

Adjectives describe only nouns and pronouns. To be certain if a word is an adjective or an adverb, decide which word it describes. Use an adjective only to describe a noun or a pronoun. Use an adverb only to describe a verb, adjective, or other adverb.

Example

Correct: They took the jobs seriously.
Not correct: They took the jobs serious.

Exercise

Tell whether each underlined word is an adjective or an adverb. Write your answers on the lines below the paragraph.

There was (1) only one ad for an office trainee in the (2) Sunday newspaper. (3) "Friendly office and (4) good benefits," it read. (5) Three applicants lined up (6) early at the office door. The (7) first person was so nervous that she spoke too (8) quickly. The next person did not have the (9) needed skills but was willing to learn. The final applicant, though, had both skills and desire and was hired.

1. _____   2. _____   3. _____

4. _____   5. _____   6. _____

7. _____   8. _____   9. _____

Check your answers on page 238.

Comparing with Adjectives and Adverbs

Sometimes you may want to compare two or more people, places, or things. To compare things, use either the comparative or superlative form of the adjective or adverb.

Example

	Adjectives		Adverbs	
	big	short	highly	slowly
Comparative:	bigger	shorter	more highly	more slowly
Superlative:	biggest	shortest	most highly	most slowly

Use the comparative form of the adjective or adverb to compare two people, places, or things. Add *-er* to one-syllable adjectives and adverbs to form the comparative. Use *more* or *less* before most adjectives and adverbs with two or more syllables to compare them.

Example

This box is heavier than the other one.
The turtle moves more slowly than the rabbit.

Use the superlative form of the adjective or adverb to compare three or more people, places, or things. Add *-est* to one-syllable adjectives and adverbs to form the superlative. Use *most* or *least* before most adjectives and adverbs with two or more syllables to compare them.

Example

Of the three subway trains due in at the same time, the "A" train will arrive the soonest.
She is the most childish of all my adult friends.

Never add both *-er* and *more* (or *less*) or both *-est* and *most* (or *least*) to an adjective or adverb.

Example

| **Correct:** | This is the hardest thing I've ever done. |
| **Not correct:** | This is the most hardest thing I've ever done. |

Exercise

Circle the correct word or words to complete each sentence.

1. Shopping on Saturdays is (harder/more hard) than shopping during the week.

2. Saturday is the day the stores are the (most crowded/more crowded).

3. Finding what you want is the (most difficult/more difficult) part of shopping.

4. Even the bundles seem (heavier/heaviest) to me on weekends.

                                    Check your answers on page 238.

Irregular Adjectives and Adverbs

Not all adjectives and adverbs have regular comparative and superlative forms. The following chart lists some of the most common irregular adjectives and adverbs.

Adjective/Adverb	Comparative	Superlative
good	better	best
many	more	most
bad	worse	worst
far	farther	farthest
ill	worse	worst
little	less	least
badly	worse	worst
well	better	best
much	more	most

Example

> Tuna is good, and shrimp is even better, but lobster is the best of all.
> Henry is ill, but he was worse an hour ago. He felt the worst yesterday.

Few and Less

Both *few* and *less* are adjectives. **Use *few* and *fewer* to compare things that can be counted. Use *less* and *least* to compare things that cannot be counted.**

Example

> I have less time for work now that I am going to school.
> There are fewer people in the audience than there were last night.

Exercise

Circle the correct word to complete each sentence.

1. Eric is not a good map reader, but Larry is even (worst/worse).

2. Chris is the (worse/worst) of all, though.

3. Li is the (best/better) of all the camp leaders, so she is in charge of giving directions.

4. The new camp site is (far/farther) from town than the last one.

5. This trail in the woods is the (farther/farthest) from town.

6. This group has (fewer/less) free time than the other group.

7. Campers who go for a month have the (more/most) time of all.

8. It's a good thing Leroy was feeling (best/better) when he awoke.

Check your answers on page 238.

Verbs

Verb Tense

Verbs are words that show action. Every verb has four main parts. The parts of a verb are used to form the different verb tenses. Tense is a form of a verb that shows when the action takes place.

Verb Parts

Present	Present Participle	Past	Past Participle
talk	talking	talked	talked
run	running	ran	run

Simple Tenses

There are three simple tenses: present, past, and future. Form the present tense by using the present part of the verb. Form the past tense by using the past part of the verb. Form the future tense by using the helping verb *will* and the present part of the verb.

Tense	Form	Use
present	talk	repeated action or habit; general truth
past	talked	action completed in the past
future	will talk	action not yet completed

Example

> **Present:** I talk to my children every week on the phone.
> **Past:** Yesterday I talked to my daughter.
> **Future:** Next week I will talk to my son.

Exercise

Circle the best way to correct the underlined part of each sentence.

1. I collect coins when I was a child.
   (1) will collect
   (2) collects
   (3) collected
   (4) collect
   (5) No change is needed.

2. I own some rare coins.
   (1) did owned
   (2) will own
   (3) has owned
   (4) is owning
   (5) No change is needed.

3. Yesterday they talk about a coin show.
   (1) talked
   (2) will talk
   (3) are talking
   (4) talks
   (5) No change is needed.

4. I go next Tuesday.
   (1) gone
   (2) did gone
   (3) went
   (4) will go
   (5) No change is needed.

Check your answers on page 238.

Perfect Tenses

There are three perfect tenses: present perfect, past perfect, and future perfect. Use the past participle and the verb *to have* to form all of the perfect tenses.

Tense	Form	Use
present perfect	have worked	a completed action or an action that continues into the present
past perfect	had worked	one action completed before another in the past
future perfect	will have worked	one future action completed before another future action

Example

> **Present perfect:** Vernon has worked here for a long time.
> **Past perfect:** He had worked at another job before he came here.
> **Future perfect:** By May 1, he will have worked here ten years.

Progressive Tenses

There are six progressive tenses. The progressive tenses show an ongoing condition or action. Use the verb *to be* and the present participle to form the progressive tenses.

Tense	Form
present progressive	am/is/are trying
past progressive	was/were trying
future progressive	will be trying
present perfect progressive	has/have been trying
past perfect progressive	had been trying
future perfect progressive	will have been trying

Example

> I can't talk right now, because I am trying to finish some work.
> He has been trying to enter the police academy for three years.
> We were trying to buy a car when we won the contest.

Exercise

Circle the correct verb to complete each sentence.

1. My sister (listened/was listening) to the radio when she heard her name called.

2. She (have entered/had entered) the contest a few weeks ago.

3. She (is listening/has been listening) to the same radio station for two years.

4. At this time tomorrow, she (driven/will be driving) a new car.

Check your answers on page 238.

Helping Verbs

A **helping verb** is a verb that is added to another verb to add to or change the meaning. *To be* is the most common helping verb. It is used to form the progressive tenses. Other verbs also can act as helping verbs.

Use the helping verbs *do* and *did* to ask a question or emphasize an action.

Example

> <u>Do</u> you want spaghetti for dinner?
> Yes, I <u>do</u> want spaghetti.

Use the helping verbs *can* and *could* to show ability.

Example

> Patricia <u>can</u> speak Spanish, Italian, and French.

Use the helping verbs *may* and *might* to show possibility or permission to do something.

Example

> Trang <u>might</u> come with us, if she can leave work early.
> My boss said that I <u>may</u> leave work early to go to the concert.

Use the helping verb *must* to show an obligation to do something or to draw a conclusion.

Example

> At ten o'clock, I <u>must</u> leave to go to the doctor's office.
> He never misses work. He <u>must</u> be sick.

Use the helping verb *should* to show that something is a good idea.

Example

> We <u>should</u> leave now if we want to arrive on time.

Exercise

Circle the correct helping verb.

1. The mayor (will be/am being/are being) running again.

2. (Does/Do/Be/Are) you think the mayor has a chance of winning?

3. Janet (did/have/has) never voted before.

4. I (am/still have/can) not gotten a chance to tell you how a ballot works.

5. (Are/Is/Does) tonight seem like a good night to go over it?

6. You (are/have/do) learned well; I am proud of you.

Irregular Verbs

Even though most verbs in English are regular, a number of common verbs have irregular past and past participle forms.

Irregular Verbs

Present	Present Participle	Past	Past Participle
am, is, are	being	was, were	been
begin	beginning	began	begun
break	breaking	broke	broken
bring	bringing	brought	brought
build	building	built	built
buy	buying	bought	bought
choose	choosing	chose	chosen
do	doing	did	done
drink	drinking	drank	drunk
eat	eating	ate	eaten
fight	fighting	fought	fought
give	giving	gave	given
know	knowing	knew	known
lay	laying	laid	laid
lie	lying	lay	lain
lose	losing	lost	lost
see	seeing	saw	seen
shake	shaking	shook	shaken
sleep	sleeping	slept	slept
speak	speaking	spoke	spoken
teach	teaching	taught	taught
win	winning	won	won

Exercise

Circle the best way to correct the underlined part of each sentence.

1. Rob <u>know</u> he wanted to work with horses.
   - (1) knowing
   - (2) knew
   - (3) have known
   - (4) was knowing
   - (5) No change is needed.

2. He <u>see</u> how to care for horses.
   - (1) saw
   - (2) seeing
   - (3) have seen
   - (4) was seeing
   - (5) No change is needed.

3. He <u>begin</u> on a farm.
   - (1) beginning
   - (2) begun
   - (3) have begun
   - (4) began
   - (5) No change is needed.

4. Last week he <u>make</u> horseshoes.
   - (1) make
   - (2) making
   - (3) has made
   - (4) made
   - (5) No change is needed.

Check your answers on page 239.

Subject-Verb Agreement

Subjects and verbs must agree in number. **A singular subject must have a singular verb. A plural subject must have a plural verb.**

Example

Singular subject and verb: A big <u>ship</u> <u>sails</u> into the harbor.
Plural subject and verb: <u>We</u> <u>are waiting</u> for the ship to arrive.

Words between the subject and verb do not affect the agreement.

Example

The <u>insects</u> on the oak tree <u>are</u> harmful.

(The subject is *insects,* not *tree.* The verb is *are.* The phrase *on the oak tree* between the subject and verb does not affect the agreement.)

Use a plural verb for subjects joined by *and*.

Example

The <u>door and the window</u> <u>are</u> both stuck.

Use a singular verb for singular subjects joined by *or* or *nor*.

Example

Each morning Juan <u>or</u> Luiz <u>buys</u> fresh rolls.

If a singular subject and a plural subject are joined by *or* or *nor*, the subject closer to the verb must agree with the verb.

Example

Neither the <u>loaf of bread</u> nor the <u>eggs</u> <u>were</u> fresh.
Neither the <u>eggs</u> nor the <u>loaf of bread</u> <u>was</u> fresh.

Exercise

Circle the correct verb to complete each sentence.

1. Most of us think that the sky (is/are) blue, but it is really black.

2. In space, the sun and moon (is/are) clearly seen during the day.

3. Many people like to (gazes/gaze) at the stars.

4. The moon and the planet Venus (glow/glows) at night.

5. The Big Dipper, along with many other stars, (shines/shine) as well.

6. Neither Pluto nor Saturn (is/are) easy to find, though.

7. The stars (provide/provides) hours of pleasure for many people.

8. Stars that shoot across the sky (is/are) a special treat.

Check your answers on page 239.

Pronoun and Verb Agreement

A pronoun used as a subject must agree with the verb in number.

These pronouns are always singular: *much, neither, anybody, no one, nothing, one, other, somebody, someone, something, another, anybody, anyone, anything, each, either, everybody, everyone, everything.*

Example

> Someone has been in the house while we were out.
> Everything is fine, thanks.

These pronouns are always plural: *both, few, many, others, several.*

Example

> Both glasses have been used.
> Several of the glasses are broken.

These pronouns are either singular or plural: *all, some, any, part, none, half.*

Example

> All of the books have been checked out.
> All of the milk was spilled on the floor.

Exercise

Circle the correct verb to complete each sentence.

1. Both Vito and Luiz (are planning/is planning) to spend the weekend looking for famous people.

2. Everyone (has told/have told) them not to be disappointed if they don't see any.

3. At 11:00 P.M. all of the actors (take/takes) their last bow and get ready to leave the theater.

4. Each of the actors (gives/give) Vito and Luiz an autograph.

5. Several of them even (stop/stops) to talk to Vito and Luiz.

6. Many famous people (is/are) this nice.

7. Several others (has/have) answered letters from Vito and Luiz.

8. Many (have/has) even sent autographed pictures to Vito and Luiz.

9. Everyone (is/are) impressed by Vito and Luiz's dedication to meeting celebrities.

10. Vito and Luiz think anything (is/are) possible if they keep trying.

Check your answers on page 239.

Active and Passive Voice

Voice refers to the form of the verb that shows whether the subject is doing the action. Only action verbs show voice. English has two voices: the *active voice* and the *passive voice*.

When the subject performs the action of a verb, the verb is in the active voice.

Example

> Ellen lost a gold ring.
> My sister took a large swallow of tea.
> I will buy a jacket for spring.

When the subject receives the action of a verb, the verb is in the passive voice.

Example

> A gold ring was lost by Ellen.
> A large swallow of tea was taken by my sister.
> A jacket for spring was bought by me.

Note that the passive voice is made up of a form of the helping verb *to be* plus the past participle of an action verb.

Write *A* in the blank if the sentence is in the active voice. Write *P* if the sentence is in the passive voice.

_____ 1. I always read the newspaper after dinner.

_____ 2. The newspaper is always read by me after dinner.

_____ 3. The front page is looked at by me first.

_____ 4. I look at the front page first.

_____ 5. Next, I scan the sports pages.

_____ 6. The sports pages are scanned by me next.

_____ 7. The ads are skimmed quickly by me.

_____ 8. I quickly skim the ads.

_____ 9. I save the comics for last.

_____ 10. The comics are saved by me for last.

Using Active and Passive Voice

Because the active voice stresses the person or thing doing the action, sentences in the active voice are more direct than passive-voice sentences. Active-voice sentences also use fewer words than passive-voice sentences. Use the active voice when possible. Compare these two sentences.

Example

> **Active voice:**　　Russ closed the door.
> **Passive voice:**　　The door was closed by Russ.

The active-voice sentence is clearer because it shows the action more directly. There are times, though, when you should use the passive voice.

Use the passive voice when you do not know who performed the action.

Example

> The lock was broken after we went out.
> At 6:00 the gates to the playing field were unlocked.

Use the passive voice when you want to stress the action, not who did the action.

Example

> My co-worker was struck by a car.
> Plans for the new village hall were revealed on Tuesday.

Use the passive voice when you do not want to name the performer.

Example

> A mistake was made.
> A check has been returned for payment.

Exercise

Each of the following sentences is in the passive voice. Write *P* if the sentence should be in the passive voice. Write *A* if the sentence should be in the active voice.

_____ 1. Around 1900, a story about a smart horse was written in a German newspaper.

_____ 2. The horse was called "Clever Hans" by its owner.

_____ 3. Answers to math problems were given by taps from the horse's hoofs.

_____ 4. Fraud was alleged by many people.

_____ 5. The trick was discovered, and the horse's method was revealed.

Check your answers on page 239.

Sentence Structure

Sentence Fragments

Not every group of words is a sentence. Some are parts of sentences, called *fragments*. Even though the fragments might begin with a capital letter and end with a period, they are not sentences.

A sentence fragment is a group of words that does not express a complete thought.

Example

Correct:	A dog ran away with the bone.
Fragment:	Ran away with the bone.
Correct:	Her friend in the diner helped her get a job as a cashier.
Fragment:	Helped her get a job as a cashier.
Correct:	The rags under the sink are dirty.
Fragment:	The rags under the sink.

Exercise

Write *C* if the sentence is correct (has a complete thought). Write *F* if it is a fragment.

_____ 1. *Roots* was the most widely-viewed TV miniseries of all time.

_____ 2. It was based on Alex Haley's book, in which he traced his family back to Africa.

_____ 3. Telling the story of Kunta Kinte, Haley's own ancestor.

_____ 4. Set down how he was brought to America as a slave.

_____ 5. Ran for twelve hours and was broadcast for eight nights from January 23 to January 30, 1977.

_____ 6. It was the highest rated series of all time.

_____ 7. Being nominated for thirty-six Emmy awards.

_____ 8. It won four awards and was so good that later there was a sequel.

_____ 9. The sequel bringing the story of the Haley family up to the present.

_____ 10. Called *Roots: The Next Generation,* it was shown on seven nights in 1979.

                                        Check your answers on page 239.

There are three ways to test if a sentence is a fragment. If you answer *no* to one of the following three questions, you have a fragment.

Test for sentence fragments

■ 1. Is there a verb?

■ 2. Is there a subject?

■ 3. Do the subject and the verb express a complete thought?

1. **Is there a verb?** If there is no verb, the group of words is a fragment. All parts of the verb must be present for a sentence to be complete.

Example

Correct:	Mark <u>is taking</u> a GED class.
Fragment:	Mark taking a GED class.

2. **Is there a subject?** If there is no subject, the group of words is a fragment. To find out if a sentence has a subject, ask *who* or *what* is doing the action.

Example

Correct:	Mark studied hard for the test.
Fragment:	Studied hard for the test. (Who studied?)

3. **Do the subject and verb express a complete thought?** Even if the group of words has a subject and a verb, it is not a complete sentence if it does not express a complete thought.

Example

Correct:	Whoever studied a lot did well on the test.
Fragment:	Whoever studied a lot. (What is the complete thought?)

Exercise

Explain why each of the following groups of words is a fragment.

1. From 1970 to 1980, the number of retired people who moved from New York to Florida.

   This is a fragment because _____

2. Was more than double the number for the past decade.

   This is a fragment because _____

3. These people who moved to New York, New Jersey, and Ohio.

   This is a fragment because _____

4. Tend to be poorer, older, and alone.

   This is a fragment because _____

Check your answers on page 239.

Run-on Sentences

A run-on sentence is two or more complete thoughts that are not correctly joined or separated by punctuation. There are two kinds of run-on sentences.

1. One type of run-on sentence is made up of two sentences that are not separated by a correct punctuation mark.

Example

> **Correct:** The storm got worse. It turned toward the land.
> **Run-on:** The storm got worse it turned toward the land.
>
> **Correct:** The Japanese subway is the fastest train. It travels over 100 miles an hour.
> **Run-on:** The Japanese subway is the fastest train it travels over 100 miles an hour.

2. The other type of run-on sentence is made up of two sentences joined with a comma when they should be joined with a semicolon or a comma and a connecting word.

Example

> **Correct:** We were not hungry; we had already had lunch.
> **Run-on:** We were not hungry, we had already had lunch.
>
> **Correct:** You can visit the White House, and you can tour many rooms.
> **Run-on:** You can visit the White House, you can tour many rooms.

Exercise

Write *RO* if the sentence is a run-on. Write *C* if the sentence is correct.

_____ 1. *Star Trek* aired on TV from 1966 to 1969 it was the first serious science-fiction show.

_____ 2. The show was set 200 years in the future it told of the adventures of a spaceship and its crew.

_____ 3. Its mission was to "seek out new life," and it was not supposed to harm any culture it discovered.

_____ 4. This warning did not stop James T. Kirk he was the captain.

_____ 5. The ship had a crew of 400 there were only eight cast members.

_____ 6. Spock was very smart, but he had no feelings.

_____ 7. His father was a Vulcan his mother was an Earth woman.

                    Check your answers on page 239.

How to Correct Run-on Sentences

Use an end punctuation mark to separate the two complete thoughts in a run-on sentence.

Example

> **Correct:** Do most people like crowds? I don't think so.
> **Run-on:** Do most people like crowds I don't think so.

Use a comma and a connecting word to combine the two complete thoughts in a run-on sentence. A comma by itself cannot connect two sentences. Use a comma with a connecting word such as *and, but, for, nor, or, so,* or *yet.*

Example

> **Correct:** The sky got dark, and it started to rain.
> **Run-on:** The sky got dark it started to rain.

Use a semicolon to connect the two complete thoughts in a run-on sentence. A semicolon is the best punctuation mark to use when the ideas in the two parts of the run-on sentence are closely linked.

Example

> **Correct:** I couldn't wait to jump in; the water looked so cool.
> **Run-on:** I couldn't wait to jump in the water looked so cool.

Exercise

Correct each of the following run-on sentences by using one of the three methods described on this page. Write your sentences in the space provided.

1. The Special Olympics was started in 1968 it is a program of sports for people with disabilities.

   _____

   _____

2. More than 4,300 athletes attend they come from fifty nations.

   _____

3. Each state competes in thirteen sporting events athletes do not have to enter every event.

   _____

4. Everyone is a winner each athlete gets a ribbon or medal.

   _____

   _____

Check your answers on page 239.

Compound Sentences

A compound sentence is made up of two or more complete thoughts. Each of these thoughts could stand alone as a sentence.

Example

> The sky turned dark gray, and the birds flew to safety.
> (The first complete sentence is: *The sky turned dark gray.*
> The second complete sentence is: *The birds flew to safety.*)
>
> She wanted to go to the club, but she knew it was very costly.
> (The first complete sentence is: *She wanted to go to the club.*
> The second complete sentence is: *She knew it was very costly.*)

There are two ways to create a compound sentence.

1. Join the complete sentences with a connecting word such as *and, but, for, or, nor, yet,* or *so.*

Example

> Jill wanted the job, yet she knew the commute would be long.
> She could accept the job, or she could reject it.
> The job had many good points, so she decided to accept it.

2. Join the complete sentences with a semicolon. Use this method only when the ideas are very closely related.

Example

> Martin read the book in two hours; he wrote his essay in three.
> Jesse liked the movie; she thought the book was better.

Exercise

Write *CS* in the blank before each compound sentence. If it is not a compound sentence, just write *S.*

_____ 1. Soap operas have earned a bad name, and they don't always deserve it.

_____ 2. Some people watch too many TV programs; other people take the plots too seriously.

_____ 3. This does not make the programs themselves bad.

_____ 4. Some people think soap opera viewers are not smart, but studies show that people from all walks of life watch soaps.

_____ 5. There are teachers, doctors, and lawyers who watch the soaps.

_____ 6. Some hospitals tell patients to watch the soaps, and some doctors tell people who feel depressed to tune in as well.

A compound sentence joins related ideas. Even though the two parts of a compound sentence can be connected by using punctuation marks, the sentence will not make sense unless the two ideas are related. Readers expect one part of a compound sentence to relate to the other part.

Example

Related:	Computers became popular in the 1970s, because they have many different uses.
Not related:	Computers became popular in the 1970s, for they are very hard to use.
	(The fact that computers may be hard to use does not relate to the idea of their popularity.)

A compound sentence creates logic between ideas. The connecting word you use helps create a logical relationship between the parts of a compound sentence. Each connecting word has a different meaning.

Connecting Word	Meaning	Function
and	also	joins ideas
but	on the other hand	contrasts
for	because	shows a reason
nor	not	joins negative ideas
or	a choice	shows a choice
so	thus	shows a result
yet	but	contrasts

Example

Logical:	I decided not to go to the party, but I planned to call you and apologize.
Not logical:	I decided not to go to the party, or I planned to call you and apologize. (The sentence does not make sense.)

Exercise

Combine the two sentences in each item below to create a logical compound sentence.

1. My first week on the job was a disaster. My boss told me so.

   _____

2. I was really upset. I knew things had to get better.

   _____

3. I tried as hard as I could. I really wanted to keep the job.

   _____

4. My co-workers gave me good advice. I felt more confident.

   _____

Check your answers on page 240.

Parallel Structure

Your writing will be clearer if all the ideas within each sentence agree or match. To make your ideas match, put them all in parallel, or similar, form. **Parallel structure** connects matching words and phrases. For example, use parallel adjectives, nouns, verbs, and adverbs when you write a list. To have parallel structure, verbs should all be in the same tense and form.

Example

Parallel:	The meal was tasty, quick, and healthful. (adjectives)
Not parallel:	The meal was tasty, quick, cheap, and the food was good for you.
Parallel:	The store is good for fruit, meat, and cheese. (nouns)
Not parallel:	The store is good for fruit, meat, and to buy cheese.
Parallel:	Doctors say I should run, swim, and walk. (verbs)
Not parallel:	Doctors say I should run, swim, and go walking.
Parallel:	In the rain I drive slowly, carefully, and defensively. (adverbs)
Not parallel:	In the rain I drive slowly, carefully, and watch out for the other drivers.

Exercise

Write *P* in the blank if the sentence has parallel structure. Write *NP* if the sentence does not have parallel structure.

_____ 1. The Statue of Liberty is the largest sculpture ever built, standing 151 feet tall and weighing 225 tons.

_____ 2. Her nose is four and a half feet long, and it measures three feet to span her mouth.

_____ 3. The Statue of Liberty appears noble and has been my favorite sight.

_____ 4. To millions, she stands for being free and friendship.

_____ 5. The artist spoke to Gustave Eiffel, who built the Eiffel Tower, and was meeting with other experts, too.

_____ 6. Bartholdi made a four-foot model as well as building a nine-foot model.

_____ 7. The workers had to take measurements, enlarge each section, and make plaster forms.

_____ 8. Then, workers fit copper sheets and were shaping the form.

In addition to using parallel words in lists, use parallel phrases in all your writing. **Write each parallel idea in the same grammatical structure.**

Example

Parallel:	The members of the council read the letter, discussed its points, and decided to ignore it.
Not parallel:	The members of the council read the letter, discussed its points, and the decision was to ignore it.
Parallel:	The letter writer stormed into the meeting, demanded to speak, and grabbed the microphone.
Not parallel:	The letter writer stormed into the meeting, demanded to speak, and was grabbing the microphone.
Parallel:	The audience stomped their feet, clapped their hands, and cheered the speaker.
Not parallel:	The audience stomped their feet, clapped their hands, and were cheering the speaker.

Exercise

Rewrite each sentence so that it has parallel structure.

1. Writing helps people think, speak, and be learning.

   _____

   _____

2. Those who can write well will be leaders in the community, state, and nationally in years to come.

   _____

   _____

3. By writing frequently, reading often, and to seek feedback, writers can improve.

   _____

   _____

4. Learning to write clearly, correctly, and be effective is a goal.

   _____

   _____

Complex Sentences

Independent Clauses

A clause is a group of words with its own subject and verb. **Some clauses can stand alone as sentences; these are called independent clauses.**

Example

> He woke up at seven o'clock, just in time to catch the bus.
> (*He woke up at seven o'clock* can stand alone as a sentence.)

Subordinate Clauses

A clause that cannot stand alone as a complete sentence is a subordinate clause. Many subordinate clauses begin with a connecting word called a **subordinating conjunction.** Here are some of the most common:

Subordinating Conjunctions

after	although	as	as if	though
when	because	before	even though	unless
if	while	since	so that	until

A sentence that has both an independent clause and a subordinate clause is called a **complex sentence.** In a complex sentence, you can place the subordinate clause at the beginning or the end of the sentence. Put the clause where it helps you state your point most clearly.

Example

> Put the cat out unless you want to let the cat shred the drapes.
> Before the rain begins, bring the laundry inside.

Exercise

Draw a line under the subordinate clause in each complex sentence.

1. After years of effort, six people climbed Mt. Everest.

2. They succeeded, even though they had a brutal time.

3. Although other people said the climb could not be done, this team made it.

4. Since the climb was so hard, they used pulleys and wedges.

5. When they reached the top, they could see four of the highest mountains on earth.

    Check your answers on page 240.

Using Subordinating Conjunctions

Use subordinate clauses to show a logical relationship between ideas. Since each subordinating conjunction has a different meaning, pick the conjunction that best links your ideas.

Categories of Subordinating Conjunctions

Choice	Time		Reason	Result	Contrast	Place
that	after	once	as	so	although	where
whether	before	since	because	that	though	
	until	when	so that			

Example

No subordinate clause:	You are late. You will not get a break.
Subordinate clause:	Because you are late, you will not get a break.

(The conjunction *because* shows why the person will not get a break.)

Use subordinate clauses to link related ideas. Make sure the ideas you link make sense together.

Example

Ideas are related:	Because of a serious illness as a child, Helen Keller was later unable to speak and hear.
Ideas not related:	Because Helen Keller was unable to speak and hear when she wrote her books, they have been in print for many years.

Exercise

Combine each pair of sentences by changing one sentence to a subordinate clause. Use a subordinating conjunction to link the ideas.

1. I went to bed. I heard a loud crash in the kitchen.

    _____

2. I pulled the blankets over my head. I was afraid.

    _____

3. I finally got up. I heard the cat's meow.

    _____

4. I knew what had happened. I saw the cat sitting by the broken plate.

    _____

Misplaced and Dangling Modifiers

Place a modifier (a descriptive word or phrase) as close as possible to the word or phrase it describes.

Example

The woman who delivered the package spoke to the man at the desk.

The batter with the red shirt hit a home run.

If the modifier is far from the word it describes, the sentence might not make sense. A **misplaced modifier** is a modifier in the wrong place in a sentence. A misplaced modifier makes a sentence confusing to readers.

Example

Misplaced modifier: The woman spoke to the man at the desk who delivered the package. (The sentence now means that the man, not the woman, delivered the package.)

Misplaced modifier: The batter hit a home run with the red shirt. (The sentence now means that the batter used the red shirt to hit the ball.)

Exercise

The modifier is underlined in each sentence. Write *C* if the modifier is in the correct place in the sentence. Write *M* if the modifier is misplaced.

_____ 1. We saw many smashed houses driving through the storm.

_____ 2. The storm even wrecked the sidewalks.

_____ 3. Scarcely people could believe the damage.

_____ 4. Broken beyond repair, Phil saw his models lying in the dirt.

_____ 5. The storm was barely over when people came to help.

_____ 6. Nearly everyone pitched in.

_____ 7. First, a list was given to each owner with many items.

_____ 8. Then, Marta picked up the clothes for the children that had been left in the box.

_____ 9. A neighbor bought a pie with a crumb crust from the store.

_____ 10. The house on the corner was rebuilt by the owners destroyed by the storm.

Check your answers on page 240.

Every modifier must describe a specific word in a sentence.

Example

> As he was coming up the stairs, the clock struck six.
> (*As he was coming up the stairs* describes what he was doing.)
>
> While we were driving down the road, we saw a bad car crash.
> (*While we were driving down the road* describes what we saw.)

A sentence cannot make sense if the modified word is missing. A **dangling modifier** is a modifier that does not describe anything in the sentence. Watch for dangling modifiers and rewrite them.

Example

> **Dangling modifier:** Coming up the stairs, the clock struck six.
> (Who came up the stairs?)
>
> **Dangling modifier:** Driving down the road, a bad car crash was seen.
> (Who was driving down the road?)

Correct a dangling modifier by adding the missing words.

Example

> **Correct:** Driving through the forest at night, we thought the trees looked eerie.
> **Dangling modifier:** Driving through the forest at night, the trees looked eerie.
>
> **Correct:** While I was speaking to a group of strangers, my knees knocked and my hands shook.
> **Dangling modifier:** Speaking to a group of strangers, my knees knocked and my hands shook.

Exercise

Rewrite each sentence to correct the dangling modifier.

1. While passing a large rock, a clap of thunder made me scream.

   _____

2. Sailing up the harbor, the boat was seen.

   _____

3. Flying over the town, the cars and houses looked like toys.

   _____

4. Do not sit in the chair without being fully put together.

   _____

Check your answers on page 240.

Revising Sentences

Wordiness

After writing a paragraph, revise your sentences to make your meaning as clear as possible. Remove any excess words that make it harder for your reader to grasp your point.

Example

> **Too wordy:** They refused to accept my phone call.
> **Revised:** They refused my phone call.
>
> **Too wordy:** Please repeat your comment again.
> **Revised:** Please repeat your comment.
>
> **Too wordy:** Is that the real truth?
> **Revised:** Is that the truth?

Exercise

Revise each of the following sentences to get rid of the extra words.

1. Henry, where will the game be held at?

   _____

2. It can't be here, because there is a heavy dew laying on the surface of the grass.

   _____

   _____

3. On their heads, the team members wore red caps.

   _____

4. When the game started to begin, they felt better since the tension was over with.

   _____

   _____

5. The pitcher he did not know to whom to throw the ball to.

   _____

6. After each inning, they repeated their signals again.

   _____

Check your answers on page 240.

Correcting Informal Speech

Another reason to revise your sentences is to get rid of words and expressions that are not correct to use in written language, even though they are used in informal speech. Here is a list of some words and expressions to avoid in your writing.

Example

Use:	What kind of <u>movie</u> are you going to see?
Avoid:	What kind of <u>a movie</u> are you going to see?
Use:	<u>Because</u> I have been here longer, I can help you.
Avoid:	<u>Being that</u> I have been here longer, I can help you.
Use:	We <u>ought</u> to leave now.
Avoid:	We <u>had ought</u> to leave now.
Use:	My <u>boss says</u> I am a good worker.
Avoid:	My <u>boss, she</u> says I am a good worker.
Use:	Try <u>to</u> work more.
Avoid:	Try <u>and</u> work more.
Use:	<u>This</u> book will help you.
Avoid:	<u>This here</u> book will help you.
Use:	The reason is <u>that</u> the bus was late.
Avoid:	The reason is <u>because</u> the bus was late.
Use:	<u>As</u> I told you, he moved to the city.
Avoid:	<u>Like</u> I told you, he moved to the city.
Use:	Please hand me <u>those</u> wrenches.
Avoid:	Please hand me <u>them</u> wrenches.
Use:	I saw on TV <u>that</u> a man was hurt.
Avoid:	I saw on TV <u>where</u> a man was hurt.

Exercise

Write *C* if the sentence is correct. Write *W* if the sentence is wrong.

_____ 1.   Being that the food is good, the place is always crowded.

_____ 2.   My friend says it is the best place to eat in town.

_____ 3.   You had ought to get there early to get a seat.

_____ 4.   The reason is that all the food is fresh.

_____ 5.   Like I told you, the fish is great.

_____ 6.   Please hand me those napkins.

_____ 7.   I heard on the radio where they are opening a new place.

_____ 8.   We have to try and get there soon.

Check your answers on page 240.

POSTTEST
Capitalization and Punctuation

Decide if each underlined part is correct. If so, write *C* in the blank. If the underlined part is wrong, write it correctly in the blank.

_____ 1. Salt Lake City is the capital of <u>utah</u>.

_____ 2. In <u>1847; the</u> Mormon pioneers entered the Salt Lake Valley.

_____ 3. Most of the land was a <u>desert,</u> and the area was short on timber and game.

_____ 4. By the end of the <u>year,</u> over 2,000 settlers had come to Salt Lake City.

_____ 5. The first winter was mild, but heavy snow and rain fell in <u>april</u>.

_____ 6. The settlers planted <u>wheat corn and potatoes</u>.

_____ 7. Other explorers traveled south and settled these <u>cities:</u> Provo, Lehi, and Payson.

_____ 8. Utah was named for the <u>ute indians</u>.

_____ 9. Mr. <u>morley</u> made peace with the Indians in 1849.

_____ 10. After a lengthy debate, <u>congress</u> made Utah a territory in 1850.

_____ 11. Besides settling the <u>land</u> the pioneers built schools, churches, and a first-class theater.

_____ 12. After the <u>civil war,</u> the first railroad across the continent was completed in Utah.

_____ 13. David Hewes of <u>san francisco</u> donated the gold spike used to join the two railroad sections.

_____ 14. The railroad brought many new settlers to <u>Utah;</u> the ranchers were unhappy with the increase in population.

_____ 15. Utah finally became a <u>state</u> in 1896.

Verb Tenses

Choose the correct verb to complete each sentence. Write the correct verb in the blank.

16. The game of Monopoly _____ introduced in the 1930s.
    is   was

17. Since then, over 70 million sets _____ sold.
    are   have been

18. The first Monopoly game was _____ on a tablecloth.
    drew   drawn

19. Each player _____ to buy properties of the same color.
    try   tries

20. If a player _____ on your property, you can collect rent.
    lands   landed

21. During an average game, you _____ land on Illinois Avenue most often.
    does   will

22. A player who _____ to jail must pay $50 or roll doubles on the dice.
    went   goes

23. When you own all the properties of one color, you can _____ houses and hotels on them.
    build   have built

24. Each time you pass "Go," you _____ $200.
    collects   collect

25. Players must buy houses before they have _____ their turns.
    took   taken

26. Expert players _____ the orange properties are always a good buy.
    know   knew

27. You can _____ deals before, during, or after your turn.
    made   make

28. You know you have _____ when the other players are out of money.
    winning   won

29. Every year, several Monopoly tournaments _____ held around the country.
    were   are

Subject-Verb Agreement

Choose the correct verb to complete each sentence. Write the correct word in the blank.

30. Children between the ages of two and five _____ an average of thirty-three hours of television a week.
watches   watch

31. They _____ little time to do anything else.
has   have

32. The average child _____ more than 13,000 deaths on television during his or her childhood.
sees   see

33. Parents and teachers _____ concerned about the amount of violence on television.
is   are

34. The government _____ studying whether television promotes violence.
is   are

35. Television _____ also popular with adults.
is   are

36. *TV Guide*, sold at supermarkets, _____ a higher circulation than any other magazine in the U.S.
have   has

37. February and November _____ two months when people watch many hours of television.
is   are

38. The TV networks _____ their best programs during those months.
shows   show

39. If many people watch a TV show, a company _____ more money to have its commercials shown during that show.
pays   pay

40. Shows with low ratings _____ sometimes cancelled.
is   are

41. A TV show with low ratings _____ less money for its network.
earns   earn

42. Studies show that most people _____ family and adventure shows.
likes   like

43. Shows about lawyers and police officers _____ also very popular.
is   are

Nouns and Pronouns

Decide if each underlined part is correct. If so, write *C* in the blank. If the part is wrong, write the correct word or words in the blank.

_____ 44. Ken <u>adams</u> is the new receptionist.

_____ 45. Please help <u>he</u> learn your names and extensions.

_____ 46. <u>We</u> also have a new phone system.

_____ 47. You will find instructions in <u>you're</u> boxes.

_____ 48. Every phone has <u>its</u> own extension.

_____ 49. All employees have <u>they</u> names in the new company directory.

_____ 50. Look up your name, and make sure <u>its'</u> right.

_____ 51. When our customers call, Ken will tell <u>them</u> the right extensions.

_____ 52. This morning, Mr. Campbell from <u>nelson supply</u> Company called our office.

_____ 53. He was angry because <u>him</u> was put on hold for fifteen minutes.

_____ 54. Customers who are on hold expect <u>there</u> calls to be answered promptly.

_____ 55. When you put customers on hold, check back with <u>they</u> often.

_____ 56. If you have any questions, talk to Ms. Whitfield at our office in <u>minnesota</u>.

_____ 57. The new company directories are <u>your's</u> to keep.

_____ 58. Take one home if you make calls from <u>their</u>.

_____ 59. I appreciate <u>your</u> hard work.

Adjectives and Adverbs

Complete each sentence by writing the correct word in the blank.

60. Many people think the _____ exciting moment in baseball history was Kirk Gibson's home run in Game One of the 1988 World Series.
more   most   mostly

61. There were two outs when Gibson walked _____ to the plate.
slow   slower   slowly

62. He had trouble swinging the bat _____ on the first few pitches.
good   well   better

63. Once, he ran _____ toward first base after hitting a foul ball.
weak   weaker   weakly

64. Gibson had an injured left leg, but the pain from his right knee was _____.
bad   worse   worst

65. Mike Davis on first base stole second base _____.
easily   easy   easier

66. First base was open, but the manager decided it was _____ to pitch to Gibson than to walk him.
good   better   best

67. Eckersley, the pitcher, threw a _____ backdoor slider.
low   lower   lowest

68. Gibson swung _____ and hit the pitch into the upper deck.
smooth   smoother   smoothly

69. Kirk Gibson limped around the bases while the crowd cheered _____.
loud   loudly   loudest

70. The Dodgers of 1988 may have had _____ talent than the Oakland A's, but the Dodgers proved to be the better team.
less   least   littler

Go on to the next page.

Plurals and Possessives

Complete each sentence by writing the correct word in the blank.

71. Since the late 1800s, detective stories have been a favorite with _____ everywhere.
    readers   reader's   readers'

72. Sir Arthur Conan Doyle wrote many short _____ and four novels about Sherlock Holmes.
    storys   story's   stories

73. _____ works have survived the test of time.
    Doyles   Doyle's   Doyles'

74. The _____ friend, Dr. John Watson, was modeled after Doyle, a medical doctor and soldier.
    detectives   detective's   detectives'

75. Sherlock is never without his magnifying glass and his pipe as he searches for clues in the

    _____ of London.
    streets   street's   streets'

76. The _____ criminals are smart, but they eventually make mistakes.
    cities   city's   citys'

77. Unlike our modern detective stories, the _____ are rarely violent.
    crimes   crime's   crimes'

78. Instead, _____ entertaining to watch Sherlock discover the meaning behind the clues.
    its   it's   its'

79. Actually, the _____ ideas led to many of our modern methods of fighting crime.
    authors   author's   authors'

80. Some _____ have formed Sherlock Holmes fan clubs.
    readers   reader's   readers'

81. They often meet to celebrate _____ birthday in January each year.
    Sherlocks   Sherlock's   Sherlocks'

Go on to the next page.

Spelling and Homonyms

Write the correct word from the list below in each blank.

Children under the age of _____ are especially prone to bumps and falls. _____ little
(82)   (83)

boy's front tooth was recently broken in a fall. He was riding a bike _____ fast. We called the
(84)

dentist _____ . She asked me about the _____ of the break.
(85)   (86)

While I was _____ the appointment, my husband put a cold cloth on our son's lip.
(87)

At the dentist's office, we had to _____ for an hour. Many other children were
(88)

_____ to see the dentist.
(89)

The dentist made sure there was not a _____ of the tooth in his lip. She also made sure
(90)

the tooth was not _____ . We made an appointment to come back in one _____ . We
(91)   (92)

were glad to _____ his tooth would be fine.
(93)

Word List

82. for	four	fore
83. Our	Are	Hour
84. to	two	too
85. imediately	immediatly	immediately
86. angle	angel	angele
87. makeing	makking	making
88. wieght	wait	weight
89. there	their	they're
90. piece	peice	peace
91. lose	loose	loos
92. weak	week	weke
93. no	know	now

Go on to the next page.

Sentence Structure

Write a word from the list below in each blank.

Every year people lose their lives in fires, _____ (94) many fatal fires can be prevented.

Parents should teach their children how to prevent fires, _____ (95) they should show them

what to do if a fire starts. Many fires start in the kitchen _____ (96) someone gets careless.

Never put water on a grease fire, _____ (97) the fire will spread. Cover the burning pan with

an air-tight lid _____ (98) fires go out when the air is cut off. Keep a fire extinguisher handy,

_____ (99) know how to use it.

Do not store papers, boxes, and old clothes, _____ (100) these items can catch fire easily.

Always throw away oily rags, _____ (101) keep flammable liquids safely stored in metal

containers.

Electrical fires are easily avoided _____ (102) you take a few precautions. Never plug

more than two appliances into one outlet, _____ (103) you may overload the circuit. A fuse may

blow _____ (104) a circuit becomes overloaded. When this happens, always find out the cause of

the problem, _____ (105) replace the fuse.

Word List

94.	because	but	or
95.	and	or	because
96.	or	so	when
97.	because	which	but
98.	unless	since	then
99.	and	or	but

100.	because	yet	and
101.	since	but	and
102.	unless	if	because
103.	but	and	since
104.	if	and	then
105.	and	or	but

Sentence Structure

Below are ten complete sentences and ten fragments. Put an *S* next to each complete sentence. Put an *F* next to each fragment.

_____106. Many children get motion sickness in cars.

_____107. Feel dizzy or tired.

_____108. Strong smells may make the child feel worse.

_____109. You should open a window.

_____110. Reading or playing with small toys.

_____111. A sick child can eat soda crackers.

_____112. In the front seat or behind the driver.

_____113. A cool cloth on the forehead.

_____114. Young children often get ear infections.

_____115. Children under four years old.

_____116. A child with an ear infection.

_____117. Small babies may get a high fever.

_____118. An ear infection is painful.

_____119. Crying and refusing to eat.

_____120. Even a mild ear infection should be treated promptly.

_____121. When they are rubbing or pulling on one or both ears.

_____122. To prevent ear infections.

_____123. A baby's head should be raised during feedings.

_____124. Needs medicine for one week to ten days.

_____125. The doctor will prescribe medicine.

Go on to the next page.

Sentence Parallelism and Clarity

Fill in the blank with one of the words or phrases listed below.

126. _____, in 1926, Warner Brothers added sound to its motion pictures.
    About 70 years ago   Start with *In*   Before modern times

127. Motion pictures have changed the way we think, talk, and _____.
    to dress   dress   are dressing

128. _____ motion pictures start out as an idea written in two or three pages.
    In this day and age,   In recent times,   Modern

129. _____ a screenplay is written by a screenwriter.
    Once the idea is written,   Next,   Following the first step,

130. The producers study the screenplay _____ plan a budget for the movie.
    to   in order to   as a way to

131. _____ making a movie is very complex, the producers hire many specialized workers.
    On account of the fact that   Due to the fact that   Because

132. Lighting technicians, production assistants, and _____ are hired to work on the movie.
    sound technicians   people to do sound   someone who knows about sound

133. The director _____ the shooting of the movie.
    tells everyone what to do during   supervises   is the boss of everyone during

134. _____ the editor combines the pictures, voices, and sound effects to make the movie.
    The next step is   Then   After the previous step,

135. _____ you watch the titles at the end of a movie, you will see that many people are needed to make a film.
    If   In the event that   On the occasion that

Posttest for Writing — Essay

This part of the Writing Skills Posttest will help you determine how well you write. You will write an essay that explains something or presents an opinion on an issue. To write your essay clearly, follow these steps.

☐   1.   Read all the directions carefully before you begin to write.

☐   2.   Read the essay topic carefully.

☐   3.   Plan what you want to say before you start to write. List your main ideas and supporting details before you write any sentences.

☐   4.   Make sure you stick to the topic.

☐   5.   Write your notes and first draft in your Personal Writing Notebook. Then write your final draft on page 215.

☐   6.   Review what you have written, and make any changes that will improve your essay.

☐   7.   Read over your essay for correct sentence structure, spelling, punctuation, capitalization, and usage.

TOPIC

More and more, goods and services are advertised on television through 900 telephone numbers. Unlike the free 800 numbers, the 900 numbers cost money to use. Many people object to these telephone numbers being advertised on television during children's programs.

Write an essay of about 200 words, stating your opinion about whether 900 telephone numbers should be advertised during children's programming on TV. Use specific examples to support your argument.

POSTTEST
Correlation Chart

Writing Skills

The chart below will help you determine your strengths and weaknesses in grammar and writing skills.

Directions
Circle the number of each item you answered correctly on the Writing Skills Posttest. Count the number of items you answered correctly in each row. Write the amount in the Total Correct space in each row. (For example, in the Capitalization and Punctuation row, write the number correct in the blank before *out of 15*.) Complete this process for the remaining rows. Then add the nine totals to get your TOTAL CORRECT for the Posttest.

Skill Areas	Item Numbers	Total Correct	Pages
Capitalization and Punctuation	1, 2, 3, 4, 5, 6, 7, 8, 9, 10, 11, 12, 13, 14, 15	_____ out of 15	77 – 79, 150 – 154, 158 – 161
Verb Tenses	16, 17, 18, 19, 20, 21, 22, 23, 24, 25, 26, 27, 28, 29	_____ out of 14	182 – 183
Subject-Verb Agreement	30, 31, 32, 33, 34, 35, 36, 37, 38, 39, 40, 41, 42, 43	_____ out of 14	66 – 67, 186 – 187
Nouns and Pronouns	44, 45, 46, 47, 48, 49, 50, 51, 52, 53, 54, 55, 56, 57, 58, 59	_____ out of 16	29, 170 – 176
Adjectives and Adverbs	60, 61, 62, 63, 64, 65, 66, 67, 68, 69, 70	_____ out of 11	42 – 43, 177 – 181
Plurals and Possessives	71, 72, 73, 74, 75, 76, 77, 78, 79, 80, 81	_____ out of 11	164 – 165
Spelling and Homonyms	82, 83, 84, 85, 86, 87, 88, 89, 90, 91, 92, 93	_____ out of 12	115, 162 – 163, 168
Sentence Structure	94, 95, 96, 97, 98, 99, 100, 101, 102, 103, 104, 105, 106, 107, 108, 109, 110, 111, 112, 113, 114, 115, 116, 117, 118, 119, 120, 121, 122, 123, 124, 125	_____ out of 32	32 – 33, 44 – 47, 54 – 55, 105, 190 – 203
Sentence Parallelism and Clarity	126, 127, 128, 129, 130, 131, 132, 133, 134, 135	_____ out of 10	54 – 55, 105, 196 – 197

TOTAL CORRECT FOR POSTTEST_____ out of 135

If you answered fewer than 122 items correctly, look more closely at the skill areas listed above. In which areas do you need more practice? Page numbers to refer to for practice are given in the right-hand column above.

ANSWERS AND EXPLANATIONS

INVENTORY

PAGE 1

1. W   Use a comma after introductory words.
2. C   Use a comma to separate two independent clauses joined by a coordinating conjunction.
3. W   Capitalize the title of important events.
4. C   Do not capitalize common nouns.
5. C   Capitalize names of countries.
6. W   Capitalize the first word of a sentence.
7. W   Do not capitalize common nouns.
8. C   Do not capitalize the continued part of a quotation.
9. W   Use commas to separate the items in a list.
10. W   Use a colon before a list of items.
11. W   Use commas to set off contrasting words or phrases.
12. C   Use a colon before a list of items.
13. W   Capitalize the first word of a quote.
14. W   Use a comma to set off opening phrases.
15. W   Capitalize a person's name.
16. C   Use a semicolon to separate two independent clauses.

PAGE 2

17. became   Use the past tense to indicate an action that took place in the past.
18. is   Use the correct form of *to be*.
19. covers   Use the present tense to indicate a continuing action.
20. has been   Use the helping verb *has*.
21. has   Use the present tense to indicate a continuing action.
22. has   Use the present tense to indicate a continuing action.
23. give   Use the correct form of the verb.
24. entered   Use the past tense to indicate an action that took place in the past.
25. is   Use the correct form of *to be*.
26. think   Use the correct form of the present tense verb.
27. accounts   Use the correct form of the present tense verb.
28. is   Use the present tense to indicate a continuing action.
29. visit   Use the correct form of the verb.

30. spend   Use the present tense to indicate a continuing action.
31. maintains   Use the singular form of the verb with the mass noun *state*.
32. travel   Use the plural form of the verb with the subject *people*.
33. has   Use the correct form of the verb.
34. link   Use the present tense to indicate the action is taking place in the present.

PAGE 3

35. was   Use the singular verb *was* with the singular subject, the infinitive *to recover*.
36. was   Use the singular verb *was* with the singular subject *no one*.
37. is   Use the singular verb *is* with the singular subject *recovery*.
38. advise   Use the plural verb *advise* with the plural subject *doctors and nurses*.
39. want   Use the plural verb *want* with the plural subject *workers*.
40. go   Use the plural verb *go* with the plural subject *patients*.
41. produce   Use the plural verb *produce* with the compound subject *exercise and physical therapy*.
42. reduce   Use the plural verb *reduce* with the plural subject *medicines*.
43. heal   Use the plural verb *heal* with the plural subject *wounds*.
44. prevent   Use the plural verb *prevent* with the plural subject *drugs*.
45. are   Use the plural verb *are* with the plural subject *rises*.
46. allow   Use the plural verb *allow* with the plural subject *methods*.
47. repair   Use the plural verb *repair* with the plural subject *doctors*.
48. are   Use the plural verb *are* with the plural subject *plastics*.
49. does   Use the singular verb *does* with the singular subject *material*.

PAGE 4

50. Kiev   Capitalize a proper noun.
51. them   Use the objective case pronoun because they are receiving the action, not doing it.

52. strength — Do not add an *s* to a collective or mass noun.
53. C — Capitalize a person's name.
54. Ivan the Terrible — Capitalize each important word in a proper noun.
55. Moscow — Capitalize a proper noun such as the name of a city.
56. Russia's — Capitalize a proper noun.
57. C — Use the pronoun *they* as the subject of the verb.
58. C — Use a possessive pronoun to show whose language it is.
59. their — Never use an apostrophe with possessive pronouns, because they are already in the possessive form.
60. C — Do not capitalize a common noun.
61. them — Use the objective case to show the pronoun is receiving the action, not performing it.
62. its — *Its'* is not a word. *Its* is the possessive pronoun. *It's* means *it is*.
63. republics — Do not capitalize a common noun.
64. C — Capitalize the name of a country.
65. C — Use a possessive pronoun to show to whom the country belongs.
66. They — Use the subject pronoun *they* to show the pronoun is doing the action.

PAGE 5

67. well — Use an adverb to describe the verb *live*.
68. worse — Use the comparative form when you are comparing two things.
69. slowly — Use an adverb to describe the adverb *very*.
70. sooner — Use the comparative form when you are comparing two things.
71. badly — Use an adverb to describe the verb *do*.
72. higher — Use the comparative form when you are comparing two things.
73. better — Use the comparative form when you are comparing two things.
74. best — Use the superlative form to compare three or more things.
75. better — Use the comparative form when you are comparing two things. Do not combine *more* or *most* with an *-er* form.
76. Most — Use the superlative form when you are comparing three or more people.

77. harder — Use the comparative form when you are comparing two things. Do not combine *more* or *most* with an *-er* form.

PAGE 6

78. mountains — Use a plural noun as the object of the preposition *in*.
79. creature's — Use an apostrophe to show ownership (the body of the creature).
80. animal's — Use an apostrophe to show ownership (the body of the animal).
81. feet — *Feet* is the plural form of *foot*. Use the plural since there is more than one foot.
82. Natives — Use the plural form of the noun as a subject.
83. Americans — Use the plural form of the noun as a subject.
84. writers — Use the plural form of the noun as a subject.
85. Reporters' — Use an apostrophe to show ownership. (The articles belong to the reporters.)
86. explorers — Use the plural form of the noun as a subject.
87. thing's — Use an apostrophe to show ownership.
88. bears — Use the plural form of the noun as the object of the preposition *by*.
89. Scientists — Use the plural form of the noun as the subject.
90. its — Use the possessive form to show ownership. *It's* is a contraction; *its'* is not a word.

PAGE 7

We <u>know</u> that diamonds are the hardest
    91

substance. Diamonds become <u>weak</u> only when they
    92

have a flaw. Then they can shatter along an <u>angle</u>.
    93

Formed by heat, diamonds are found in <u>holes</u> in the
    94

ground. Value is based on clarity, color, and <u>weight</u>.
    95

Did you know that most diamonds <u>are</u> not
    96

used in jewelry? <u>Except</u> for a small number of
    97

stones, that is. Most diamonds have a <u>different</u> use.
    98

They are used in <u>making</u> things. This is because
    99

they're hard. They do not <u>break</u> easily. Diamonds
  100   101

are used to drill <u>metals</u>. <u>Pieces</u> of diamonds are
102   103
pressed together. These are used to make home

<u>knife</u> sharpeners. Nearly all the world's diamonds
104
come from <u>foreign</u> countries.
105

PAGE 8

    People used to avoid the sun, <u>because</u> they
106
tried to keep their skin untanned. They wore hats,

<u>or</u> they stayed inside on sunny days. Women even
107
wore gloves, <u>and</u> they carried small umbrellas.
108

    Today, doctors warn people about the sun, <u>but</u>
109
many people still want to get a tan. Some people go

to beaches and pools to "catch some rays," <u>and</u>
110
smear on gobs of suntan lotion. They lie in the sun

for hours, <u>because</u> they think it will make them
111
look good. Many people also go to suntan parlors,

<u>even though</u> that costs a lot of money. People do not
112
see how harmful the sun's rays are, <u>but</u> doctors
113
warn us. Doctors say the sun causes skin cancer,

<u>and</u> cancer can kill you.
114

    You should see your doctor if a mole changes

shape, <u>since</u> this can be a warning sign of skin
115
cancer. Also watch if a mole changes color, <u>because</u>
116
this is dangerous, too. The sun also dries out your

skin, <u>since</u> it takes away the moisture. The sun
117
feels good, <u>but</u> it's not good for you.
118

PAGE 9

119. F   no verb
120. F   no subject
121. S
122. F   not a complete thought
123. F   no verb
124. S
125. S
126. F   not a complete thought
127. S
128. S
129. S
130. S
131. F   no verb
132. S
133. S
134. F   not a complete thought
135. F   not a complete thought

136. S
137. F   no verb
138. S

PAGE 10

139. start with *In*   The first choice is too wordy and unclear; the second choice is untrue.
140. small, flat piece of wood   The other choices are too wordy and unclear.
141. which   *Which* refers to a thing (wood) and can be the object of the preposition *to*. *Whom* refers to a person.
142. under   The other choices are unclear.
143. cleaning   Use parallel structure. *Cleaning* parallels *twisting* and *spinning*.
144. sorting fibers   Use parallel structure. *Sorting fibers* parallels *carding* and *combing*.
145. satin   Use parallel structure. *Satin* parallels *plain* and *twill*.
146. on   *By means of* is too wordy; *in order to* is incorrect.
147. If   The other choices are unclear and too wordy.
148. Because   The other choices are unclear and too wordy.
149. variety   Use parallel structure. *Variety* parallels *speed* and *accuracy*.
150. making   The other choices are unclear and too wordy.

INVENTORY FOR WRITING—ESSAY
PAGE 12

Below is a sample essay by a student who <u>supports</u> gun control.

    Gun control will reduce the number of violent crimes. First, making it harder for people to obtain guns will force people to think before they use a gun. Second, registering guns will allow the police to know who has guns, which will also help prevent crimes of passion.

    In many places, people can just walk into a gun store, buy a weapon, and use it later while they are raging. If a government law forces people to wait two weeks—or more—before they can buy a gun, people will have a chance to "cool off" after an argument and think about the results of their actions.

Lawmakers have also proposed making people register all their guns. This will also help prevent violent crime because it will keep a record of anyone who owns a gun. People will realize that the police can much more easily locate them if they use their guns to harm others. This will prevent some violent crime because it will also force people to think before they act.

Creating a waiting period before someone can buy a gun and registering all guns are two methods of gun control that will help reduce violent crimes. Since guns are responsible for the bulk of all crimes, controlling their sale and distribution will save millions of lives every year. One of those lives may be yours.

Below is a sample essay by a student who <u>opposes</u> gun control.

Gun control will have no effect on the number of violent crimes. First, gun control will not decrease the number of guns in the hands of criminals. Second, making it harder for law-abiding citizens to obtain arms violates the Bill of Rights.

A criminal usually does not walk into a gun shop, buy a weapon, and use it to rob a bank. Guns used in crimes are almost always obtained illegally. Criminals do not want to register guns that can be easily traced. A network already exists on the street for criminals to obtain all the guns they need and want.

On the other hand, gun control would make it more difficult for law-abiding citizens to protect themselves. Imagine that your family has been threatened repeatedly by gang members. You want to buy a gun to protect your family but are forced to fill out forms and wait several weeks to buy a gun. Meanwhile, your family is in danger daily.

The Bill of Rights guarantees your right to bear arms to protect your family and your property. Gun control interferes with that right. The enforced waiting period and government red tape of gun control will encourage law-abiding citizens also to buy guns illegally. So gun control will not reduce the number of crimes nor the number of guns in the hands of criminals.

PART A: WRITING SKILLS

SECTION 1

PAGE 17, GUIDED WRITING

Sample answers:
1. Sports Topic 1: How to Play Soccer, Topic 2: Keeping Score in Bowling
2. Exercise Topic 1: Avoiding Injuries, Topic 2: Running in a Race
3. Movies Topic 1: Favorite Movie of All Time, Topic 2: Favorite Movie Character
4. Animals Topic 1: Favorite Animals, Topic 2: Hunting Should Be Outlawed

PAGE 18, GUIDED WRITING

Sample answer: Advantages of a large family: never lonely, learn to get along with others, support one another

PAGE 18, JOURNAL WRITING

Sample map:

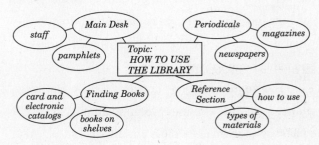

Sample answer:
- I. Never lonely
     - A. When young you have someone to play with
     - B. When older you have someone to go out with

- II. Learn to get along with others
     - A. Learn to share
     - B. Learn to solve arguments
     - C. Learn to compromise

- III. Support one another
     - A. Have people to call on when you need help
     - B. Have people to borrow money from
     - C. Have people to talk to about your problems

PAGE 20, EXERCISE

1. Sentence A gives the best support to the main idea. Sentence B tells only one side and may not attract the reader's interest. Sentence C simply restates the topic.
2. Sentence A is the best answer. It makes a strong statement about the main idea. Both Sentences B and C are vague statements that do not clearly support the topic.
3. Sentence B is the best answer. It clearly states the author's purpose. Sentence A does not clearly support the topic. Sentence C is a supporting detail.

PAGE 21, EXERCISE

Paragraph 1
1. fact/reason
2. compare/contrast
3. example

Paragraph 2
1. fact/reason
2. compare/contrast
3. order of importance

PAGE 22, EXERCISE A

Paragraph 1: 1, 5, 3, 2, 4
Paragraph 2: 4, 5, 1, 3, 2 or 3, 2, 1, 5, 4

PAGE 22, EXERCISE B

Paragraph 1: time order
Paragraph 2: facts/reasons

PAGE 22, JOURNAL WRITING

Sample answers:
1. Morning people and night people are like oil and water. Morning people wake up with the sun, smile, and start talking. When night people have to get up early, they grumble and refuse to talk. Night people come alive at the end of the day. They are ready to party just as morning people are about to turn in for the night.
2. Learning to organize your time will change your life. You can begin by writing down how you spend every hour of the day. Do this for one week and you will begin to see where your time is going. Next, make a list of the time wasters you can avoid. Then figure out how much time you have left for the things you have been putting off.
3. Friendship is one of the most important things in life. If you know how to be a good friend, then you know how to be loyal. Friendship also teaches you how to keep secrets and how to make sacrifices for

someone else. Friendship is supposed to be a two-way street. If this is true, then all the good you give will come back to you.

PAGE 23, EXERCISE

1. question
2. prediction
3. recommendation

PAGE 25, EXERCISE

b	1.	The first sentence logically belongs directly in front of sentence 7.
d	2.	Sentence 2 is the sentence that states the main idea of the paragraph.
g	3.	No error.
f	4.	The sentence is missing a subject.
a	5.	The word *attacks* should be taken out the first time it appears.
e	6.	The idea in this sentence is vague and unclear. The same idea is stated clearly in sentence 7.
c	7.	*Nonsmokers* is plural, so the plural verb *are* should replace the singular verb *is*.

PAGE 25, JOURNAL WRITING

Edited version:

(1) There are far fewer smokers today than there were in the past. (2) The time has come to outlaw smoking in all public places. (3) Smoke is a hazard to the healthy nonsmoker. (4) In public places it pollutes the air and irritates the eyes. (5) It can also cause sneezing ~~attacks~~ and allergy attacks. ~~(6) Non-smokers should stand up and be counted.~~ (7) Since nonsmokers ~~is~~ are the majority, they must push for laws that protect their rights.

PAGE 27, EXERCISE

Proofread version:

¶ I am enclosing a copy of my resume in response to 𝑠𝑝 your ad in the Boston Journal on June 26, 1992. I hope you will find my ~~exereience~~ experience and skills in line 𝑠𝑝 with the qualifications for the telemarketing sales position. ¶ I am available to come to your office for a job interview. please call me at 555-6242.

PAGE 27, JOURNAL WRITING

Final version:

I am enclosing a copy of my resume in response to your ad in the Boston Journal on June 26, 1992. I hope you will find my experience and skills in line with the qualifications for the telemarketing sales position.

I am available to come to your office for a job interview. Please call me at 555-6242.

SECTION 2

PAGE 29, EXERCISE A

1. he   her (Sam is the subject; Alice is the object.)
2. He   their (Tomás is the subject; Sam and Alice's are possessive nouns.)
3. them   (Sally, Keisha, and Corinne are objects of the preposition to.)
4. him   (Diego is the object of the preposition to.)
5. They   (Sam and Alice are subjects.)

PAGE 29, EXERCISE B

1. me (Me is the object of the preposition to.)
2. We (We is the subject.)
3. mine (Mine is a possessive pronoun taking the place of a possessive noun.)
4. I (I is the subject.)
5. us (Us is the object of the preposition to.)
6. our (Our is a possessive pronoun telling whose friends.)
7. We (We is the subject.)
8. Our (Our is a possessive pronoun telling whose goal.)

PAGE 31, EXERCISE A

1. Some people like to give parties.
2. Joanne and I gave a New Year's Eve Party.
3. Alex invited everyone over for his birthday.
4. Barbara cooked and packed a picnic lunch for eight.

PAGE 31, EXERCISE B

1. My sister plans to be a track star.
2. She runs and exercises every day.
3. Our father trains and coaches her for track meets.
4. My mother and I attend and give our support.
5. She runs for the Ohio State University track team.

6. Last week the team won a meet against Memphis State.
7. My sister competed in three events.
8. She got first place in two events.

PAGE 32, EXERCISE

1. F (needs a subject)
2. S
3. F (needs a verb)
4. S
5. S
6. F (needs a subject and a verb)

PAGE 32, GUIDED WRITING A

1. Judy plays practical jokes all the time.
2. My boss is a smart person.
3. They dropped crumbs all over the floor.

PAGE 32, GUIDED WRITING B

Sample answers:

1. She waited two hours and left.
2. These pink, white, and yellow flowers need water.
3. Irv stayed home as long as he could.

PAGE 33, EXERCISE A

1. because/since
2. but
3. if/since/because
4. although/but
5. when/if

PAGE 33, EXERCISE B

Sample answers:

1. Last year I took a trip to Florida. My sister's two kids went with me.
2. I took all their games and toys, but the kids still drove me crazy.
3. They were never sleepy at the same time. One of them was always crying.

PAGE 34, EXERCISE

1.	2.	3.
1 - F	1 - C	1 - B
2 - C	2 - B	2 - C
3 - A	3 - A	3 - D
4 - D	4 - D	4 - A
5 - B	5 - F	5 - E
6 - E	6 - E	6 - F

PAGE 35, GUIDED WRITING

Sample answers:

1. Before I was in high school, I had attended six different schools. My mother was an entertainer, so my family moved a lot. We lived with relatives or friends, although

sometimes we rented our own apartment. Most people don't like to move and make changes all the time. For me, it was a way of life because we had done it since I was born.

2. Denise and Carol got caught in a terrible snowstorm. They were on their way home from a weekend trip. They made a wrong turn and ended up on a deserted road. The road had not been plowed, and they got stuck in a huge snowdrift. Luckily there was a house nearby. A kind family let them spend the night and helped them dig their car out the next day.

3. My last birthday was the best one I have ever had. Two of my friends gave me a surprise birthday party. The landlord let them use a vacant apartment in our building, so there was plenty of room. They invited everyone we know. Most of the guests brought food. I realized how lucky I am to have so many friends.

PAGE 35, JOURNAL WRITING

Sample answer:

Topic: A Childhood Memory

Looking back at some of the things I did as a teenager makes me break out in a cold sweat. The purpose of each adventure was always fun, but sometimes things got out of hand. In my search for good times, I was part of several pranks, ranging from fairly harmless to fairly serious.

The first prank proved that good, clean fun does not have to be dull. As a high school student, I was credited with making the world's largest dessert. With several friends, I spent an entire year collecting boxes of Jell-O. Late one night we entered our school's indoor pool. We turned the water temperature up as high as it would go and poured in box after box of the strawberry powder. The next morning, school officials arrived to find the pool filled with 13,000 gallons of the quivering, rubbery stuff.

SECTION 3

PAGE 38, GUIDED WRITING

Sample answers:

1. The car has a blue and red racing stripe.
2. The streetlight had a blinking yellow light.
3. My birthday cake had pink icing.
4. The old oak tree was over six feet tall.
5. The bright blue bowling ball had holes too big for my fingers.

PAGE 39, EXERCISE

1. e
2. c
3. d
4. b
5. a
6. g
7. j
8. f
9. i
10. h

PAGE 39, GUIDED WRITING

Sample answers:

1. He has a two-year-old son.
2. After dinner we had vanilla ice cream and apple pie.
3. I gave my daughter a fluffy gray kitten.

PAGE 40, EXERCISE

1. sight
2. touch
3. hearing
4. smell
5. taste

PAGE 40, GUIDED WRITING

Sample answers:

The sunset was a brightly colored stage.

The rhythms of several beating drums came from the open window at the factory.

The hamburger was so hot that it burned my tongue.

Her handshake was sweaty and cold.

The new baby had the smell of sweet cream.

PAGE 40, JOURNAL WRITING

Sample answer:

Going to the movies is my favorite pastime. I love to sit in a cozy dark theater and munch on freshly popped popcorn. The seats are soft and comfortable, and everything is quiet as you wait for the previews to start. After that, you can forget about all your troubles and relax, as you watch a good car chase, shootout, or love scene.

PAGE 41, GUIDED WRITING

Sample answers:

1. My apartment is the size of a matchbox.
2. Rich has hair like silk.
3. The wind howled all night long.
4. The lemonade was like a cold shower.
5. The smell of her perfume met me at the door.

PAGE 41, JOURNAL WRITING

Sample answer:

When my family goes to the park, we usually take along a full meal. We look for a large empty space of grass, because we need a lot of room. After we rub sunblock on each other, we sit down and begin to eat. We usually have fried chicken, potato salad, cole slaw, baked beans, and homemade oatmeal cookies. All of this gets washed down with ice-cold lemonade or soda.

PAGE 42, EXERCISE

1. fine
2. fresh
3. brightly
4. beautifully
5. delicious
6. regularly

PAGE 43, EXERCISE

1. hottest
2. newest
3. more quickly
4. most important
5. easy

PAGES 44–45, EXERCISE

1. The skies opened up, and lightning streaked across the sky.
2. Last year we had floods, but this year was not as bad.
3. The storm caused severe damage, and several people were injured.
4. Windows were shattered by the wind, so we went into the basement.
5. We read books, or we played cards.

PAGE 45, GUIDED WRITING

Sample answers:

1. The steak was tender, but it was too well done.
2. The street was deserted, and I was afraid to go out alone.
3. The couch was new, so we tried not to get it dirty.
4. The soldiers marched bravely, but their mission failed.
5. The sky looked threatening, so we left the beach early.
6. The fruit was ripe, and we picked as much as we could.
7. The snow was knee-deep, but it was not cold outside.
8. I should get gas soon, or I will run out.
9. We could see this movie, or we could see a different one.

PAGE 46, EXERCISE

1. Whenever
2. when

3. Whenever
4. If
5. as though
6. because
7. Even if
8. Unless
9. Whichever
10. After

PAGE 47, EXERCISE

1. The bus driver signaled, turned into the traffic, and slowly made her way along the street.
2. Jose's red car has bucket seats and chrome trim.
3. The sofa was old, plaid, and had worn-out cushions.

SECTION 4

PAGE 51, EXERCISE

First, go north to the corner. Second, turn right at the food store. Meanwhile look for the sign for Smith Street. When you see the sign, walk a block more. Then turn left. Last, stop at the dress shop. Our apartment is on the second floor.

PAGE 52, GUIDED WRITING

Sample answers:

First, walk one block to Price Street. When you pass the gas station, turn left. Next, turn right at the train tracks. After you see the post office, there is a bank. Then walk four more blocks. We are the third house on the right.

PAGE 52, EXERCISE A

First, the peanuts are shelled. Second, they are sorted for size and value. Next, they are roasted. After they are cooked, the red outer skin is removed. Then the nut is split and the small piece called the "heart" is taken off. The heart makes the peanut butter sour. Last, the nuts are mashed. During the last step of mashing, workers add honey, sugar, and salt.

PAGE 52, EXERCISE B

____4____ Next, I have a cup of tea and a piece of toast. ____1____ When I wake up, I jog for half an hour. ____6____ Before I leave, I call my friend. ____5____ While I eat, I watch the news. ____3____ Third, I get dressed. ____7____ Last, we meet on the street. ____2____ Second, I take a bath.

PAGE 53, EXERCISE A

1. future
2. present
3. past

PAGE 53, EXERCISE B

1. (1) have grown (present perfect, action still going on)
2. (1) had cleaned (past perfect, action completed before another past action)
3. (2) has visited (present perfect, third person singular)
4. (2) had swum (past perfect, action completed before another past action)

PAGE 54, EXERCISE A

1. Circle Sentence 1: Save a room with a bath for the couple.
2. Circle Sentence 2: I found a letter that is not mine in the mailbox.
3. Correct
4. Circle Sentence 4: We bought a cat we call Fluff for my son.

PAGE 54, EXERCISE B

1. 3
2. 1

PAGE 55, EXERCISE

1. Incorrect: "a good job" and "to pay me a fair wage" are not parallel.
2. Incorrect: "carefully" is an adverb and is not parallel with "intense" or "driven."
3. Incorrect: "resting" is a verb and is not parallel with "kindly" or "friendly."
4. Correct—circle.
5. Incorrect: "to shop" is not parallel with "watching football" or "playing baseball."

PAGE 55, GUIDED WRITING

1. It is good for people to run, swim, and jog.
2. Running, for example, helps you stay fit and healthy.
3. Swimming can help in toning your muscles and lowering your blood pressure.
4. You can start by walking a block a day and eating good food.
5. Exercise can help you look better, be stronger, and be wiser.

PAGES 56–57, EXERCISE

Put an X by sentences 1, 3, 5, 7, and 8.

PAGE 57, GUIDED WRITING

Sample answers:

1. The place I feel most at home is at the beach in the winter.
2. Getting a good job depends on dressing neatly for an interview.
3. One way to stay healthy is to eat a lot of leafy green vegetables.
4. After work, I like to cuddle on my sofa, with a fluffy blanket around my shoulders.
5. One of my problems is losing my temper over small problems.
6. The game was good because the Yankees scored five runs in the bottom of the ninth inning to win the game.
7. When I think of my past, I recall the sweet smell of honeysuckle.
8. One reason people give up smoking is because they do not want to get lung cancer.
9. One of my strengths is my patience.
10. One of my hobbies is bowling.

PAGE 57, JOURNAL WRITING

Sample answers:

1. Many people throw out things that other people can use. Some people throw away food that would be a nutritious meal to others. Some people throw away items that can be recycled, such as newspapers, bottles, cans, and plastic containers. Some people throw away things that are dangerous to the environment.
2. It is helpful to have the correct change ready. Always know the route the bus travels, or ask the driver. Offer elderly people a seat. Be careful not to block the aisle with bulky packages.
3. The high salt content of chips and other snack foods can be harmful to the heart. Foods such as processed meats often have a high fat content. Many junk foods are more expensive than healthful foods. Junk foods can contain additives that may be unhealthy.
4. Set reasonable goals for each week. If you don't change your eating habits, you can gain back the weight you lose. Read food labels and learn the calorie and fat contents of what you are eating. Keep a diary of what you eat in order to understand your habits.
5. Many people believe that dreams tell us about our subconscious. Many people dream about what they think will happen in the future. Dreams can be about a person's past. Everyone needs to dream to be healthy.

SECTION 5

PAGE 60, GUIDED WRITING

Sample answers:

1. appeal to emotions: After I got fired from my last job, I cried all night. I felt sorry for myself!
2. appeal to ethics: People deserve the chance to fail. When we deny people the right to fail, we cheat them out of a chance to learn how to solve their own problems.

PAGE 61, EXERCISE

1. Therefore
2. so
3. In brief

PAGE 62, EXERCISE

1. contrast (shows the difference between people who are working and those who are not)
2. compare (shows one way that peanuts and ice cream are the same)
3. contrast (tells one way Japan is different from France)
4. contrast (tells one way *As the World Turns* is different from other soap operas)

PAGE 62, GUIDED WRITING

Sample answers:

1. I liked the last movie I saw, but the ending was too obvious.
2. The movie was as exciting as my friends had said.
3. The movie had great action scenes, yet there were too many car chases.
4. The movie told the ending in the first scene, in contrast to the movie I saw last week.

PAGE 63, GUIDED WRITING

Sample answers:

1. compare: Marie is like Helen because they both enjoy watching movies, dancing, and bowling.
   contrast: Unlike Helen, Marie does not like jogging.
2. compare: New York and Boston are both cold in the winter and warm in the summer.
   contrast: Boston is much smaller than New York, and I can walk around the whole city in a day.

PAGE 64, GUIDED WRITING

Sample answers:

1. Sabrina's new poodle is cuddly.
2. My leg was broken in the crash.
3. Mr. Mori drives a moving van from 4:00 P.M. until 8:00 P.M.
4. The shop steward stalked into the boss's office for an answer.
5. They were gobbling candy in the next row and making a huge racket.

PAGE 65, EXERCISE

1. through thick and thin
2. as American as Mom's apple pie
3. selling like hotcakes
4. tried and true
5. raining cats and dogs
6. sick and tired
7. as hard as nails
8. as gentle as a lamb
9. take the bull by the horns

PAGE 65, GUIDED WRITING

Sample answers:

1. I've had some good and bad experiences today.
2. "Now it's time to suffer the results of your actions," Mr. Wright said.
3. If you eat well, get enough rest, and have a good outlook, you will live a long life.
4. A summer cold is horrible.
5. The fly was dead.

PAGE 65, JOURNAL WRITING

Sample:

There are several reasons why the space program should not be ended. Many scientific advances are made in order to improve the space program. In addition, people can learn more about the universe through the experiments conducted in _____ space program gives the United States _____ ity to work with scientists from other _____ oint projects. The space program is _____ ut the money it costs is well spent.

_____ XERCISE A

PAGE 66, EXERCISE B

1. A (salad) ~~with extra carrots~~ <u>is</u> my usual lunch.

2. The (people) ~~in the back of the crowd~~ <u>need</u> to be heard.

3. (Ned) ~~, with his three dogs,~~ <u>runs</u> around the block after work.

4. The (leader) ~~of the unions~~ <u>says</u> profits are down this year.

PAGE 67, EXERCISE A

1. leak (plural subject with *and*)
2. gives (singular subject with *or*)
3. bring (plural subject with *and*)

PAGE 67, EXERCISE B

1. spend (*Americans* is plural.)
2. eat (The subject is plural.)
3. loves (The subject is singular.)
4. take (The subject is plural.)

PAGE 68, EXERCISE

1. F   2. O   3. O   4. O   5. F   6. F

PAGE 69, EXERCISE

1. jumping to conclusions
2. quoting false experts
3. switching cause and effect
4. jumping to conclusions

SECTION 6

PAGE 72, JOURNAL WRITING

Sample answer:

Dear Aaron,

    How are you? I've been thinking about you lately and wondering when you might be able to come for a visit. It's only a two-hour ride by train, and I could meet you at the station. I'm free almost every weekend. Just let me know in advance so I can plan some interesting things for us to do.

    I hope to hear from you soon.

Regards,
Sandra

PAGE 74, JOURNAL WRITING

Sample Answer:

201 Lowell Avenue
Overland Park, MA 00910
October 10, 1992

Ms. Joyce Hawkins
Overland Medical Center
39000 South Oak Drive
Overland Park, MA 00990

Dear Ms. Hawkins:

    I received your letter about the winter training program at Overland Medical Center. Thank you for getting in touch with me.

    A copy of my resume is enclosed. As you can see, I worked as a clerk/typist at the Lenox Hill Hospital for the past two summers. Working at the hospital helped me decide that I want to pursue a career in the health field. I feel that your program offers the kind of training I need to achieve my goal of becoming a medical professional.

    I am pleased that you are considering me for entry into the program. If there is anything else I can do, please let me know.

Sincerely,
Antonio Torres
Antonio Torres

PAGE 74, GUIDED WRITING

Sample answers:

1. Dear Kareem,
   I have been calling you but did not get an answer. I was calling to ask you to repay the $5.00 I loaned you a couple of weeks ago. Please give me a call so that we can arrange to meet.
2. Ms. Chen:
   If it is all right with you, I would like to take five days of vacation July 10–14. I'm sure that the backlog of orders will be cleared up by then. It should be a slow week since it's right after the holiday. I would appreciate your letting me know soon. Thank you.

PAGE 76, EXERCISE

1.
P.O. Box 32
Eden Prairie, MN 55344
October 20, 1992

Dear Aunt Frances,

Your nephew,
Danny

2.

222 East 24th St.
Philadelphia, PA 20035
June 14, 1992

Mr. Bernard Adams
Travelworld
901 Harrison Avenue
Philadelphia, PA 20039

Dear Mr. Adams:

Sincerely,
Elaine Evans

PAGE 78, EXERCISE A

1. Last year I worked on Senator Smith's campaign.
2. The campaign office was on Fifth Avenue in the Chrysler Building.
3. The victory party was sponsored by the Independent Voters of America.
4. The party was held at their building on the Hudson River.
5. Laura Washington, Vice President of the organization, made a speech.

PAGE 78, EXERCISE B

may 20, 1992

supreme computer, inc.
958 alexander street
river tower bldg.
columbus, oh 30921

dear mr. potter:

my supervisor, doris healy, director of sales here at bradley associates, asked me to send you the enclosed brochure. the brochure gives details on the services our company provides to computer stores like yours. if you are interested in our services, please call me within the next ten days to take advantage of our free trial offer. the offer ends on may 31. we are closed next monday, due to memorial day weekend.

sincerely,

James Hobson

james hobson
sales assistant

PAGE 79, EXERCISE

1670 Evergreen Road
Houston, TX 80023
January 25, 1992

Ms. Vanessa Lewis
Lewis and Evans Assoc.
Houston, TX 80025

Dear Ms. Lewis:

¶ I attended your career planning workshop at the Valley College Library on December 15, 1991. Your presentation was just what I needed to organize myself. Would it be possible for you to send me a resume writing worksheet? Unfortunately, you ran out of handouts before you got to me.

Sincerely,

Joseph Wallach

Joseph Wallach

PAGE 81, GUIDED WRITING

Sample answer:

It was a pleasure meeting you during my interview at the day-care center last week. Thank you for considering me for the position of administrative assistant.

Following are the names, addresses, and telephone numbers of two people you can contact for references:

1. Mr. Henry Banks, 1800 Doheny Drive, Los Angeles, CA 90003 (555-7390)
2. Mrs. Mary Kirby, 1600 Maple Avenue, Long Beach, CA (555-0079)

Mr. Banks was my basketball coach, and Mrs. Kirby is a family friend.

I look forward to hearing from you, and I hope your decision will be positive.

Sincerely,

Calvin Simpson

Calvin Simpson

SECTION 7

PAGE 87, GUIDED WRITING

Sample answers:

1. Conduct a survey by telephone or by questionnaire; collect firsthand information by visiting the human resources department of local companies.
2. local, regional, or trade magazines, want ads in local newspapers
3. **General questions:** What do you think are the most important skills for employees to have? Do you think reading, writing, and math are the most important? What skills must employees have to be hired?

   Specific questions: What skills are the most important for employees who are hired by your company? Rank the importance of the following skills using this scale:

   1 = good to have   3 = very important
   2 = important   4 = must have

   basic skills (reading, writing, math); ability to learn; ability to listen; ability to think fast; good people skills; ability to solve problems; specific job skills

PAGE 88, GUIDED WRITING

Sample answers:

1. Correct grammar and a good vocabulary are very important in business settings.
2. Sentence structure is one important thing to keep in mind.
3. If you are dressed well, you will have more confidence in yourself, and this will show when you speak.
4. Image is very important in business.

PAGE 89, GUIDED WRITING

Sample answers:

Paragraph 1

Learning is now a fact of life in the workplace. Even routine jobs are changing as the demands of businesses change. Often employees are moved from one job to another. They must be able to absorb information quickly. They must be able to move to another task with little supervision. The first step in adapting to this demand is losing the fear of the unknown. Most new situations are not as different as they seem at first. Learn to look at the big picture. Then you can apply what you already know to the new situation.

Summary

Learning is necessary because jobs and businesses are changing. Employees are moved and must absorb new information and tasks quickly with little supervision. Adapting involves being unafraid of new ideas. Look at the big picture, and apply what you already know.

Paragraph 2

When you are faced with a problem on the job, your first reaction should be to think about it. Thinking about the problem means trying to figure out *why* something is going wrong. Knowing why will usually help you come up with a solution. Most problems have more than one solution. Don't always think that you have to have the *right* answer. Most bosses are grateful for an employee who suggests a way to solve a problem, even if they don't always think the employee's way is the best way.

Summary

When you have a problem on the job, figure out why and come up with a solution. There is usually more than one solution to a problem. Bosses prefer employees who look for ways to solve problems, whether the employee has the right answer.

PAGE 90, GUIDED WRITING

Sample answers:

1. Communication Skills
   Warren, Dorothy. "Communication Skills: A Key to Success." *Careers*, April 1992, page 35. Good communication skills are the key to getting along with others and being successful on the job. What you say makes a lasting impression. "We never get a second chance to make a good first impression."
2. Communication Skills
   Warren, Dorothy. "Communication Skills," page 35
   Informal language, such as slang or poor grammar, is not acceptable at work. An example of informal language is saying "Hi" when you're introduced to someone. Saying "How do you do?" is more appropriate when meeting someone in a business setting.
3. Communication Skills
   Warren, Dorothy. "Communication Skills," page 35
   Correct grammar and a good vocabulary are important in creating a positive image. Sentence structure — subject-verb agreement, using correct parts of speech, tone, and tense — is important.

PAGE 93, EXERCISE A

1. spoken
2. written
3. taught
4. fallen
5. begun

PAGE 93, EXERCISE B

1. saw
2. went
3. drove
4. slept
5. eaten
6. caught
7. froze
8. fried
9. swam
10. took

PAGE 93, GUIDED WRITING

Sample answers:

1. I bought a new car.
2. John has done all his work.
3. Hector came to the game with Vicki.
4. You are dropping food all over your new clothes.

PAGE 95, JOURNAL WRITING A

Sample answer:

Introduction

    My supervisor, Shirley Jones, asked me to prepare the weekly report on service calls covering the week of April 4–8.

Body

    The customer service department received a total of eight calls. Of five total calls for repairs, two calls were for VCR's; two calls were for CD players; and one call was for a tape player.

    Two calls concerned problems with repairers—one did not show up and another was late.

    We received one other call about a remote control that was missing from a TV delivery.

Conclusion

    A total of eight calls were received and processed. Please let me know if you need any additional information.

PAGE 95, JOURNAL WRITING B

Sample title page:

> James Baldwin: Life in France
>
> Prepared by
> (Your Name)
>
> Submitted to
> Carol Rivera
> American Literature
>
> (Current Date)

Sample Bibliography:

Baldwin, James. "No Man's Land." *Esquire*, January 1980, pages 15–17, 89–92.

Goldberg, Leon J. *The Life of James Baldwin*. New York: Random House, 1988.

McMillan, William. "Mr. Baldwin: An Interview." *Look*, March 1970, pages 24–27.

Williams, Alice. "A Native Son Returns." *The New York Times*, March 25, 1980, page 35.

SECTION 8

PAGE 98, GUIDED WRITING

Sample answers:

1. the right to choose; liberty; free will; independence
2. a paved road, named after its inventor, the Scottish builder J. L. McAdam (1756–1836)

PAGE 99, EXERCISE A

Sample answers:

1. in addition, what is more, also, furthermore, besides, moreover, anyway
2. then, next, after that, later, afterward, after a while
3. as a result, thus, because of this, therefore, hence, for this reason

PAGE 99, EXERCISE B

Sample answers:

1. , and
2. , but
3. , so
4. ; as a result,

PAGE 100, GUIDED WRITING

There are many ways to make this paragraph flow more smoothly. Here is one sample:

People who win big prizes in the lottery often find that the money does not make them happy. First, they have to deal with lots of people trying to get a piece of the pie. What is more, winners find that their friends expect them to hand over some of the winnings. Because of this, they have to be on guard all the time. After a while, lottery winners find that they cannot trust anyone. All this pressure takes the fun out of winning. They can no longer relax and enjoy life. Nonetheless, I am willing to give it a try!

PAGE 101, EXERCISE

Sample answers:

1. maroon, scarlet, wine, ruby, crimson, cherry, rose, flame, communist
2. succeed, master, conquer, overcome, earn, gain, attain
3. stroll, amble, trek, march, hike, saunter
4. cash, funds, coins, bucks, riches, income, bills

PAGE 101, GUIDED WRITING

Sample answers:

1. The sky was a <u>crisp</u> blue and the air had the <u>tang</u> of autumn.
2. For dinner we had <u>juicy</u> hamburgers, <u>sweet</u> corn, and <u>tart</u> lemonade.
3. The new baby <u>curled</u> its <u>tiny</u> finger around my uncle's <u>fat</u> thumb.
4. My <u>fiery</u> sunburn turned my face <u>scarlet</u>.

PAGE 102, EXERCISE A

1. neat
2. racket
3. mansion
4. decrease
5. gentle
6. scorn

PAGE 102, EXERCISE B

1. (A) hostile
2. (C) distinguished
3. (B) Super Bowl
4. (A) nutritious
5. (C) captain

PAGE 103, EXERCISE A

1. passive (action done to the subject, *pill*)
2. active (subject, *We*, performs action)
3. passive (action done to the subject, *news*)
4. active (action done by the subject, *I*)
5. passive (action done to the subject, *New York*)

PAGE 103, EXERCISE B

1. (B) 2. (B) 3. (A) 4. (A)

PAGE 104, EXERCISE A

1. After four o'clock, the thief broke the lock.
   (The subject, *thief*, did the action, *broke*.)
2. The crew of *Apollo 11* landed on the moon.
   (The subject, *crew*, did the action, *landed*.)
3. They left a plaque on the moon.
   (The subject, *they*, did the action, *left*.)

PAGE 104, EXERCISE B

1. (A) 2. (B) 3. (A) 4. (B)

PAGE 105, EXERCISE

1. (B) 2. (A) 3. (A) 4. (B)

PAGE 105, GUIDED WRITING

1. In the distance, we could see the small ships.
2. Modern cars can be driven faster than older cars.
3. I asked the speaker to repeat what he had said.
4. The wilted plant was on the floor.

PAGE 106, GUIDED WRITING

Sample answers:

1. I like to read forecasts of the future, but I have to wonder if any of them are true.
2. Preferred: When people are treated with respect at work, they feel better about their work. Or: When a person is treated with respect at work, he or she feels better about his or her work.
3. Correct
4. When you look for a loan, you find who has the best rate. Or: When one looks for a loan, one finds who has the best rate.

PAGE 107, EXERCISE

1. **(1)** The word *backgrounds* was misspelled without the letter *g*.
2. **(3)** The word *they*, the first word in the sentence, was not capitalized.
3. **(3)** The word *language* was misspelled; the letters *a* and *u* were switched.

SECTION 9

PAGE 110, JOURNAL WRITING

Sample answer:

Pet owners must keep their animals safe! Unless you live on a farm or other open land, you must not let your pet run loose. How many times have you heard about pets that ran onto roads or highways and were struck by passing cars? Don't leave pets alone in cars, either. On hot days, cars can heat up inside very quickly with all the windows closed. Animals can suffocate in minutes. Don't let this happen!

PAGE 111, EXERCISE

Sample answers:

1. plopped, fell, lay, collapsed
2. Fear, Horror, Terror
3. chugging, roaring, racing
4. stomped, fled, flew, stormed
5. fifty dollars, an extra check, a cash bonus
6. beating down on, pelting, pinging on, pummeling, bombarding
7. screamed, yelled, shouted, bellowed
8. overjoyed, thrilled, elated
9. exhausted, drained, unenergetic, worn out
10. gulped, bolted, inhaled

PAGE 112, EXERCISE

Sample answers:

1. very poor, terrible, awful
2. wasted gas
3. out of money
4. did not do their work, wasted time
5. stolen
6. lose interest
7. handsome, masculine, virile
8. fond of, interested in, involved with
9. pretty, attractive, appealing
10. try to fool me

PAGE 112, JOURNAL WRITING

Sample answer:

You made me very angry when you yelled at me about the wood that was stolen. I'm not the one who took the wood. This whole matter is very unfair! I feel you have been treating me poorly all week over this. I know I am not the best worker in the plant, but I don't waste time. Please do not blame me for this anymore; let the matter rest.

PAGE 113, EXERCISE

1. hidden
2. showy
3. pretend
4. dismal
5. nimble
6. biting
7. stiff
8. confuse
9. cleanse
10. squeeze

PAGE 113, GUIDED WRITING

Sample answers:

1. My nosy neighbor is always spying at us from her window.
2. Fred slammed the front door shut after he lost the fight.
3. The movie star emerged from her limo to greet her fans.
4. Maria commented on the new boots Alba wore to work.
5. The spoiled child grabbed the candy from his friend's hand.

PAGE 114, EXERCISE

Sample answers:

1. vital
2. hurt
3. prying
4. slender
5. uproar
6. budge
7. schedule
8. a slob
9. chubby
10. pushy

PAGE 114, JOURNAL WRITING

Sample answer:

Hi Everyone,

Greetings from our cozy vacation cottage. I'm becoming a good carpenter as I repair the window frames. But protecting ourselves from the driving rain passes the time. Besides, the wet weather has chased away the flies and filled the pond.

PAGE 115, EXERCISE

1. buy
2. hear
3. board
4. piece
5. pain
6. meat
7. bear
8. read

PAGE 116, EXERCISE

Sample answers:

Cross off: no money (same as "money problems")
Possible groups:

pros of divorce	cons of divorce
children better off	money problems
no more fights	cost a lot
	children hurt
	people judge you badly
	fights
	being alone
	pressure from parents

PAGE 116, JOURNAL WRITING

Sample answer:

The best place to live

live in a city	live outside a city
close to work	quiet
public transportation	children have lots of
opportunities for night	room to play
school	not crowded
more to do	outdoor recreation
close to shopping	
movie theaters	

PAGE 117, EXERCISE

Sample answers:

1. in the want ads, by calling friends
2. want more money, want a chance to get ahead
3. when they lose the old one, when they are unhappy
4. people who are laid off, people who are fired, people who left school
5. good skills, a polite manner

PAGE 117, JOURNAL WRITING

Sample answer:

Day-Care Centers
Where are day-care centers located?
Why do people use day-care centers?
When can children be left at day-care centers?
Who works in day-care centers?
What do day-care centers cost?
How are day-care centers regulated?

SECTION 10

PAGE 122, PERSONAL DATA SHEET

Sample objective:

Nurse's aide in a hospital or nursing home

PAGE 125, EXERCISE

1. Typed
2. Handled
3. Completed
4. Operated

PAGE 126, EXERCISE

Sample answers:

1. Repaired equipment, such as photocopier.
2. Created signs for window displays.
3. Scheduled covering the reception desk.
4. Managed newsstand in owner's absence.
5. Won awards for running track.

PART A REVIEW (PAGES 134–139)

1. They (plural subject)
2. He (subject)
3. Her (possessive)
4. him (object of preposition)
5. me (object of preposition)
6. he (subject)
7. her (object of verb)
8. I (subject)
9. Diana started her new job on Friday.
10. Bob and she work at the baseball stadium.
11. They sell peanuts and ice-cream sandwiches.
12. Bob's friends attend most of the games.
13. The employees can buy tickets for half-price.
14. F (no verb)
15. S
16. S
17. F (no subject or verb)
18. F (no subject)
19. S
20. unless
21. but/and/although
22. and/so/since/because
23. when/if
24. George completed the form. He gave it to Ms. Golov.
25. She liked his resume. It was neat and well-organized.
26. Ms. Golov offered George a job. He would have to work Saturdays.
27. The job pays well. The company offers good benefits.
28. large (adjective, describes library)
29. fine (adjective, describes paintings)
30. carefully (adverb, tells how displayed)
31. beautiful (adjective, describes garden)
32. easily (adverb, tells how to get to)

33. gladly (adverb, tells how they will give you directions)
34. fastest (compares three or more)
35. well (no comparison; adverb describes the verb)
36. harder (compares two people)
37. quickly (no comparison; adverb describes the verb)
38. highest (compares three people)
39. past
40. future
41. present
42. past
43. present
44. future
45. had been cooking (past perfect progressive tense)
46. started (past tense)
47. has been (present perfect tense)
48. will have worked (future perfect tense)
49. had told (past perfect tense)
50. Bob and Angela went to the Kentucky Derby last year.
51. They stayed at the Middletown Hotel on Main Street.
52. On Wednesday they crossed the Ohio River and visited Bob's aunt in Indiana.
53. Aunt Mary works as a travel agent for American Travel Incorporated.
54. On Friday Angela wanted to go to the Louisville Zoo.
55. Afterward, they ate dinner at Clarke's Cafe on South Fork Road.
56. Is Stan coming to Nita's Halloween party?
57. She is serving hot dogs, potato salad, and baked beans.
58. Sheila was born on May 25, 1965.
59. Kham's boss, Charles H. Garrett, is from Boise, Idaho.
60. Do you want red, blue, or gold ribbon?
61. Discount Photo Company put an ad in the newspaper.
62. The last conference was held in Denver, Colorado.
63. Jesse, Lupe, Rita, and Anna are Dodgers fans.
64. written (past perfect tense)
65. begun (present perfect tense)
66. cost (past perfect tense)
67. knew (past tense)
68. found (future perfect tense)
    went (past tense)
    took (past tense)
    (present perfect tense)
    (past tense)
    (past perfect tense)

74. A (locked)
75. P (was broken)
76. P (was found)
77. A (sprained)
78. P (was made)
79. Aretha made the chicken soup.
80. Mr. Kington wrote the letter.
81. The Chicago Cubs won the pennant.
82. Early this morning, someone broke the pay phone.
83. It's (contraction for *it is*)
84. here (adverb, tells where)
85. our (possessive pronoun)
86. There (adverb, tells where)
87. know (verb)

PART B: HANDBOOK

PAGE 150

1. ?
2. .
3. .
4. !

PAGE 151

1. The cute, cuddly Teddy Bear is a popular toy.
2. Reader, do you know how the Teddy Bear was named?
3. Well-liked, athletic Theodore Roosevelt loved to hunt.
4. However, while hunting in 1902 he would not shoot a bear that had been tied to a tree.
5. The man who drew a picture of the tense, exciting scene started a fad: the Teddy Bear.

PAGE 152

1. Born in Texas in 1905, billionaire Howard Hughes led a sad life.
2. His mother, who kept him from playing with other children, died when Howard was sixteen.
3. His father died two years later, and Howard took charge of the family business.
4. Howard was a great businessman, but he soon became restless.
5. Lured by the movies, Howard went to Hollywood.
6. Over the next few years, he produced many famous movies.

swers and Explanations

7. Hughes, who loved flying, formed the Hughes Aircraft Company.
8. By 1938 he was a hero, having set three world speed records.
9. Not a happy man, he spent the rest of his life alone in a hotel.

PAGE 153

1. Martin Luther King, Jr., was a very famous leader.
2. After he earned his last degree, people called him Martin Luther King, Ph.D., or Dr. King.
3. He worked in Montgomery, Alabama to improve civil rights.
4. On April 3, 1968, he gave his last public speech.
5. He was shot and killed April 4, 1968, in Memphis, Tennessee.
6. On June 8, 1968, his killer was arrested in London, England.
7. More than 150,000 people were at his funeral in the Ebenezer Baptist Church in Atlanta, Georgia.
8. On May 2, 1968, a poor people's march began to honor Dr. King.
9. The march ended on June 24, 1968.

PAGE 154

1. Many Americans like the British Royal Family; this is shown by the number of people who view royal events.
2. People like to watch royal weddings the best; they also watch shows about royal birthdays.
3. Over 750 million people watched the wedding of Prince Charles and Lady Diana; this was the most popular royal event ever.
4. The wedding took place July 29, 1981; it was held at 4:30 P.M.
5. There were TV shows on the following topics: parties, cost, and guests.
6. The bride went to the church in a glass coach; it is part of the family's custom.
7. Diana was nervous; she said Charles' names in the wrong order.

PAGE 155

1. On June 3, 1965, astronaut Ed White left the space capsule to go on a twelve-minute space walk.
2. When the twelve minutes passed, White's partner said, "It's time to come in."
3. "I'm not coming in because I am having fun," said White.

4. "Come in!" McDivitt ordered.
5. "Get back in here before it gets dark," McDivitt pleaded.
6. White said that it would make him sad to come back in.
7. "Get him back in now!" ground crew workers ordered.
8. McDivitt answered, "He's in his seat now."

PAGE 156

1. Sunburn, snakebite, and arrow wounds—people going west in the 1800s faced all these dangers.
2. There were some cures—if you could call them that.
3. Women—already working very hard—made up most of the potions.
4. Salt, goose grease, and skunk oil—these were the main parts of many salves and creams.
5. Toasted onion skins and raw chicken—if you can believe it—were used to treat snakebite.
6. People put salt pork in their ears to cure an earache—I can't stand it!
7. Wild herbs, seeds, and plants—these were the key to healers.
8. Some cures were more harmful than the sickness—that's no surprise.
9. Records show that ammonia and paint cleaner—of all things—were used to cure aches and pains.

PAGE 157

1. Being an actor calls for (1) talent, (2) a thick skin, and (3) luck.
2. Actor Edward James Olmos (famous for his role in *Miami Vice*) surely has talent.
3. Olmos is also well known for his role as Jaime Escalante (a teacher).
4. Pedro Olmos (Edward's father) left Mexico to marry Eleanor Huizar.
5. Mr. Olmos (1925–1988) couldn't speak English when he arrived in the United States.
6. As a result, he tried many different jobs (at least a dozen).
7. Mr. Olmos had these skills: (a) dancing, (b) singing, (c) playing music.
8. Edward learned how to jitterbug and cha-cha (old-time dances).
9. Olmos sang and danced at clubs on Sunset Strip (located in Hollywood).

PAGE 158

1. many people stay up late at night to watch talk shows.
2. the first talk show was the *Tonight Show*.
3. it started on September 27, 1954.
4. the first host, Steve Allen, said, "this is sort of a mild little show."
5. on the show, Steve Allen played music, talked to people, and did funny skits.
6. three years later, *The Jack Parr Show* took over in the same time slot.
7. "this is an hour and forty-five minutes a night," Parr said, "and I can't figure it out."
8. in 1962, Parr stepped down, and Johnny Carson was made the host.
9. this show became one of NBC's biggest moneymakers.
10. many people think the show is such a success because of Carson's great skits and jokes.

PAGE 159

1. harriet quimby was the first Woman to earn a pilot's license.
2. She was a writer in new york city before she became a Flyer.
3. She fell in love with Airplanes in 1910 when she saw her first Flying meet.
4. harriet became a pilot and toured in mexico with a troupe of Pilots.
5. She decided she would be the first Woman to cross the english channel.
6. She took off on april 16, 1912, sitting on a wicker Basket in the cockpit.
7. After a scary flight, she landed on a french Beach.
8. The *new york times* was not on her side; a writer said that her flight did not prove anything at all.

PAGE 160

1. ed j. smith reports people are taking cheaper trips in the summer.
2. mr. and mrs. jenks got a room in orlando, florida, and went camping.
3. Last year, the jenkses would have gone to sea world instead.
4. This year, dr. Perez and his family went hiking instead of going to mt. rushmore in south dakota.
5. ms. Wills went to see her friend rather than flying to the island of st. kitts.
6. miss e.k. link from new town, long island, spent two days in maine.
7. She went to lake meade last year.
8. busch gardens in tampa, florida, is still very busy, though.
9. mr. hunt said that he wants to go to the middle east and see the dead sea.

PAGE 161

1. As of friday, april 16, martin luther king's birthday will be a holiday.
2. This holiday is in the place of columbus day, which we took as a day off on october 10.
3. The plant will, of course, still be closed on the fourth of july, labor day, and new year's eve.
4. But if any of these holidays falls on a monday or a friday, you will have a long weekend.
5. This year the company's fourth of july picnic will be on sunday, july 7.
6. I will be back at work on tuesday, september 6, the day after labor day.
7. Some people want to have the party on flag day, june 14, instead.
8. There has also been talk of a halloween party for october 31, which is a thursday this year.
9. We could hold the party on friday, november 1, if that is a better time.

PAGE 162

1. chief
2. ancient
3. succeed, seize
4. heir
5. Their
6. hopeful

PAGE 163

1. received
2. delayed
3. paid
4. writing
5. worrisome

PAGE 164

1. businesses
2. holidays
3. nieces, nephews
4. bushes
5. peaches
6. teeth
7. memories

PAGE 165

1. Tran's
2. children's
3. friends'
4. factory's
5. bodies
6. workers'
7. everyone's
8. workers'
9. friend's

PAGE 166

1. I have
2. did not
3. There is
4. was not
5. were not
6. will not
7. Let us
8. did not

PAGE 167

1. their
2. It's
3. they're
4. You're
5. Who's
6. it's
7. their
8. They're
9. you're
10. Who's

PAGE 168

1. week
2. accept
3. fair
4. aisles
5. fourth
6. know
7. break
8. lessen
9. close
10. whole

PAGE 169

1. who
2. good
3. well
4. among
5. bring
6. who

PAGE 170

1. common nouns: program, air, history
   proper nouns: *Gunsmoke,* September
2. common nouns: fall
   proper nouns: *Gunsmoke*
3. common nouns: show (*adult* is used as an adjective here)
   proper nouns: Western
4. common nouns: program, radio, spring
   proper nouns: William Conrad
5. common nouns: man
   proper nouns: Conrad, Marshal Matt Dillon, Dodge City, Kansas

PAGE 171

1. collective: team
   mass: water
2. collective: committee
3. mass: spirit, strength
4. mass: power
5. collective: audience
   mass: gravel, water
6. mass: time
7. collective: families
   mass: gold
8. collective: jury, team
9. collective: crowd
10. mass: courage, cold

PAGE 172

1. We
2. He
3. We
4. She

PAGE 173

1. us
2. me
3. us
4. them
5. us

PAGE 174

1. his
2. his
3. His
4. my
5. mine, yours
6. our
7. your
8. his

PAGE 175

1. Diego
2. shirt
3. Annette
4. machine
5. Fitzpatricks
6. horse
7. women
8. Sharon and Danielle
9. neighbor
10. couple

PAGE 176

1. our
2. their
3. he
4. their
5. his

PAGE 177

1. skilled
2. Irish, Russian, early, hunting
3. work, long
4. German, English, big
5. good, strong

PAGE 178

1. ever, really
2. how, warmly
3. often, quite, seriously
4. very, badly
5. barely
6. almost, quickly
7. completely

PAGE 179

1. adverb
2. adjective
3. adjective
4. adjective
5. adjective
6. adverb
7. adjective
8. adverb
9. adjective

PAGE 180

1. harder
2. most crowded
3. most difficult
4. heavier

PAGE 181

1. worse
2. worst
3. best
4. farther
5. farthest
6. less
7. most
8. better

PAGE 182

1. (3) collected
2. (5) No change is needed.
3. (1) talked
4. (4) will go

PAGE 183

1. was listening
2. had entered
3. has been listening
4. will be driving

PAGE 184

1. will be
2. Do
3. has
4. still have
5. Does
6. have

PAGE 185

1. (2) knew
2. (1) saw
3. (4) began
4. (4) made

PAGE 186

1. is
2. are
3. gaze
4. glow
5. shines
6. is
7. provide
8. are

PAGE 187

1. are planning
2. has told
3. take
4. gives
5. stop
6. are
7. have
8. have
9. is
10. is

PAGE 188

1. A
2. P
3. P
4. A
5. A
6. P
7. P
8. A
9. A
10. P

PAGE 189

1. P   The sentence stresses the action, not the performer.
2. A   The sentence should stress the performer of the action.
3. A   The sentence should stress the performer of the action.
4. A   The sentence should stress the performer of the action.
5. P   The sentence stresses the action, not the performer.

PAGE 190

1. C
2. C
3. F
4. F
5. F
6. C
7. F
8. C
9. F
10. C

PAGE 191

1. it is missing a verb.
2. it is missing a subject.
3. it is missing a verb.
4. it is missing a subject.

PAGE 192

1. RO
2. RO
3. C
4. RO
5. RO
6. C
7. RO

PAGE 193

Sample answers:

1. The Special Olympics was started in 1968; it is a program of sports for people with disabilities. *or*
   The Special Olympics was started in 1968. It is a program of sports for people with disabilities.
2. More than 4,300 athletes attend, and they come from fifty nations.
3. Each state competes in thirteen sporting events, but athletes do not have to enter every event.
4. Everyone is a winner, for each athlete gets a ribbon or a medal.

PAGE 194

1. CS
2. CS
3. S
4. CS
5. S
6. CS

PAGE 195

Sample answers:

1. My first week on the job was a disaster, and my boss told me so. *or*
My first week on the job was a disaster; my boss told me so.
2. I was really upset, yet I knew things had to get better. *or*
I was really upset, but I knew things had to get better.
3. I tried as hard as I could, for I really wanted to keep the job. *or*
I tried as hard as I could, because I really wanted to keep the job.
4. My co-workers gave me good advice, so I felt more confident.

PAGE 196

1. P
2. NP
3. NP
4. NP
5. NP
6. NP
7. P
8. NP

PAGE 197

1. Writing helps people think, speak, and learn.
2. Those who can write well will be leaders in the community, state, and nation in years to come.
3. By writing frequently, reading often, and seeking feedback, writers can improve.
4. Learning to write clearly, correctly, and effectively is a goal.

PAGE 198

1. After years of effort
2. even though they had a brutal time
3. Although other people said the climb could not be done
4. Since the climb was so hard
5. When they reached the top

PAGE 199

Sample answers:

1. After I went to bed, I heard a loud crash in the kitchen.
2. Because I was afraid, I pulled the blankets over my head.
3. When I heard the cat's meow, I finally got up.
4. When I saw the cat sitting by the broken plate, I knew what had happened.

PAGE 200

1. M
2. C
3. M
4. M
5. C
6. C
7. M
8. M
9. C
10. M

PAGE 201

Sample answers:

1. While I was passing a large rock, a clap of thunder made me scream.
2. Sailing up the harbor, we saw the boat.
3. As we flew over the town, the cars and houses looked like toys.
4. Do not sit in the chair without putting it together fully.

PAGE 202

1. Henry, where will the game be held?
2. It can't be here, because a heavy dew is on the grass.
3. The team members wore red caps.
4. When the game started, they felt better since the tension was over.
5. The pitcher did not know to whom to throw the ball.
6. After each inning, they repeated their signals.

PAGE 203

1. W
2. C
3. W
4. C
5. W
6. C
7. W
8. W

POSTTEST

PAGE 204

1.	Utah	Capitalize the name of a state.
2.	1847, the	Use a comma after introductory words.
3.	C	
4.	C	
5.	April	Capitalize the name of a month.

6.	wheat, corn, and potatoes	Use commas to separate three or more items in a list.
7.	C	
8.	Ute Indians	Capitalize the name of a people.
9.	Morley	Capitalize a person's name.
10.	Congress	Capitalize a government body.
11.	land,	Put a comma after introductory words.
12.	Civil War,	Capitalize the title of important events.
13.	San Francisco	Capitalize the name of a city.
14.	C	
15.	C	

PAGE 205

16.	was	Use the past tense to indicate an action that took place in the past.
17.	have been	Use the present perfect tense to indicate a past action continuing to the present.
18.	drawn	Use the past tense.
19.	tries	Use the present tense to indicate a continuing action.
20.	lands	Use the present tense to indicate a continuing action.
21.	will	Use the future tense to show an action that will happen in the future.
22.	goes	Use the present tense to indicate a continuing action.
23.	build	Use the present tense to indicate a continuing action.
24.	collect	Use the singular form of the verb with *you*.
25.	taken	Use the present perfect tense to indicate a past action continuing to the present.
26.	know	Use the present tense to indicate a continuing action.
27.	make	Use the present tense to indicate a continuing action.
28.	won	Use the present perfect tense to indicate a past action continuing to the present.
29.	are	Use the present tense form of *to be* to indicate a continuing action.

PAGE 206

30.	watch	Use a plural verb with the plural subject *Children*.
31.	have	Use a plural verb with the plural subject *They*.
32.	sees	Use a singular verb with the singular subject *child*.
33.	are	Use a plural verb with the plural subject *Parents and teachers*.
34.	is	Use a singular verb with the singular subject *government*.
35.	is	Use a singular verb with the singular subject *Television*.
36.	has	Use a singular verb with the singular subject *TV Guide*.
37.	are	Use a plural verb with the plural subject *February and November*.
38.	show	Use a plural verb with the plural subject *networks*.
39.	pays	Use a singular verb with the singular subject *company*.
40.	are	Use a plural verb with the plural subject *Shows*.
41.	earns	Use a singular verb with the singular subject *show*.
42.	like	Use a plural verb with the plural subject *people*.
43.	are	Use a plural verb with the plural subject *Shows*.

PAGE 207

44.	Adams	Capitalize a person's name.
45.	him	Use the objective case to show the pronoun is receiving the action, not performing it.
46.	C	
47.	your	Use the possessive pronoun *your* to show ownership. The contraction *you're* means *you are*.
48.	C	
49.	their	Use the possessive pronoun *their* to show ownership.
50.	it's	The contraction *it's* means *it is*; *Its'* is not a word.
51.	C	

52. Nelson Supply — Capitalize all important words in a proper noun.

53. he — Use the subjective case to show the pronoun is doing the action, not receiving the action.

54. their — Use the possessive case pronoun to show ownership. *There* is an adverb telling where something is.

55. them — Use the objective case to show the pronoun is receiving, not performing the action.

56. Minnesota — Capitalize the name of a state.

57. yours — Never use an apostrophe with possessive pronouns, because they are already in the possessive form.

58. there — Do not confuse the possessive pronoun *their* with the adverb *there*.

59. C

PAGE 208

60. most — Use the superlative form to compare three or more things.

61. slowly — Use an adverb to describe the verb *walked*.

62. well — Use an adverb to describe the verb *swinging*.

63. weakly — Use an adverb to describe the verb *ran*.

64. worse — Use the comparative form to compare two things.

65. easily — Use an adverb to describe the verb *stole*.

66. better — Use the comparative form to compare two actions.

67. low — Use an adjective to describe the noun *slider*. No comparison is being made.

68. smoothly — Use an adverb to describe the verb *swung*.

69. loudly — Use an adverb to describe the verb *cheered*.

70. less — Use the comparative form to compare two teams.

PAGE 209

71. readers — Use the plural form to agree with *everywhere*.

72. stories — Use the plural form to agree with *many*.

73. Doyle's — Use the singular possessive to show ownership (the works of Doyle).

74. detective's — Use the singular possessive to show ownership (the friend of the detective).

75. streets — Use the plural form to show London has many streets.

76. city's — Use the singular possessive to show ownership (the criminals of the city).

77. crimes — Use a plural subject to agree with the verb *are*.

78. it's — Use the contraction *it's*, which means *it is*.

79. author's — Use the singular possessive to show ownership (the ideas of the author).

80. readers — Use the plural form to agree with *Some*.

81. Sherlock's — Use the singular possessive to show ownership (the birthday of Sherlock).

PAGE 210

Children under the age of <u>four</u> [82] are especially prone to bumps and falls. <u>Our</u> [83] little boy's front tooth was recently broken in a fall. He was riding a bike <u>too</u> [84] fast. We called the dentist <u>immediately</u> [85]. She asked me about the <u>angle</u> [86] of the break.

While I was <u>making</u> [87] the appointment, my husband put a cold cloth on our son's lip. At the dentist's office, we had to <u>wait</u> [88] for an hour. Many other children were <u>there</u> [89] to see the dentist.

The dentist made sure there was not a <u>piece</u> [90] of the tooth in his lip. She also made sure the tooth was not <u>loose</u> [91]. We made an appointment to come back in one <u>week</u> [92]. We were glad to <u>know</u> [93] his tooth would be fine.

PAGE 211

Every year people lose their lives in fires, but[94] many fatal fires can be prevented. Parents should teach their children how to prevent fires, and[95] they should show children what to do if a fire starts. Many fires start in the kitchen when[96] someone gets careless. Never put water on a grease fire, because[97] the fire will spread. Cover the burning pan with an air-tight lid since[98] fires go out when the air is cut off. Keep a fire extinguisher handy, and[99] know how to use it.

Do not store papers, boxes, and old clothes, because[100] these items can catch fire easily. Always throw away oily rags, and[101] keep flammable liquids safely stored in metal containers.

Electrical fires are easily avoided if[102] you take a few precautions. Never plug more than two appliances into one outlet, since[103] you may overload the circuit. A fuse may blow if[104] a circuit becomes overloaded. When this happens, always find out the cause of the problem, and[105] replace the fuse.

PAGE 212

106.	S	
107.	F	The subject is missing.
108.	S	
109.	S	
110.	F	The subject and verb are missing.
111.	S	
112.	F	The subject and verb are missing.
113.	F	The verb is missing.
114.	S	
115.	F	The verb is missing.
116.	F	The verb is missing.
117.	S	
118.	S	
119.	F	The subject and verb are missing.
120.	S	
121.	F	The subject and verb are missing.
122.	F	The subject and verb are missing.
123.	S	
124.	F	The subject is missing.
125.	S	

PAGE 213

126.	Start with *In*	The other choices are too wordy and unclear.
127.	dress	Use parallel structure with verbs.
128.	Modern	The other choices are too wordy.
129.	Next,	The other choices are too wordy and unclear.
130.	to	The other choices are too wordy.
131.	Because	The other choices are too wordy and unclear.
132.	sound technicians	Use parallel structure with subjects.
133.	supervises	The other choices are too wordy and unclear.
134.	Then	The other choices are too wordy and unclear.
135.	If	The other choices are too wordy and unclear.

PAGE 215

Following is a sample essay that opposes advertising 900 numbers during children's programming.

Advertisers should not be allowed to offer 900 telephone numbers during children's TV programming. These numbers are designed only to sell goods and services. Children are too young to understand what they are doing when they respond to these costly ads.

Advertisers use 900 numbers to sell many products, from daily horoscopes and sports information to investment offerings and romance services. Rarely are these items offered to children. Instead, vendors built on their success with adults to target a series of products for children. These include phone calls to Santa Claus, the Easter Bunny, and cartoon characters. They also include offers for games, toys, and contests. Most of these products have little value, but children find them hard to resist, and so they place the calls.

What children do not understand is that 900 numbers are expensive. In just a few minutes, a child can run up a phone bill of more than $10.00. Some 900 ads carry a warning: "Kids, ask Mom and Dad before you call." Most children are not mature enough to resist a call to Santa or their favorite cartoon character. As a result, children can run up huge phone bills that parents are responsible for paying.

Since the calls are expensive and the products are of little value, 900 phone numbers should be banned during children's programming. Children should not have access to these numbers.

Following is a sample essay that supports advertising 900 numbers during children's programming.

Advertisers should be allowed to promote 900 telephone numbers during children's programming. There is no reason to treat 900 number services differently than any other product.

Children's programming depends upon funding from advertisers. The advertisers pay high fees to have their commercials shown. They hope that interested children will ask their parents to buy the products. There is no reason to deny the owners of 900 number services this same free enterprise opportunity.

One might argue that 900 number services are of little value. However, commercials for candy, sugary breakfast cereals, and the latest toys and fads are shown during children's viewing hours. Do these products have greater value than these 900 number services? No, they do not; we are simply used to seeing them.

Advertisers know that the parents make the buying decisions. It is also the parents' task to raise responsible children. By the time children are old enough to remember and dial the 11 digits in a 900 number, they are old enough to be taught to make good decisions about spending money.

Although 900 numbers may be an expensive nuisance for some people, there is no reason to ban them. We should not expect the government to do a parent's job.

Index

future perfect tense, 53, 183
future progressive tense, 183
future tense, 53, 136–137, 182

G

gerunds, 174
good/well, 169
grammar, editing, 24–25,
144–146
See also individual topics

H

have, 183
helping verbs, 92, 184, 188
holidays, capitalization of, 77,
161
homonyms, 115, 139, 168
inventory, 7
posttest, 210
how-to writing, 52
hyphens, 177

I

ideas
generating, 17–18, 116–117,
142
mapping or outlining, 18, 36,
48, 82, 84–85, 97, 108,
116, 142–143
independent clauses, 46, 198
index cards for notetaking, 89,
97
indirect object, objective case
pronoun as, 173
informal speech, correcting, 203
information
adding, and commas, 151
classifying, 91, 97
informational writing
See explanatory writing
inventory, 1–12
irregular adjectives and
adverbs, 181
irregular plurals, 164
irregular verbs, 92–93, 185

italic type, 87

J

job application form, 130–133
journal writing, 18, 22, 25, 27,
29, 30, 35, 39, 40, 41, 61,
65, 72, 74, 91, 95, 100, 102,
106, 110, 111, 112, 114,
116, 117

L

language
as expression, 111
formal and slang, 112
literal, 41
specific versus vague, 64–65,
145
less/few/fewer, 169, 181
letterhead stationery, 75
letter writing, 15, 72–85
business, 72–76, 80, 154
capitalization/punctuation,
77–79, 154
formal and informal style, 74
formatting letter parts, 75,
82, 85
for job interview, 84
letter to the editor, 70–71
personal, 72, 74–76
literal language, 41

M

main idea, 19, 24, 36, 48, 56,
58, 68–69, 70, 82, 84, 85,
94, 97, 108, 118, 143
mapping ideas, 18, 36, 48,
82, 84, 85, 97, 108, 116,
142–143
mass nouns, 171
may/can, 169
mechanics handbook, 150–169
modifiers
dangling and misplaced,
200–201
months, capitalization of, 77,
161, 204

N

names, capitalization of, 77,
137, 160
narrative writing, 15, 28–37
nominative case, 172
notetaking, 89–91, 97
nouns, 29, 31, 47, 55, 134, 159,
170–171, 196–197
and adjectives, 42, 177, 179
inventory, 4
plurals of, 164–165
possessives, 165
posttest, 207

O

objective case, 173
object of a preposition, objective
case as, 173
opinions, 68, 70
order of importance, 20–22, 58
outlining ideas, 18, 36, 82, 84,
85, 91, 97, 143
ownership, showing
See possessives

P

paraphrasing, 88–89
parentheses, 157
passive voice, 103–104, 139,
188–189
past participle, 92, 182–183,
185
past perfect progressive tense,
183
past perfect tense, 183
past progressive tense, 183
past tense, 53, 92, 136, 182, 185
perfect tenses, 53, 183
periods, 33, 79, 138, 150
personal data sheet, 122–124
personal letters, 15, 72, 74–76
personal narrative, 28–30
personal pronouns, 28–29, 134,
172–174, 176
persuasive writing, 15–16,
60–71

place names
  and capitalization, 160, 177
  and commas, 138, 153
plagiarism, 88
plurals, 66–67, 164–165,
    186–187
  inventory, 6
  posttest, 209
point of view, 28, 60–62, 64,
    68–69, 106, 119
possessives, 28–29, 134, 165,
    167, 174
  inventory, 6
  posttest, 209
posttest, 204–215
precise words, 39, 50, 98, 111,
    119, 169
predicates, 31, 44, 134
predictions, writing, 23
prefixes, 163
preposition, 173
present participle, 92, 182, 185
present perfect progressive
    tense, 183
present perfect tense, 53, 183
present progressive tense, 183
present tense, 53, 92, 136–137,
    182, 185
prewriting, 14, 16–18, 36, 48,
    58, 70, 82, 84, 96, 108, 118,
    128, 142
pronouns, 172–174
  and adjectives, 42, 177, 179
  agreement, 176
  antecedents, 175–176
  inventory, 4
  object, 28–29, 134
  possessive, 28–29, 134, 167,
    174
  posttest, 207, 209
  subject, 28–29, 31, 134, 187
  and verb agreement, 187
proofreading, 26–27, 37, 49, 59,
    71, 78, 83, 85, 97, 109, 119,
    146–149
proper adjectives, 159, 177
proper nouns, 159, 165, 170
publishing final drafts, 15, 27,
    37, 49, 59, 71, 83, 85, 97,
    149

punctuation, 33, 77, 79, 138,
    147–157, 192–193, 195
  inventory, 1
  posttest, 204
purpose
  defining and identifying, 16,
    36, 48, 58, 70, 82, 84, 85,
    96, 108, 118, 142

Q

question marks, 79, 138, 150
questions
  about a writing topic, 17,
    117–118
  writing, 23
quotation marks, 155, 158
quoting false experts, 69

R

recommendations, writing, 23
report writing, 15, 86–97
  formal and informal, 94
  parts of a report, 94, 97
request, letter of, 73
research, for writing topics, 17
research report, 86
resumes, 120–129
revising
  polishing work, 107
  sentences, 15, 105–106,
    202–203
  written work, 24–25, 37, 49,
    59, 71, 83, 85, 97, 109,
    119, 129, 144–146
run-on sentences, 33, 135,
    192–193

S

second-person pronouns, 28,
    172, 176
semicolons, 62, 154, 192–194
sensory details, 40
sentence structure
  clarity, 54
  compare and contrast
    sentences, 62–63

complete sentences, 32, 135,
    190–191
complex sentences, 46,
    198–199
compound sentences, 44–45,
    194–195
fragments, 32, 135, 190–191
handbook, 190–203
inventory, 8–10
parallel structure, 10, 55,
    196–197
posttest, 211–213
revising, 105, 202–203
run-on sentences, 33, 135,
    192–193
sharing final drafts
  See publishing final drafts
simple tenses, 53
slang, 112
special writing situations, 15,
    120–133
spelling, 147–149, 162–163
  inventory, 7
  posttest, 210
style, editing, 24–25, 144–146
subjects, 31, 44, 66, 134, 186,
    188, 191
  compound, 67
subject-verb agreement, 66, 186
  inventory, 3
  posttest, 206
subordinate clauses, 46,
    198–199
suffixes, 163, 180
summary, writing, 23, 87–90,
    144
superlative form, 43, 180–181
supporting details, 19–25, 37,
    49, 56–57, 80, 109, 119,
    143–146
surveys, 86
synonyms, 101–102, 109, 115,
    119

T

take/bring, 169
that/who/whom, 169
thesaurus, 101

third-person pronouns, 28–29, 172, 176

time order, 20–22, 34, 51–52

title page, of report, 94

titles
    capitalization of, 77, 137, 160
    and commas, 153

topic
    defining, 16, 36, 48, 58, 70, 82, 84, 85, 96, 108, 118, 142
    discussing, 17, 116

topic sentence, 19–24, 34–35, 37, 48, 58, 70, 96, 109, 118, 119, 143

transition words, 51–52

usage handbook, 170–189

verbs, 31, 47, 55, 125–126, 179, 191, 196–197
    active/passive voice, 103–104, 109, 139, 188–189

and adverbs, 42, 178–179
helping, 92, 184, 188
inventory, 2–3
irregular, 92–93, 138, 185
posttest, 205–206
pronoun-verb agreement, 187
subject-verb agreement, 66–67, 186
verb tenses, 53, 92–93, 103–104, 136–138, 145, 182–183

vocabulary, 101–102

voice, active and passive, 103–104, 109, 139, 188–189

well/*good*, 169

who/*whom*/*that*, 169

wordiness, correcting, 105, 109, 202

words, choosing, 39, 64, 113, 169

words in a series, 47, 151

writing process
    editing and revising, 24–25, 37, 49, 59, 71, 83, 85, 97, 109, 144–146, 202–203

final draft, 26–27, 37, 49, 59, 71, 83, 85, 97, 109, 119, 129, 146–149

first draft, 19–23, 37, 49, 58, 70, 82, 85, 97, 109, 118, 128, 143–146

models, 142–149

prewriting, 14, 16–18, 36, 48, 58, 70, 82, 84, 96, 108, 128, 142

publishing, 15, 27, 37, 49, 59, 71, 83, 85, 97, 109, 119, 149

writing skills
    creative writing, 110–119
    descriptive writing, 38–49
    explanatory writing, 50–59
    expository writing, 98–109
    how-to writing, 52
    inventory skills test, 11–12
    letter writing, 72–85
    narrative writing, 28–37
    overview, 14–15
    persuasive writing, 60–71
    report writing, 86–97
    special writing situations, 120–133
    writing process, 16–27

Editing Checklist

		YES	NO
Content	Does the content reflect your original purpose?	☐	☐
	Is the content right for your intended audience?	☐	☐
	Is the main idea stated clearly?	☐	☐
	Does each paragraph have a topic sentence?	☐	☐
	Are topic sentences supported by details?	☐	☐
	Are details written in a logical order?	☐	☐
	Is the right amount of information included? (Check for details that are missing or not needed.)	☐	☐
Style	Will the writing hold the reader's interest?	☐	☐
	Are thoughts and ideas expressed clearly?	☐	☐
	Are any ideas repeated?	☐	☐
	Are some words used too many times?	☐	☐
Grammar	Are all sentences complete sentences?	☐	☐
	Are any sentences too long and hard to understand?	☐	☐
	Are any sentences too short and choppy?	☐	☐
	Are nouns and pronouns used correctly?	☐	☐
	Are verbs used correctly?	☐	☐
	Are adjectives and adverbs used correctly?	☐	☐

Proofreading Checklist

	YES	NO
Is correct punctuation used in every sentence?	☐	☐
Is correct capitalization used in every sentence?	☐	☐
Are all words spelled correctly?	☐	☐
Are new paragraphs clearly shown? (Check to see if paragraphs are either indented or have an extra line space in between.)	☐	☐
If handwritten, is the handwriting as neat as possible?	☐	☐
If typed, is the typing neat and without errors?	☐	☐
Is there enough space between words and lines?	☐	☐
Are the margins too wide or too narrow?	☐	☐

Proofreader's Marks

b̲ B	change to a capital letter
B̸ b	change to a lowercase letter
the end○	insert a period
red, white∧ and blue	insert a comma
Will you go ?	insert a question mark
and Sue Will you∧go?	insert word(s)
(Sp) (there) car	check spelling
end.¶We will	insert a paragraph indent
end.⌒ We will	remove a paragraph indent
go on away	delete a word
an# d∧a half	add a space between words
to͡day	delete a space between words